THE ENCYCLOPEDIA OF OCCULT AND SUPERNATURAL MURDER

THE ENCYCLOPEDIA OF OCCULT AND SUPERNATURAL MURDER

Brian Lane

LONDON NEW YORK SYDNEY TORONTO

This edition published 1995
by BCA
by arrangement with Headline

First published in 1995 by
HEADLINE BOOK PUBLISHING

CN 3393

Typeset by
Letterpart Limited, Reigate, Surrey

Printed and bound in Great Britain by
Mackays of Chatham PLC, Chatham, Kent

For Bela
Walk with care, walk in safety . . .

Contents

Acknowledgements

Regular readers of my books will know that, without the same loyal and supportive back-up team I would be lost. I have sung their praises so often that to do so again could be embarrassing.

They know who they are, and I hope they know how grateful I am.

Brian Lane
London, October 1994

Author's Introduction

The planning of a thematic book, no matter how 'encyclopedic', is usually a fairly simple matter; the only problem in my experience lies in what to *ex*clude from a vast amount of available material. *The Encyclopedia of Occult and Supernatural Murder* presented exactly the opposite problem – of what should be *in*cluded. In other words, what defines the subject matter of occult and supernatural murder? Apart from the obvious, there are clearly areas where the edges are blurred enough to merit inclusion or not, and to readers who feel that their 'favourites' have not been included, I apologise. In the end this has had to be a very subjective piece of decision-making. However, it is also, I hope, representative of a tantalisingly elusive subject.

Although each of the entries which comprise this book must be taken on its own merit, as narratives of crimes and times, of beliefs and disbelief, certain inescapable patterns do emerge which seem to have given a rudimentary 'boundary' to what is either 'occult', or 'supernatural', or both.

Psychic attack

There are very few recorded instances of this type of murder. One of the reasons is that level-headed criminologists are rarely willing to admit the possibility of the psychic element in crime; and another is that workers with the paranormal tend not to become involved with criminology. One notable exception was the tragic death of **Norah Farnario**. Quite what frightened poor Norah to death we will never know, but her involvement with powerful occult groups of the time was no coincidence. Nor is it any coincidence that serious occult training always provides instruction on neutralising deliberate psychic attack. These remedies range from seeking refuge in a circle 'drawn' with consecrated water to putting saucers of vinegar in which exorcised salt has been dissolved at strategic points around the building. One particularly gruesome protection against malevolent spirits was revealed at the trial of **St Clair Daniel** in the Virgin Islands. It is a belief among the followers of voodoo that the shades of the dead (called 'jumbies') hover around for seven days, during which time they are capable of turning people into zombies. The only protection, apparently, is to cut off the deceased's head.

However, matters do not always proceed so straightforwardly with sacred circles. Not infrequently the demons, or spirits, or whatever any religion calls these malevolent entities, enter the body and soul of the hapless victim. It is a job now for the exorcist. Exorcism is employed in one form or another by most of the world's faiths, and at its simplest is no more than a piece of rudimentary 'sympathetic magic'. That is to say, the exorcist makes things so uncomfortable for the demons that they depart the host's body; being of a wicked nature most of these hob-goblins respond to prayers, consecrated water, incense and all those other trappings of a Good God. But what if the devils prove persistent? Then tougher measures are called for.

The Muslim faith, for example, has special exorcists – the *pir* – trained to make the *body* of the victim so uncomfortable that the infestation flees. Unfortunately, this involves considerable physical torment – starvation, sleep deprivation, beatings and so on – and on occasion although the *djinns* may be banished, so is the victim's life. A fate suffered by one young woman at the hands of **Mohammed Bashir**. **Maria Magdalena Kohler**, self-styled 'Holy Mother' of an offbeat group calling itself the International Association for the Preservation of World Peace, also went in for exorcism by mortification of the flesh. In fact she battered and ill-treated one of her followers for five years, without success. In the end, not surprisingly, the poor woman died of her injuries. The **Vollmer** family and their friends similarly indulged in a spot of DIY exorcism – but being Christian Charismatics they called it 'deliverance'. Whatever it was the ritual beatings resulted in Alice Vollmer's untimely and excruciating death; for what comfort it may have been to her, Mrs Vollmer's husband was able to report that at the moment before death the evil spirits were banished.

Lest it be thought that exorcisms only take place among weird cults in far-away places, the following story, set in the heart of London occurred at the end of August 1994. Following an epileptic fit, a seven-year-old child lost his use of speech, and despite every effort made by his desperate mother, the boy still could not speak. In the end a local social worker recommended 'healing' by a minister of the Pentecostal Church. This old-fashioned exorcism consisted of the usual Bible-thumping, chanting and 'speaking in tongues'. Then, according to the mother: 'He got me up and started spinning me round, talking in this weird language and put his hands on my head. I started thinking, "What's going on here?" ' What indeed? According to the pastor, the reason for the child's affliction was that he had been possessed by the devil; and the reason why he had been possessed by the devil was because his mother wore gold jewellery: 'He said to me, "Give me your jewellery and I will throw it into the pit of hell." ' The woman wisely refused, and her son is now undergoing more conventional treatment at Great Ormond Street Children's Hospital, where doctors are confident that they will be able to restore his speech.

The shades of the dead
Ghosts, the shades of the dead, are frequently associated with incidents of violent death, and a number of murder locations are said to be haunted. One of the most celebrated, though the house no longer stands, was **'Castel-a-Mare'**, a large residence in the peaceful town of Torquay. The haunting was investigated by the foremost medium of her day, Violet Tweedale, who was able to communicate with the spirits involved in the murder of the master of the house and his maid. There have been a number of attempts to rationalise the phenomenon of ghosts, perhaps the most convincing being the 'psychometric hypothesis'. This proposes that powerful emotions and images are able to imprint themselves on to their surroundings in such a way that they can be picked up and re-created at a later point in time by a person of sufficient sensitivity – such as Violet Tweedale.

Another famous murder site that is said to be haunted is Hilldrop Crescent in London, where **Dr Hawley Harvey Crippen** killed his wife. Some claim that, on the anniversary of Mrs Crippen's death, the shade of her husband can be seen walking from the house, with Cora's head wrapped up in a parcel.

Psychic detection

If it is possible for 'sensitives' to communicate with the dead, then it should reasonably be possible to put this rare gift to practical use in helping to solve crimes. And this is just what has happened with increasing success over the past few decades. While this aspect of crime detection is a long way from the 'ghosties and ghoulies' normally associated with the supernatural, the possession of paranormal powers is sufficient to earn the so-called 'psychic detectives' a place in this book.

One of the earliest examples of the phenomenon was in the case of the murder of Irene Wilkins by **Thomas Henry Allaway**, in 1921. Over the course of several seances the spirit medium, Mrs Charlotte Starkey, was entered by the spirit of the victim, who was able to give an account not only of the circumstances of her death, but of the man responsible for the murder. A similar successful communication with a deceased victim was undertaken by Estelle Roberts over the disappearance of ten-year-old Mona Tinsley in 1937. Mrs Roberts was able to tell police officers where and how little Mona had died, and where her body had been dumped; **Frederick Nodder** was later charged with the murder, convicted and hanged.

There have been, more recently, a number of what we might call 'professional' psychic detectives. Clairvoyants such as the late Peter Hurkos and Gerard Croiset, who have made a career combining parapsychological research and helping the police with their enquiries. Both men were Dutch, which is less a matter of coincidence than that the Netherlands has a history of taking parapsychology seriously, and that their police forces have a more open mind than most in using the 'gift of unseen powers'. Although he helped police in the search for missing persons (his specialty) in half a dozen countries, Gerard Croiset was quite unable to explain how his gift worked. On one occasion he described it as like seeing a fine powder which gradually resolved itself into shapes, first two-dimensional, then three-dimensional.

These images were usually seen in black and white – except where a dead body was involved, where they would be in colour. Although he was more successful at finding missing persons (80 per cent), Croiset was involved with such murder investigations as that of **Fred Thompson** in 1961.

Although he made no attempt to explain it, Peter Hurkos could pinpoint exactly the time he 'received' his psychic powers. It was 10 July 1941, when he fell off a high ladder while working as a house painter. When he recovered consciousness after a brain operation, Hurkos began to make predictions, and to reveal intimate details of other people's lives. Hurkos's 'method' was to 'see' people and events, by holding an object or piece of clothing personal to the subject – murder victim, lost person, or in his early days as a stage psychic, a member of the audience. This technique is called 'psychometry' and is in wide use among psychic detectives and clairvoyants. In later years Peter Hurkos spent much of his time in America, and it was there that he became involved in the most controversial murder case of his career – that of the **'Boston Strangler'**. After a series of remarkable visions Hurkos was convinced that he had identified the Strangler; unfortunately the police had another suspect, Albert De Salvo, who confessed to the crimes. Until his death, the clairvoyant lost no opportunity to claim that the police were wrong and that he was right – a claim being taken increasingly seriously.

A different type of 'psychic detection' is presented by those individuals who have been given information in the form of dreams – ordinary people for the most part, who have no connection with the paranormal. One famous recipient of a nocturnal prophesy was old Mrs Martin, who dreamt that her daughter Maria's body would be discovered in the notorious **Red Barn Murder**. Another was Eric Tombe's mother who correctly dreamt that her son's body would be found at the bottom of a well, cruelly murdered by his friend **Ernest Dyer**.

Death by witchcraft

When a witch makes a waxen image or some such thing in order to bewitch somebody; or when an image of someone appears by pouring molten lead into water, and some injury is done upon the image, such as piercing it or hurting it in any other way, when it is the bewitched man who is in imagination being so hurt; although the injury is actually done to the image by the witch or some other man, and the devil in the same manner invisibly injures the bewitched man, yet it is deservedly ascribed to the witch.

Malleus Maleficarum (Part II), Kramer and Sprenger, 1486

It is difficult to understand, in these comparatively enlightened times, that there was at one period an almost tangible madness spreading throughout Europe resulting from a fear of 'witches'. A time during which thousands of helpless old crones suffered torture and execution for the crime of 'bewitching to death', and who were in reality no more than the victims of spite and blind superstition. For this reason including the witch trials in this study posed certain problems. In the end it was thought proper to present some of the more notorious cases – such as the **Warboys Witches** – because it became clear that the significant factor was an unshakeable belief that it was *possible* to bewitch a person to death, by some pact or other with Dark Forces.

Though there is evidence of strict laws governing the practice of witchcraft from early Anglo-Saxon times, the concept of its evil was based on the purely practical expedient of punishing crimes against man and against his property. However, the spread of the Church of Rome throughout western Europe ensured that witchcraft would eventually be seen as a heresy and an offence against God, and the suppression of heretics – real or imagined – became a crusade. The Holy Inquisition was established in Castile with royal assent in 1478, and with Thomas de Torquemada as Grand Inquisitor, started its operations over the whole of Spain in 1483. Its initial programme was the complete eradication, by any means, of all heretical beliefs and practices – aimed especially at the Jews and the Moors. By a Bull of Pope Sixtus V in 1505, however, the Inquisition was rendered sufficiently elastic to embrace all forms of 'Sorcery and Divination' – including astrology and 'witchcraft'. In 1486 two Dominican friars, Jakob Sprenger and Heinrich Kramer, composed the terrifying treatise on 'Witchcraft, Its Discovery, Treatment and Cure' called the

Malleus Maleficarum. It became the indispensable companion of all judges, magistrates and priests during the years of fury of the Inquisition, being both a theological self-justification and a practical handbook on each step in the denunciation, trial and execution of 'heretics'. It is impossible to compute the numbers of the Spanish Inquisition victims, but in 1481 it is said that three thousand were burned in Andalucia alone, and seventeen thousand others tortured.

At first the insular nature of Britain protected it in large measure from the worst excesses of the Inquisition, and although 'sorcery' was still legislated against, penalties were mild. Witchcraft first became a heinous crime in England under a 1563 statute of Queen Elizabeth I, arising in part from her own insecurity and in part from pressure by the clergy. This Act of Elizabeth made the invocation of spirits 'whereby any persons shall be killed or destroyed, or wasted, consumed or lamed in his or her body or matter' an offence punishable by death. The steady growth of superstition during Elizabeth's reign is exhibited by the spectacular nature of some of the contemporary trials – at **Chelmsford** in 1566, the first major witch-hunt in England; at St Osyth in 1582.

In 1604 James I increased the severity of the punishments for all kinds of witchcraft, and the eastern counties trembled before the name of Matthew Hopkins, the self-styled Witchfinder-General of England, responsible for the executions of more than a hundred so-called 'witches' and the imprisonment and torture of countless others. Hopkins masterminded the lurid trials of the Manningtree Witches in 1645, and the **Bury St Edmunds Witches** later in the same year.

Earlier, a number of local witch-hunts had resulted in the executions of the Witches of Northamptonshire on 22 July 1612, and the deaths of many of the **Lancashire Witches** tried in August of the same year. The last witch to hang in England was Alice Molland at Exeter in 1684, though with the restoration of the Stuart Line in 1660 there were few executions, and most indictments for witchcraft were charged only with the more serious crimes of murder and destruction. The last recorded witch trial was in 1712 when Jane Wenham was convicted at the Hertford Assizes but not executed.

The Black Arts

Although they are often connected in the popular mind, when it comes to murder 'witchcraft' and Satanism are two very different things. It can be said, certainly in my experience, that those who adhere to the old religions, to witchery, have a mainly benevolent approach to their working practices. Not so the Satanists, at the base of whose practice is the concept of blood sacrifice. True, in most instances the only blood shed is that of a few hapless chickens, but there is ample evidence for much more sinister goings-on at a higher level in some of the more organised international cults.

The first distinction to be made, then, is between the serious devil-worshipper and the, mainly, American high-school kids for whom a flirtation with the devil is just part of growing up – like drugs, sex and heavy-metal music. Such a case was that of **Richard Kasso**, a youth whose murderous attack, despite his exhortation to the victim to 'Tell Satan you love him', was more to do with the real or imagined theft of drugs than it was to do with the occult. That said, the growing threat of black-magic-inspired killings has so alarmed some police forces that officers are receiving special instruction – such as the eighty New York state police officers who attended a seminar on Satanism and the occult in 1989, in order to 'respond to the growing incidence nationwide of cult-related crimes and rituals'. An initiative being taken up across the country.

One of the major influences to emerge from any study of Satanism-related crimes, is the number of killers who claim to have become involved in devil-worship as a result of reading *The Satanic Bible*, by Anton LaVey. This book above all others has been found in the possession of young cult killers – **Stanley Dean Baker**, **Lloyd Gamble**, **Scott Waterhouse**, and the unlovely **Richard Kasso** among the dozens. LaVey was born in 1930, and in his youth took easily to the life of the travelling carnival, where he rose from cage-boy to lion tamer and picked up all manner of tricks from the stage illusionist which would one day pepper his appearances as the high priest of devil-worship. He began to attract a following to his 'esoteric' meetings around 1960, and by 1966 proclaimed the 'Age of Satan' and founded the First Church of Satan. And the Church grew, spawning the inevitable break-away groups and offshoots. Mad as a hatter? Perhaps, but nobody can deny the power and influence that LaVey has over the minds of an alarming number of America's disaffected youth – could it even be as the High Priest claimed, that before he dies, LaVey and an elite brand of Satanists will rule the world?

But however we may belittle the Anton LaVeys as fairground charlatans, there are some very sinister facts beginning to emerge about the spread of cults that have, mafia-like, become engaged on a large scale in drug trafficking, prostitution and murder. And there is evidence that just one of these powerful groups could have been responsible for at least some of the killings for which **David Berkowitz**, the 'Son of Sam' killer, was arrested.

Conclusion
These are just some of the excursions into the macabre and mysterious that I invite you to take in this book; there are many more wild tales to be discovered between its pages. Above all, the sheer bewildering variety of cases will highlight the difficult choices that had to be made in compiling *The Encyclopedia of Occult and Supernatural Murder*.

Brian Lane
London, October 1994

A

'ACID BATH MURDERER', *see* **HAIGH, John George**

ALEXANDER, Harald and Frank   Everybody is entitled to be a little bit crazy – in fact most of us are, it is what makes us interesting. However, nobody would deny that we must stop short of criminal madness; and that, it seems, is what possessed the Alexanders.

It all started in a 'harmless crazy' sort of way, in the 1960s, when the Hamburg-based Alexander family – father Harald, mother Dagmar, elder daughter Marina, twins Petra and Sabine, and son Frank – became attached to a religious cult called the Lorber Society. The sect grew up in Germany around the teachings and preachings of the nineteenth-century wandering cleric and prophet Jacob Lorber and was based on total withdrawal from society and self-sacrifice, coupled with a belief that all non-members were owned by Satan. Before Lorber died in 1864, he passed his wisdom on to a wheelwright named Georg Riehle. When Riehle fell fatally sick, he in turn passed the learning on to his constant companion Harald Alexander, along with the coveted portable organ which accompanied most sect activities. Mrs Alexander fully supported her husband's self-bestowed religious authority, and when their son Frank was born in 1954, Harald anointed him 'Prophet of God', and thenceforth the child's every whim was law.

In his early teens Frank was introduced to sex – not the normal healthy kind of activity with local girls his own age because they, after all, were considered sinful and unclean. Instead, Harald generously gave the boy access to Dagmar, and to the elder daughter Marina too. In fact, Harald not infrequently joined in. There was nothing, it seemed, that the Alexanders would not do for their in-house Holy Prophet. And it might have stayed in the family for a while longer had the younger girls not innocently mentioned the goings-on at home, and had their friends' parents not alerted the Hamburg police.

Prudently, in February 1970, Harald removed his family, Prophet and all, to an apartment in the Calle Jesus Nazareno in Santa Cruz, capital of Tenerife in the Canary Islands. Here life continued much as before, Frank and his sisters supporting the family through a succession of dreary clerking and domestic jobs.

And so it went on, just as in Hamburg, for the following eleven months. Then, on 20 December 1970, Harald and Frank went to collect young Sabine Alexander from her employment as a general housekeeper to a local doctor's family. According to one account they greeted her with the words: 'We wanted you to know at once that Frank and I have just killed your mother and your sisters.' They need not have bothered, the agonised screams of the dying women had forced neighbours to call the police to 37 Calle Jesus Nazareno, and the place was already alive with detectives and forensic experts.

The sight which greeted their horrified eyes will live in their heads for ever. Every inch of the small apartment was dripping with blood – ceiling, walls, floors, all the furniture. Everything belonging to the women had been destroyed, including their bodies. In an orgy of desecration their breasts and vaginal area had been hacked off and nailed to the walls; Dagmar Alexander's heart had been ripped out and impaled on a wooden stake.

Horrifying? Yes, of course it was. But worse was to come. Worst of all was hearing the disgusting Alexanders' crowing of their 'act of cleansing' – of the 'holy time', the 'hour of killing'. It appeared that Frank, the 'Prophet of God', had decided that 20 December was 'the time' and, while Harald struck up some suitable hymns and psalms on the portable organ, he battered his family to death with a heavy coathanger. Then, while the Prophet took his turn at the organ, Harald performed the mutilation, the while shouting the Lord's praises.

It is no surprise that Harald and Frank Alexander were considered too mad even to stand trial – after all, they could never feel guilt at having helped purify the world. And so they were committed to, and remain in, a secure prison for the criminally insane. As for Sabine, the remaining female of the

Alexander clan, she begged to be allowed to suffer alongside her father and brother but was refused. Instead she was placed in the care of a convent, from the walls of which she has never ventured.

ALLAWAY, Thomas Henry On 20 December 1921 an advertisement appeared in *The Morning Post* which would result in one of south-west England's most notorious murder cases. It read:

> LADY COOK, 31, requires post in a school. Experienced in a school with forty boarders. Disengaged. Salary £65. Miss Irene Wilkins, 21 Thirlmere Road, Streatham, London SW16.

The address was where Miss Wilkins, a single lady, lived with her parents, and where she eagerly awaited a reply; she did not have long to wait. At midday on the 22nd, a Thursday, Irene Wilkins received this telegram:

> MORNING POST. Come immediately 4.30 train Waterloo Bournmouth Central. Car will meet train. Expence no object. Urgent. Wood. Beech House.

What Irene could not have guessed as she hurriedly dispatched a telegram of acceptance before leaving home with her few portable belongings in an attaché case, was that there was no such person as 'Wood' and no such place as 'Beech House'. Although her telegram was returned the following day 'Address unknown', it was not until the evening when Mr and Mrs Wilkins read of the discovery of a young woman's body in Bournemouth that they put two and two together and took their fears to the officers at Streatham police station.

It had been at 7.30 on that Friday morning, 23 December, that Charles Nicklen had been on his regular morning stroll around a patch of ground known locally as Fifteen-Acre-Meadow – probably for obvious reasons. Close to the edge of the field Nicklen saw a couple of cows worrying at a bundle on the ground. With little better to occupy him, Charlie Nicklen investigated, and found it was the body of a woman.

By 8.00 a.m. the police had arrived, and at nine o'clock police surgeon Dr Harold Summons was beginning his scene-of-crime examination. Aside from superficial bruising consistent with blows from a clenched fist, Dr Summons concluded that the cause of death had been severe head injuries delivered with a heavy implement such as a hammer. Estimated time of death was between 7.45 and 8.20 the previous evening. Detectives working at the scene determined from the signs of a struggle on the path leading to the field, and a trail of blood, that the victim had been attacked before being dumped in Fifteen-Acre-Meadow. The muddy conditions provided footprints made by both a man's and a woman's shoes and tyre-prints made by Dunlop Magnums. It did not take long for the Bournemouth and the Streatham inquiries to be linked, and Mr and Mrs Wilkins' identification of their daughter's gold watch, engraved with her initials 'IMW', resolved the question of identity. All that remained was to track down the savage killer who had cut short Irene's innocent life.

In the course of investigating the telegram from 'Wood' at Bournemouth officers learned of two similar wires sent from the same location and responding to similar 'appointments wanted' ads. It was their great good fortune that neither of the other recipients of telegrams kept their appointment. In the case of one of these communications the post office clerk who had taken the form over the counter recalled the sender's unusually 'rough' voice, and thought that he might be a chauffeur. Which was more than slightly interesting because officers questioning people who had been on the 4.30 train with Irene Watkins found a man who saw her get into a chauffeur-driven grey Mercedes at the station. This Mr Humphris had thought nothing of the matter at the time, and had not taken a note of the car's registration number. However, by a remarkable coincidence he saw the same man, in the same car, on 4 January 1922. Aware of its significance Frank Humphris took down the number and passed it on to the murder incident room. For reasons of carelessness or misfortune this vital clue was ignored.

However, reports of the 'grey Mercedes' had panicked one local chauffeur sufficiently to cause him to vacate his lodgings at nearby Boscombe with unseemly haste, taking with him for good measure a cheque book belonging to his employer. Thomas Allaway was picked up eight days later in Reading and in his pockets police found

a number of betting slips, the handwriting on which matched the
script on the telegram forms. As if to confirm his guilt, although
Allaway tried to disguise his handwriting when asked by detectives
to write out the text of the telegrams, he proceeded to reproduce
faithfully the 'Bournmouth' and 'expence' of the Wilkins telegram,
as well as other obvious inaccuracies.

On 3 July 1922, Thomas Allaway stood at the Winchester
Assizes before Mr Justice Avory. His alibi that he had been in his
lodgings on the night of the murder and had spoken to his
landlord, was flatly refuted by that gentleman, who said that not
only had he not been in conversation with the prisoner, but that it
would have been impossible as he had been out of the house since
early evening. Also lined up among the ranks of prosecution
witnesses were the three post office clerks and Mr Humphris, all
of whom confirmed their identification of Allaway, and a railway
signalman who had seen him standing at Bournemouth station on
the day of the murder.

Thomas Henry Allaway was convicted of Irene Wilkins' murder, and on 19 August 1922 he was hanged at Winchester after
making a last-minute confession to the prison governor.

Although there was never any suggestion that the cruel murder at
Bournemouth was eventually solved by spiritual intervention,
there was no shortage of offers from mediums and psychics
willing to throw their various talents behind the police effort. One
of the most startling advances was made by a 'sensitive' named
Mrs Charlotte Starkey and published privately under the title *The
Great Bournemouth Mystery*.

A colleague of Mrs Starkey later wrote:

I have a friend who is born Clairvoyant and Psychometrist, and I
repeatedly tried to persuade her to see if she could get anything that
would throw light on the state of darkness existing. I might not have
been so persistent had Mrs S not declared *from the time the murder took
place that she felt the murderer was in Boscombe or its immediate
neighbourhood*. She demurred to my repeated suggestion, saying that as
she had not done any psychic work for several years (having had to give
it up through a prolonged illness) she was not sure such sittings would

prove of value; also pointing out that there was no article left behind by the murderer, and she did not see how she could get in touch with the case unless she could handle *something he had handled*. I suggested getting the originals of the telegrams, and she countered this suggestion by pointing out that these had been handled by so many persons and she would get so many influences that it would be next to impossible to pick out with any degree of certainty the writer of the missives. Readers may wonder what handling an article would have to do with the matter. Well, there is a psychic gift known as Psychometry or Soul reading, and persons who possess this gift can, by handling an article, describe the person to whom such article has belonged, go into his movements, and sometimes (but rarely) get names connected with it. In this particular case it looked as if matters were a bit hopeless owing to this lack of articles and I fully realised the difficulties. However, I got the lady to walk down with me to view the spot where the body was found, and while she stood passively gazing at the place with every sympathy aroused in her for the murdered woman, I began to look around hoping against hope to find some little trifle – if only a bit of cloth that had been left behind. As Sir A. Conan Doyle says, in his *Wanderings of a Spiritualist*: 'A piece of clothing is, as a rule, to a psychometrist what it would be to a bloodhound – the starting point of a chase which runs down its victim.'

All I could find was a quantity of matchsticks; that struck me as strange, for they were all at a rounded corner of the curbing of the path opposite the spot where the body was found. And this would be about the position where the motor car stood that conveyed the body of the murdered woman to the spot. These I carefully collected up – there were about fifty in all – and I noticed that there seemed no signs of matches either up or down the roadway, hence the possibility was that they *might* have been handled by the murderer.

Mrs S had also been busy as she said she had got a vision of a man standing inside the wire fencing near where the cut furze bushes lay. We took the matches home and she placed the little parcel on her pillow – she got influences of three men but could not get one to stand out plainer than another. But she said, 'The man who did the deed has not left Boscombe, he is close by us – and I cannot go further than Fisherman's Walk on one side and Boscombe Gardens on the other.' When I tell you that Allaway stored the car he drove about a hundred yards from our house and that his employer's son where he constantly attended was about 500 yards away, and that Allaway lived within about 500 yards of us, readers will realise how true Mrs S's statement proved to be.

B

BAKER, Stanley Dean It began as a routine traffic violation. There had been a hit-and-run smash between two cars around California's Big Sur area, and Highway Patrol officers had just circulated the description of the two 'long-haired hippy-types' who sped away from the site of the accident. Within the hour two suspects were picked off the street and taken in for questioning. Stanley Dean Baker was twenty-two years old, his buddy Harry Allen Stroup just twenty; both admitted being involved in the hit-and-run. So far a normal everyday misdemeanour, one of a countless number of such humdrum incidents that would waste police time. But soon 13 July 1970 would become a day that the officers involved would not forget in a hurry.

A routine search of Stan Baker's pockets turned up a well-thumbed copy of LaVey's *Satanic Bible* and a human finger bone. This latter was explained by Baker with the disarmingly straightforward statement: 'Yeah, I'm a cannibal.' The devil-worshippers' handbook was also simple to explain. When he had been at college in Wyoming Baker had joined a Satanic cult called the 'Four P Movement' – and he had the tattoos to prove it.

Four P is one of the more notorious groups originally founded in California, but later spreading across the western states via college-campus recruitment. It is alleged that cultists graduated from the sacrifice of animals to the sacrifice of human beings, the blood from which was ritually drunk by participants in the ceremony. Among the better known multiple killers said to have been involved with the Four P are Charles Manson and various members of his 'Family) (see page 166), David Berkowitz, the 'Son of Sam' killer, and Fred Cowan, the Nazi sympathiser whose shooting spree on St Valentine's Day 1977 left five dead in New York State.

And Stanley Dean Baker, of course, who was now claiming to have sacrificed numerous lives at the request of Four P's leader, the 'Grand Chingon'. One he remembered particularly well; it had taken place the previous 20 April, when forty-year-old designer Robert Salem was butchered in his San Francisco apartment. Baker obligingly left his fingerprints on the walls in the victim's blood. And what of that other grisly relic found in Stanley's pocket – the finger bone? That, apparently, had been harvested from a more recent sacrifice up in Montana. Showing no evidence of remorse for his evil ways, Baker considerately gave detectives detailed directions to the isolated spot on the Yellowstone River where James Schlosser's body could be found – or most of it anyway. The unfortunate Schlosser's heart and several more fingers had been removed to provide Stanley and his chum Harry with a light snack.

On 20 July 1971, Stanley Baker and Harry Stroup were convicted by a Montana jury of first-degree murder and ordered to be confined in the state prison. Stroup behaved himself inside and was released in 1979. Baker continued his affair with Satan, and formed a devil-worshipping coven in prison. His behaviour became so disruptive that he was eventually removed to a high-security institution in Illinois. Stan Baker earned parole in 1985 and faded into obscurity until he was found by a journalist six years later living in Minneapolis.

BASHIR, Mohammed   Many tragic and unnecessary deaths are caused in the name of 'religion', and this does not apply solely to offbeat cults such as devil worshippers. One of the most awful cases in recent years was the killing of a young Asian girl while being subjected to exorcism by a Muslim *pir* or holy man, and his assistant.

In the spring of 1991, twenty-year-old Kusor Bashir was depressed; not, it must be said, a momentary fit of despair, but something deeper. It was suggested that her failure to pass her driving test was the final blow. At any rate Kusor's parents, devout Muslims, decided that she had become inhabited by *djinns*

– and that to them was very bad news indeed. These *djinns* – some are good, some bad – are believed by Muslims to be invisible spirits 'created by smokeless flame', and although many in the Asian community have departed from such superstition, even some less orthodox Muslims believe in the *djinns* and in the power of the holy Koran to dispel them. The more fanatical among the religion's believers are convinced that stronger measures are necessary to rid the body and soul of the unwelcome demons. Such believers were Mr and Mrs Bashir.

A jury at Manchester Crown Court in April 1992 heard how the Bashirs had called in the local *pir*, sixty-three-year-old Mohammed Nurani, who in turn introduced his assistant, a 'priest' named Mohammed Bashir (no relation of Kusor Bashir). Between the holy men and the family a decision was made to exorcise Kusor of the *djinn* called John Wayne (yes, really!). Mr Richard Henriques QC, Crown prosecutor, told the court that over the next eight days there took place an orgy of violence. First Nurani visited the family at Oldham and placed Kusor Bashir inside a circle drawn with chalk and forced her to inhale the fumes of burning mustard oil. Then the exorcism got under way. Deprived of food and sleep for the following week, Kusor was repeatedly beaten with heavy sticks and was subjected to having hot chilli powder forced down her throat to expel the *djinn* John Wayne. When the spirit refused to leave quietly, the jury was told, Kusor Bashir was kicked, stamped on and jumped on.

Perhaps that did the trick; perhaps it was the last straw for John Wayne and he fled. We will never know, because after eight days of torture Kusor Bashir died when one of sixteen fractured ribs perforated one of her lungs. When her body was eventually examined by a pathologist he found, apart from the fractured ribs and lung damage, a fractured breastbone, extensive bruising to her arms and legs and lacerations across her face, head and breasts.

Little wonder, then, that the Manchester jury, who had sat horrified by the descriptions of this outrageous ritual, should return a verdict of guilty of murder against the 'holy man' Mohammed Bashir. His spiritual leader, the *pir* Mohammed Nurani was convicted of 'plotting to cause grievous bodily harm'.

They received, respectively, life imprisonment and five years.

Perhaps the saddest epitaph is that Kusor Bashir's family, distraught at her suffering, had repeatedly been told 'the girl is not in pain; it is the *djinn* who feels the pain' – and they had believed it.

BATEMAN, Mary   Until her marriage to John Bateman, Mary had been in service with a number of wealthy families in the area around Leeds and York, and had been summarily dismissed by each of them as soon as the family silver started to disappear.

Bateman, a wheelwright by trade, joined the army in around 1804, and with Mary by his side moved to several bases located around the British Isles. Mary, who had now begun to supplement her stealing with fortune-telling, pursued her own career. One recorded example of Mary's enterprise was this. A large factory in Leeds having burned down, killing a number of its workers and leaving their families destitute, Mrs Bateman set up a 'fund' for their support – collecting money, food and other comforts door-to-door. The cash she pocketed, the goods she sold. The success of this ruse was to prove the incentive to many more scams in the future.

In 1806 she met the Perigo family, William and his wife Rebecca. Poor superstitious Rebecca, frightened out of her wits by the belief that a curse, or 'evil wish', had been laid upon her, readily accepted the services of 'Miss Blythe', a non-existent wise-woman who, through Mary Bateman, promised to lift the curse. Having swindled the Perigos out of most of their money and possessions in return for this bogus occult protection service, Mary prepared for them, in the name of Miss Blythe, a special pudding, after eating which William Perigo became very ill, and Rebecca died.

Mary Bateman, known as the 'Yorkshire Witch', was put on trial at York Castle on 17 March 1809. She was convicted and sentenced to death, and, in a final irony, when Mary was cut down from the gallows her skin was flayed from her body and sold as good-luck charms.

There exists a transcript of Mary Bateman's trial which, long-winded as it is, highlights not only Mary's wickedness, but also the almost unbelievable gullibility of the Perigos: 'Credulity and vice were Mary's best friends.'

'Miss Blythe,' through Mary Bateman, sent William Perigo a number of letters during 1806–7 making demands of either money or goods – for example, around the middle of October 1806, she wrote:

My dear friend,
You must go down to Mary Bateman's at Leeds on Tuesday next and carry two guinea notes with you and give her them, and she will give you other two that I have sent to her from Scarbro'; and you must buy me a small cheese about 6 or 8 pound weight, and it must be of your buying, for it is of particular use, and it is to be carried down to Mary Bateman's and she will send it to me by coach – this letter is to be burnt when you have done reading it.

These 'requests' arrived at the rate of about one every two weeks, and insisted that William send various articles of furniture, clothing, food and other property or money to Bateman. The following list accounts for the greater part of what the Perigos parted with between December 1806 and the beginning of April 1807:

1 Goose
2 pairs of Men's Shoes
A Goose Pie
A Tea Caddy
Several Shirts
A Counterpane
A piece of Woollen-cloth
A Silk Handkerchief
A Silk Shawl
A light-coloured Gown Skirt
A light-coloured Cotton Gown
2 Pillow-slips
A new Waistcoat
60 pounds of Butter
7 strokes of Meal
6 strokes of Malt

A quantity of Tea and Sugar
2 or 3 hundred Eggs
A pair of Worsted Stockings
A pair of new Shoes
A pair of black Silk Stockings
3 yards of Knaresboro' Linen-cloth
10 stones of Malt
A piece of Beef
3 bottles of Spirits
2 Tablecloths
2 Barrels
2 Napkins

In addition Perigo paid Mary various amounts of money adding up to about £70 – a small fortune in 1807.

Later, in April of that year, the screw was turned even tighter when Mary Bateman needed a new bed:

My dear friends,
I will be obliged to you if you will buy me a camp bedstead, bed and bedding, blanket, a pair of sheets; and a long bolster must come from your house – you need not buy the best feathers, common ones will do – I have lain on the floor for three nights, and I cannot lay on my own bed, owing to the planets being so bad concerning your wife. And I must have one of your buying or it will not do: you must bring down the china, the sugar and the caddy, the three silver spoons and the tea at the same time, when you buy the bed, pack them all up together – my brother's boat will be up in a day or two, and I will order my boatman to call for them all at Mary Bateman's. And you must give Mary Bateman one shilling for the boatman, and I will place it to your account. Your wife must burn this as soon as it is read, or it will not do.

At the end of the month Mary delivered Miss Blythe's final letter:

My dear friend,
I am sorry to tell you that you will take an illness in the month of May, either one or both of you, but I think both. But the work of God must have its course. You will escape the chambers of the grave and though you seem to be dead, yet you will live. Your wife must take half a

pound of honey to Mary Bateman, and it must remain there until you go down yourself, and she will put in such-like stuff as I have sent from Scarborough to her. You must eat pudding for six days, and you must put in it such stuff as I have sent to Mary Bateman, and she will give your wife it, but you must not begin to eat of this pudding until I let you know . . .

This, of course, was the pudding which robbed poor Rebecca Perigo of her life and nearly put paid to William; the 'such-like stuff sent from Scarborough' was mercuric chloride.

BEECHOOK, Mirella   At 4.20 on the afternoon of Wednesday 18 September 1985, Lynn Kavanagh gave her daughter one final warning not to talk to strangers. Then she watched as four-year-old Stacey went out to play in the central area between the blocks of flats on the Swan Lane housing estate in Rotherhithe, south-east London. Mrs Kavanagh had been particularly vigilant since reading reports of the savage killing of little Leoni Keating who had been abducted from a caravan site at Great Yarmouth just the previous Friday.

Two hours later Mrs Kavanagh opened her front door in response to an urgent knocking. Outside she found twenty-five-year-old Mirella Beechook looking very agitated and clutching one of Stacey's shoes. Lynn Kavanagh knew Mrs Beechook as a resident of one of the neighbouring blocks on the estate; in fact her daughter Tina was Stacey's best friend. Barely able to speak through her anguish, Mrs Beechook said that Stacey had been round and she had taken both the girls with her to the local shops. She had gone to make some purchases in one shop, and when she came out Mirella Beechook found the children had gone. Assuming they had become bored and gone back home she returned to the flats in Rotherhithe Street; the girls were not there. On the way back to the shops, she said, she had found Stacey's red shoe.

Not surprisingly, both mothers imagined the worst; and when they heard, the whole estate shared their obvious fears. Within the hour friends and neighbours were organising themselves into search parties to comb the immediate area. With increasing desperation the boundaries of the search widened to the nearby

Thames dockland, and the loyal local searchers were soon joined by specialist teams of police officers equipped with helicopters and tracker dogs. It was just before midnight that one of those dogs confirmed everybody's worst fears. Beneath a thin covering of leaves behind some undergrowth in Southwark Park lay the body of poor Stacey Kavanagh; she had been strangled.

The hunt was now on for seven-year-old Tina Beechook, and nobody that dark night could feel much optimism. By dawn even Detective Chief Superintendent Roy Gregg of Scotland Yard was saying: 'Every minute that passes makes me more anxious about Tina. I must be drawn to the conclusion that some harm has come to her.' Mr Gregg also noted that: 'It could have been someone who was known to the children.'

Later that same day, a distressed Mirella Beechook tearfully appealed on television that whoever had abducted Tina: 'Leave her somewhere that she can find her way home.'

By Saturday, less than three days after Stacey Kavanagh's body had been found, detectives had compiled a dossier on Mirella Beechook. Born on the island of Mauritius, she had already absorbed much of her family's obsession with voodoo and its practices before she arrived in England in 1974 at the age of fourteen. Indeed, Mirella still adhered to the off-shoot cult of Gris-Gris while living in London, and her flat was practically a temple to such gods as Baron Samedi, Lord of the Graveyard, Doctor of Death. In 1977 she married Ravi Beechook who, having made her pregnant with Tina, wandered off, returning occasionally to the flat in Rotherhithe for 'company'. During one of these periods Mirella became pregnant again; in October 1979 Sabrina was born.

Now, it may just be a piece of wild imagination, but Ravi was convinced all the while that his estranged wife was trying to bewitch him. Perhaps it was the occasional effigy stuck with nails and pins that was left on the doorstep; or his photograph with a needle piercing the head. This behaviour, Ravi supposed, was some form of revenge against him for not returning home.

But if this was sinister, there was worse to come. Less than a month after her birth, baby Sabrina was back in hospital with stomach trouble. After one of Mirella's visits, nurses became worried about the infant's drowsiness; they became even more worried when they found a sleeping pill under Sabrina's cot. An urgent blood test revealed a dangerously high level of the drug Mogadon. The result was that Mirella Beechook was examined by a psychiatrist before being put on trial. Although the expert advice was that Mirella was not seriously mentally ill (she had insisted that the voodoo curse of the evil eye had caused her to harm her baby), she was not imprisoned or referred to a psychiatric hospital, but simply put on probation. Tina and Sabrina were placed in local authority care; Sabrina was subsequently adopted and in 1980 Tina was allowed back to her mother.

Five years later Mirella Beechook was convicted of shoplifting and sentenced to three months' imprisonment. Shortly after her release she was again arrested for shoplifting. Less than a week afterwards, while Mirella was still awaiting trial, Stacey Kavanagh was murdered.

All this the police now knew, so it is with little surprise that on the morning of 21 September we find plainclothes detectives keeping a close watch on number 7 Sandwich House, the home of Mirella Beechook. From their position they saw the arrival of Ravi, the errant husband. They saw him knock on the door, talk briefly with his wife and then accompany her on a walk in the central square. Then they saw Ravi turn and run back towards the flat. At this point the officers intercepted him. With almost uncontrollable anger and distress, Ravi told them what his wife had just said – that Tina was dead; that she, her own mother, had strangled her . . .

It was true. When both Ravi and Mirella Beechook had been secured, investigating officers entered the flat and found the body of little Tina, tied up in a bag and stored under her mother's bed.

When she appeared before Sir James Miskin, the Recorder of London, at the Central Criminal Court in June 1986, Mirella Beechook entered a plea of diminished responsibility. Once again she blamed the 'voices' for telling her to kill, but the jury would have none of it. When they returned from their deliberations, the seven men and five women had decided that Mirella Beechook was guilty not of manslaughter (the diminished responsibility verdict), but of murder. It was a decision entirely supported by the judge for, in sentencing Mirella Beechook to two life sentences, he observed that although she could not have been acting normally at the time, her mental disorder did not amount to diminished responsibility.

BEESON, Joseph, and **BENNETT, Edward**   Just read these few lines – a fragment from a song composed by a young man named Bennett, Ed Bennett:

Death is rising through the air as thunderbolts strike;
Blood is dripping from the walls, someone's gonna die;
You hear screams of pain and agony as children are nailed on crosses.
Kill 'em, let's kill 'em dead.

Not, you might think, the poetry of an average eighteen-year-old. Funny thing was, Ed was just about everybody's idea of the average, wholesome eighteen-year-old – a former boy scout and Little Leaguer, he was an enthusiastic Mormon. And if he had never been too brilliant at school, Ed Bennett had a good reason. At the age of fourteen he was diagnosed dyslexic and enrolled at a special school. This was the point at which fate, Ed's personal kismet, took over. To no great surprise, the trickle of public funds ran dry and progressive projects like Ed Bennett's special school closed down on him after the first year. Bewildered by this apparent betrayal, Ed dropped out of the education system altogether. For a while, a very short while, he worked on a mink farm, but quit when he learned the animals were being turned into fur coats. That's the kind of boy Ed was; until around the beginning of 1987 when his chum Lewis Ivey introduced him to Joe Beeson.

Joseph's background was everything that Ed's was not. Joe was what you might call, without much fear of contradiction in his home town of American Fork, bad . . . At age eleven he was taken into custody after stealing from a shop. Six years later he had committed just about every petty crime in the book and been committed to just about every juvenile detention institution in the area. He had also picked up along the way a fascination for Nazism and black magic. Not bad for a seventeen-year-old. Worse was to come.

It was 1987, then, and Edward Bennett had been introduced to Joseph Beeson by their mutual friend Lewis Ivey. One of the first things they did was throw together a rock band, Rigor Mortis – with Ed writing those memorable lyrics under the sobriquet 'Eddie the Rotting Corpse': 'Kill 'em, kill 'em dead.' All in good time . . .

About now Beeson and Bennett had officially joined a bunch of pseudo-Satanists practising in the derelict buildings that once were host to the aspirations of the Brigham Young University. Kids' stuff really – drugs, booze, heavy-metal music and, to be devastatingly grown-up, the ritual sacrifice of a few small animals. So far, strictly high-school naughty.

Then the police got interested. Not in the mumbo-jumbo, the Satanic graffiti and the chicken blood, but in the amount of drugs that was circulating in this small community. The police might never have guessed, had it not been for one of the cult tipping them off. Anyway, Joe Beeson and Ed Bennett were in the frame, arrested, charged, and bailed to appear in court.

But Joe and Ed were too far down the road to self-destruction now, and not caring very much who they dragged into the pit with them. The first stop in their flight from justice was Las Vegas, where they held up a convenience store, killing the till-girl and wounding a customer. Then, presumably thinking their trail had cooled, the amateur Satanists drove back into Utah and met up with their fellow chicken-stranglers. Of course, Joe and Ed wanted to boast. Of course they did – they'd killed somebody! Sure, it was only a defenceless twenty-one-year-old girl behind a corner-store counter, but what the hell, all Satanists had to start somewhere.

The man's name, so I am told, was Jeff Chandler. He had informed on Satan's drug cult once before, which is why Joe and Ed had to flee. Now he had squealed again. And Joseph Beeson and Edward Bennett were back in custody again.

The trial of Beeson and Bennett was neither lengthy nor memorable. The result, however, restored faith for a few people trying to live their modest lives in the state of Utah. In June 1988, Joseph Beeson pleaded guilty to murder and attempted murder, and was given two life sentences. In 1990 he proved too unpleasant even for the inmates of the Utah state prison at Ely – they stabbed him to death. Edward Bennett was sentenced to be executed, and waits his turn on Death Row.

BELCHER, Terry, and **McINTYRE, Robert** In the early hours of the morning of 26 January 1988, highway patrolmen pulled over a van which had jumped a stop sign outside Gonzales, Louisiana. The vehicle was carrying Georgia registration plates, and the driver, sixteen-year-old Terry Belcher, told officers that he and his passengers – Robert McIntyre, also sixteen, and seventeen-year-old Malisa Earnest – were out of Douglasville and heading for New Orleans on vacation. A routine computer check on the car, however, rather spoiled that story – the vehicle had been reported stolen, by Bob McIntyre's parents.

So far just the average sort of mischief that teenage kids get into, and the patrolmen were probably thinking it was better they stole the van from their own folks rather than a stranger. Back at the station the three youngsters were held pending contacting parents.

Later that day Malisa Earnest's cell-mate, who had been overnighting after being picked up on a loitering charge, asked to see a detective. Malisa, she told him, had spent the morning rambling on about devil worship and human sacrifice and a murder back at Douglasville. Malisa's story was that she and another girl (later identified as Theresa Simmons) had hitched a lift with Belcher and McIntyre and ended up in an abandoned house where they all drank a little booze and smoked a bit of weed. High on both, the boys started yelling the praises of Satan – as such kids are not unknown to do. It was only when McIntyre and Belcher decided to offer up Theresa as a blood sacrifice that Malisa began to worry. According to her, they buried Theresa Simmons in some woods.

Whatever the truth or fantasy of Malisa Earnest's tale of devilry, the police at Gonzales, La, decided to call through to the police at Douglasville, Ga, and check on their three 'guests'. And what they learned was most enlightening. It seemed that Malisa had recently absconded from a home for disturbed juveniles with her friend, seventeen-year-old Theresa Simmons. On 22 January one of Theresa's friends received a telephone call from her saying that they had met up with these two weird boys. She had not been heard from since.

The two weird boys, clearly Belcher and McIntyre, were transferred to Atlanta and the interviewing skills of the Georgia police force. While Bob McIntyre had little enough to say for himself, Terry Belcher was unstoppable in his praise for the Prince of Darkness. Of course he was a Satanist! He had joined a proper devil-worship cult the previous year and had dedicated himself to a study of the dark powers. He also went in for sacrifices – nothing big to start, a few small birds and animals – and blood-drinking; just the average Satanist behaviour. But having recruited Bob McIntyre to his 'coven' and ensnared Malisa Earnest, Terry decided to go for the big one – for 'full power'. Yeah, OK, Malisa was persuaded to bring Theresa along with them, and then they killed her. Apparently the three drug-crazed children of Lucifer took it in turn to strangle her with a leather thong; then after appropriate prayers lifted from a copy of the ubiquitous *Satanic Bible*, they buried Theresa Simmons' body in the scrub behind the house.

Belcher, McIntyre and Malisa Earnest were jointly charged with first-degree murder. Belcher lectured the court on the pleasures and profits of Satanism and was sentenced to life. McIntyre – with ironically, his friend Terry as chief prosecution witness – also picked up a life sentence. As for Malisa, she was found guilty of being an accessory and given the relatively lenient sentence of three years.

BERGAMINI, Joseph With a loud cry of 'Don't worry, I won't die, Satan', twenty-three-year-old Joe Bergamini stabbed his mother to death and badly wounded his father with the same kitchen knife. The date was 22 November 1990, Thanksgiving Day, and neighbours were alerted by Kathleen Bergamini's agonised screams coming from the family home at Ozone Park, in the Queens district of New York. Arrested by police close to the scene of his matricide, Bergamini refused to respond when charged with murder and assault.

Joseph Guadagno, whose family occupied the apartment above the Bergaminis, told the press later how he and his wife had been watching the Thanksgiving parade on television when they became aware of an increasingly heated row in the flat below: 'There was a lot of screaming . . . Somebody said "Stop it! Stop it!" Then I heard "Don't do it!" Then I heard Joseph yell "Don't worry, I won't die, Satan".' Moments later the Bergaminis' twenty-five-year-old daughter was pounding on the door sobbing that her parents had been stabbed.

Although Arthur and Kathleen Bergamini were respected locally as friendly, helpful people, Joseph had always been a bit on the peculiar side – 'erratic' was how some neighbours described him – and there were regular disagreements with his parents over his not coming home until the early hours of the morning. One close neighbour recalled that Joe was in the habit of attacking his nineteen-year-old brother Michael, sometimes violently, and described him as 'a bit abnormal'. To find out quite how abnormal Joe Bergamini's head is, and quite how his apparent dialogue with the Prince of the Darkness helped lead to his awful crime, we can only await the verdict of the psychiatrists.

BERKOWITZ, David It was only when they found the letter addressed to the New York Police Department that detectives realised that they were dealing with worse than an ordinarily weird killer. Up to that point he was just another serial slayer leading the NYPD a merry dance and putting the city into a state of terror. The letter read, in part:

> I am deeply hurt by your calling me a wemon [woman]-hater. I am not. But I am a monster . . . I love to hunt. Prowling the street looking for fair game – tasty meat. The wemon of Queens are prettyist [prettiest] of all . . . I live for the hunt – my life. Blood for Papa . . . I say goodbye and goodnight. Police: Let me haunt you with these words: I'll be back! I'll be back! To be interpreted as – Bang Bang Bang Bang Bang – Ugh!! Yours in murder,
>
> Mr Monster

There were also rambling references to blood-drinking and cannibalism; and the writer referred to himself variously as 'Beelzebub' and the 'Chubby Behemoth'. The hand-scribbled letter had been left in an envelope at the scene of Mr Monster's sixth attack, the fatal shooting of Valentina Suriani and Alexander Esau – killed as they sat in their car in the Bronx. The pattern was becoming dreadfully familiar.

The terror had begun at one o'clock on the morning of 29 July 1976, as Donna Lauria, a young medical technician, and her friend, Jody Valente, a student nurse, were sitting in their car outside Donna's home in the Bronx. As they were talking a man walked calmly out of the darkness, took a gun from a brown paper bag and started shooting; he left Donna dead and Jody with a thigh wound. On 23 October of the same year, Carl Denaro and Rosemary Keenan were shot at and wounded as they sat in their car outside a bar in Queens and then, at midnight on 27 November, Donna DeMasi and Joanne Lomino were shot and wounded while sitting on the steps outside Joanne's home in the same district.

By now ballistics experts were working on bullet-mark comparisons, and the result of their tests established that all three attacks had been carried out with the same .44 Bulldog – giving the murderer the provisional name 'The .44 Killer'. Then on 30 January 1977, another couple, John Diel and Christine Freund, were fired on in their car in Queens – the bullets killed Christine but left her companion unharmed. Further senseless, random attacks were made on 8 March when nineteen-year-old student Virginia Voskerichian was shot dead in the street, and on 14 April when Valentina Suriani and Alexander Esau were killed. And now the 'Chubby Behemoth' was taunting them.

Aside from the letter found by members of the 'Operation Omega' team formed to investigate the series of killings, he also wrote a letter to New York *Daily News* columnist Jimmy Breslin on 1 June. He concluded his letter: '. . . Not knowing what the future holds I shall say farewell and I will see you at the next job? Or should I say you will see my handiwork at the next job? Remember Ms Lauria. In their blood and from the gutter, "Sam's Creation" .44.'

'Sam's Creation'? Now the *Daily News* had a new name for the killer, 'Son of Sam'. Breslin, through his column, replied to the letter goading the killer into making another move; it was a dangerous game, and there were still more attacks and one death to come. The first, on 26 June, was in Queens, where Salvatore Lupo and Judith Placido were wounded while they sat in a car. Then on 31 July Stacey Moskowitz and Robert Violante became Son of Sam's last victims; shot in their car, twenty-year-old Stacey died in hospital, Robert Violante was blinded.

But like many before him, the mystery killer known as Son of Sam had made his one big mistake. While he was at the last shooting he left his yellow Ford Galaxie blocking a fire hydrant, and was given a traffic violation ticket. When he returned to the car he took the ticket off the window and threw it in the gutter – a gesture of defiance which was seen by a passing motorist. She might have thought no more of it had she not seen the young man later while she was out walking her dog; this time he was carrying something up his sleeve that looked as though it might be a gun. When the police were informed, they ran a check on the car that the ticket had been issued to and came up with the name David Berkowitz, resident in the suburb of Yonkers. When police found his car there was a loaded .44 pistol on the seat, so they settled down to wait until Berkowitz came out of his apartment to claim it. Now confronted by armed officers, Berkowitz was taken from the car and asked, 'Who are you?' 'I'm Sam,' he replied. David Berkowitz went quietly to the police station where he made a full confession. It was all very much of an anti-climax, with the pudgy twenty-four-year-old cutting a most unlikely figure as a dangerous multicide.

David Berkowitz had been born in June 1953, and had suffered the kind of deprivation, rejection and insecurity shared by many multiple killers. As his paranoia grew over the years he began to entertain the notion that women despised him and thought him ugly. In 1974, so he later claimed, Berkowitz became aware of 'the voices' as he lay in the darkness of his squalid apartment; the voices were telling him to kill. When police searched the Yonkers flat after his arrest, they found the walls covered with scribbled messages such as 'Kill for My Master' – a sinister clue to

Berkowitz's involvement in Satanism.

The origin of the name 'Sam's Creation' seems to have been Berkowitz's neighbour Sam Carr, whose black labrador, Harvey, kept Berkowitz awake at night with its barking. Worse still, so Berkowitz later claimed, the dog was possessed by demons, which the creature sent into his head ordering him to kill. He began sending a series of hate letters to Carr, and in April 1977 Berkowitz shot and wounded the dog; it had been his intention to kill Harvey, but apparently the demons spoiled his aim.

An obvious paranoid schizophrenic, Berkowitz was thought sane enough to stand trial, though that process was pre-empted by his pleading guilty. On 23 August 1977, he was sentenced to 365 years, which he serves at the Attica correctional facility. On 10 July 1979, Berkowitz was attacked in prison and his throat slashed with a razor. Although the wound required fifty-six stitches he refused to name his assailant, but hinted that it was connected with an occult group with which he had once had dealings, and whose members were trying to silence him.

Then, from his prison cell, David Berkowitz began to send out letters elaborating on his membership of a killer cult which was responsible for some of the Son of Sam murders. One, dated October 1979 reads, in part:

> I don't really know how to begin this letter, but at one time I was a member of an occult group. Being sworn to secrecy or face death I cannot reveal the name of the group, nor do I wish to. This group contained a mixture of satanic practices which included the teachings of Aleister Crowley and Eliphas Levi. It was (still is) totally blood orientated and I am certain you know just what I mean. The Coven's doctrines are a blend of Druidism, the teachings of the Secret Order of the Golden Dawn, Black Magick and a host of other unlawful and obnoxious practices.
>
> As I have said, I have no interest in revealing the Coven, especially because I have almost met sudden death on several occasions (once by half an inch) and several others have already perished under mysterious circumstances. These people will stop at nothing, including murder. They have no fear of man-made laws or the Ten Commandments.

Ironically, two of Sam Carr's sons, John and Michael, were members of the same group. There is some evidence for the fact that the Son of Sam killings were the work of more than one person when one looks at the witness statements describing a tall, thin man with long fair hair – almost the exact opposite of the black-haired 'Chubby Behemoth'. In fact the former description fits John 'Wheaties' Carr almost perfectly.

One person who noticed these inconsistencies very early in the case was New York journalist Maury Terry, for whom the pursuit of the occult involvement in the Son of Sam killings became little short of obsessional. Terry's extensive study, *The Ultimate Evil* (Doubleday, New York, 1987), is too complex to précis here, but there is little doubt that the series of murders for which David Berkowitz has been held solely responsible, is far wider reaching in its occult implications than the official version credits. In particular, Maury Terry warns that the so-called 'Twenty-two Disciples of Hell' of which Berkowitz and the two Carr brothers (both now dead in mysterious circumstances) were members, still exists. Terry concludes his book with a list of recent cases which seems to indicate that they are still actively killing.

BOOHER, Vernon   It was around 8.30 on the evening of 9 July 1928 and Harley Heaslip, a prominent physician in Mannville, Alberta, was just settling down to relax when he received a telephone call from twenty-one-year-old Vernon Booher, the younger son of a local farmer, pleading with him to come quickly because, he said, 'something terrible has happened'. Dr Heaslip drove out to the farm and met Vernon Booher outside the house, the wretched youth trembling and gibbering that 'murder has been done'. Booher said that a little while earlier he had gone to the house to investigate the sound of gunshots and found his mother and brother dead.

When they entered the house, they first found the body of Mrs Eunice Booher, still sitting in a chair in the living room, looking for all the world as though she was just having a nap, until they saw the head wounds. In the kitchen lay the corpse of the elder Booher son, Frederick, who had also been shot in the head. The body of a hired hand, Gabriel Goromby, was discovered in an outhouse; he had been shot twice through the head and once in the chest. Later that same night, when the Royal Canadian Mounted Police had become involved, Vernon Booher remembered that another hired man, Bill Rosyk, was 'missing'. At Vernon's suggestion, a search was made of the barn and Rosyk's body was found; he had died from gunshot wounds to the head and stomach.

Ballistics experts soon confirmed that all four victims had been shot with a .303 rifle, and RCMP crime-files were able to add that just such a weapon had been stolen from Charles Stephenson's nearby farm on the previous Sunday. It was also recalled that Vernon Booher had been hanging around the same farm at the same time. On 17 July, a little more than a week after the massacre, the police felt confident enough to arrest Booher and charge him with the murders.

Up to this point it had been a fairly routine, if somewhat gruesome and apparently motiveless murder. The matter of the motive was eventually solved by one of those exercises in dogged questioning and analysis without which few police forces would be able to function. Constable Frederick Olsen, attached to the Alberta Division of the RCMP, had been detailed to look into the background of the Booher boy; and what he learned explained a lot. It appeared that Vernon had been intending to marry a girl, the daughter of a local farmer, of whom his mother did not approve; indeed, Mrs Booher made her dislike so obvious that the unhappy girl, unable to cope, broke off their engagement. Vern had not been pleased. So, according to officer Olsen's reasoning, Eunice Booher had been the prime target, brother Fred and the two hired hands had simply been 'silenced'. The only thing missing was the murder weapon, the one piece of evidence which might provide the tangible clues that would put Vernon Booher's head in a noose.

But if it had been the patient research of Constable Olsen which provided the motive, it was the sharp mind of Inspector Hancock which led indirectly to the .303 rifle. Hancock had read in his local paper that a certain Dr Maximilien Langsner, a psychic originally from Vienna now living in Vancouver, had successfully helped the police there to identify a burglar by using telepathy. Prepared to try anything once, Inspector Hancock invited Dr Langsner to Edmonton. Two days later, the psychic and the suspect faced each other in a cell at the Alberta Provincial Police headquarters. It was some hours before Langsner penetrated the mind of Vernon Booher, but when he did it was with quite spectacular results. 'The object you are seeking [the rifle],' Langsner told Inspector Hancock, 'will be found in a clump of bushes, a few hundred feet from the house,' and he proceeded to make a diagram of the bushes and trees around the farm yard. And there, as the psychic had predicted, Hancock found the murder weapon. The rifle was shown to Booher in his cell, and he obligingly confessed.

Vernon Booher stood trial at the Supreme Criminal Court of Alberta on 24 September 1928, where his counsel fought to have the confession ruled out on the grounds that he had been hypnotised by Dr Langsner at the time, and on this point the judge ruled in favour of the defence. However, the evidence was still enough to persuade the jury to return a verdict of guilty, and for Chief Justice Simmons to sentence him to death.

On appeal, Booher was granted a new trial on technical grounds, and his second trial opened on 21 January 1929 before Mr Justice Walsh. In the main it followed the pattern of the earlier trial with additional evidence from the Warden of Alberta Jail who testified that Booher had admitted his guilt to him in the previous September, before the trial began. There could be no objection that this statement had been made under hypnotic influence, and following a five-hour retirement, the jury again found Booher guilty and again he was sentenced to death. Vernon Booher was hanged in Fort Saskatchewan Jail on 29 April 1929.

BOSEGGIA, Lina, *et al.*   What happened to Serge Boseggia was a mystery. He vanished into thin air on 31 December 1962, and the police were unable to find any trace of him. A wealthy man, Boseggia could have paid to engineer his own disappearance to any part of the world had he been so inclined. As it was, the official line was that the tycoon had 'fallen into a deep hole'.

He left a beautiful wife, Lina, and two teenaged sons. The boys grew up, left home, got married. Lina stayed alone at the family's elegant villa in an exclusive suburb of Milan. By January 1981 it seemed pretty unlikely that her husband was coming home, and Lina had him declared legally dead. She thus became absolute owner of the estate.

And there the matter would have rested. But one day in June 1986 Lina Boseggia got into her Lancia sports car, drove the hundred-odd miles to Verona, parked near the Porta Nuova, and threaded her way through the streets to the salon of Elisa Veronese, the fortune-teller. It was a consultation Elisa would never forget. When she looked into her crystal ball she saw blood; she saw a heavy blade, an axe, cleaving the skull of a dapper dark-haired man. She saw murder.

Far from seeming perturbed, the stylish woman sitting opposite her appeared satisfied, even vindicated; she paid her fee, and left. The astounded Elisa threw off her fortune-teller's gown and ran out into the street. Her client was just rounding the corner.

Nothing in Elisa Veronese's forty-seven years prepared her for what she found herself doing next. She stalked the mysterious woman across the city; witnessed her drive off in a car registered in Milan, and noted its licence number, MI 268-47; went home, packed her overnight case, and took the train to Milan. There she called at the Automobile Club, saying she had run into the Lancia while it was parked, and wanted to contact the owner. The obliging young clerk wrote down the crucial details: Lina Boseggia, 8 via Palmanova.

It was Elisa's instinct to go to the police, but what would she tell them? They would never take her seriously. Instead, she took a cab to via Palmanova, and rang at the door of a house across the road from number 8. She used to have a friend who lived there, she improvised; did they remember her? Emma Venturini invited her in, and told Elisa what she was beginning to suspect. Signor Boseggia had disappeared twenty years ago.

Now, our amateur sleuth felt confident, there was something to put before the police. And Inspector Lino Mantinelli took what she had to say very seriously. Seriously enough to apply for a search warrant for the grounds of the villa, where the metal detector picked up something rather substantial a few feet under the surface. It was the blade of an axe, which shared its resting place with the bones of the man it had killed.

It didn't take long to put the story together. While Serge Boseggia was drunk after a New Year's Eve party, his wife and sons took the opportunity to rid themselves of the tight-fisted, overbearing man. Lina, Damiano and Dario each took one swing of the axe; and a quarter of a century later, on 15 May 1987, they were each sent down for twenty years.

BOSTOCK, Paul   Paul Bostock once wrote to a girlfriend: 'I am an animal who should never walk the streets again.' The letter was sent from prison, and it is mercifully unlikely that it will ever be felt safe to release its writer.

In June 1986, Bostock, a body-building fanatic whose time was mostly spent worshipping Satan and studying the occult, was arrested after a particularly savage sexual attack on a young nurse; she had been stabbed thirty times. It was only under police questioning that Bostock revealed that he was a *double* killer.

The first murder, which followed another sadistic sexual assault, had taken place slightly less than two years previously – when Paul Bostock was only sixteen years old. The victim had been bound and gagged and repeatedly stabbed; her body was left just outside Leicester along with a sheet of paper scribbled with what were described as 'occult' drawings. For almost twelve months, Bostock made regular pilgrimages to his victim's grave, and it was on one of these macabre trips that he encountered, and killed, the second woman. This time, however, he was seen and shortly afterwards taken into custody, when a notebook removed from his Leicester home gave ample evidence of his involvement both in black magic and the earlier unsolved murder.

'BOSTON STRANGLER', *see* **DE SALVO, Albert**

BOUCK, Claude and Nicole   It was every parent's nightmare; a child who just seems to vanish into thin air.

Michel and Denise Devilet had arrived at the Belgian seaside town of Coxyde with their three children, Frédéric, Michel and Christel, on the evening of 7 August 1987. The following morning Christel, an independent nine-year-old, left her two brothers and set off alone to explore the attractions of the promenade. She was last seen by Frédéric and Michel at the entrance to the Luna Park amusements – she was talking with a fat woman. Now it was late evening and Christel had not returned. Despite extensive police inquiries around the resort's entertainment spots and a painstaking local hunt by search teams, there was no clue to the child's whereabouts. Except for the fat lady.

There were no developments for a seemingly endless six days. Then the Coxyde police received a telephone call from their counterparts in Dunkirk, across the border in France. Christel Devilet's body had been found floating in the Canal de Bourbourg. A medical examination of the terribly mutilated remains offered the real possibility that Christel had been raped and ritually tortured to death – a missing child inquiry had become a murder case, of a particularly horrific kind. The full autopsy report listed numerous cuts and burns, often of a design and configuration suggesting an occult significance. It also seemed that a small fire had been lit on her abdomen, indicating that the victim had been used as an altar in some form of black mass.

Meanwhile the police at Dunkirk had estimated, from the length of time the body had been in the water and the strength of the current, just about where Christel Devilet had been put into the canal. It was here that they ran into a piece of much-needed good luck. A man had been walking his dog along the towpath at this point on the previous Saturday night – the night Christel was killed – and he had noticed a white Peugeot car with a Belgian number plate. This information was relayed back to Coxyde, and an immediate trace revealed that twenty-nine white Peugeots had been locally registered. By a process of logical elimination, this list was reduced to four.

One of the registered owners on this shortlist was thirty-five-year-old Claude Bouck; but it was not Claude who attracted the eye of the police, it was his wife Nicole. Nicole was a rather fat lady.

A search of the Boucks' home revealed a basement temple-cum-torture-chamber, equipped to carry out just such infamous treatment as that suffered by their human sacrifice Christel Devilet. Besides, traces of blood matching Christel's group were found on the floor of the cellar. Although they initially denied having anything to do with the killing, Claude and Nicole Bouck finally confessed – though without much remorse. After all, they pointed out to the police, they were Satanists, and that's what Satanists do!

It was not an explanation that satisfied the court, and without hesitation the Boucks were sent to prison for life.

BRADY, Phoebe and Verren, and **HARMSWORTH, Michael**
The body was found on a desolate, treeless moor on the road from Cork to Dublin, buried in a shallow grave. So shallow that one foot protruded above ground, which is what had caught the attention of passing motorist Thomas Gilligan, on the morning of 23 December 1979. The Homicide Squad was alerted, and the body taken down to the morgue where the extent of the injuries became apparent. The man had been gagged and bound, beaten with a dog whip on the back and buttocks, and with iron bars on the chest and head, fracturing his skull, smashing his face and rib cage, rupturing several of the vital organs; his testicles were bruised. He was thirty-six years old, and his name was Eric Willmot.

Willmot had been a tinker who etched a living at the fairs and markets, which is where he had come under the spell of Phoebe Brady in 1973. He had gone to her caravan to have his fortune told, fell for her stunning good looks, and ended up in her bed. A bit of casual fun for the tinker, perhaps, but not for the High Priestess of the Devil Worshippers, the title Phoebe Brady had inherited on the death of her mother. She ruled a sect of twenty or thirty members, who put into practice the laws she ordained. And one of those laws was that having slept with her, Eric Willmot had to wed her.

He did so unwillingly, 'with the sanction of the Devil and beneath an arch of crossed clubs', and received a wedding ring from Phoebe for his troubles. The honeymoon was an extended sojourn in Phoebe's bed, an exhausting effort to satisfy her lusty appetite.

Over the years Willmot tried to run away a number of times – as had his several predecessors – only to be returned to the fold with a good beating for his pains. On the last occasion, six months before the murder, he had sustained a broken arm and three cracked ribs.

Wisely, Willmot planned to make good his escape. Unwisely, he spread it around the bars in Cork that he was saving his money, was emigrating to Canada, and had sold the wedding ring. That last indiscretion was a heinous offence against the sanctity of the Devil Worshippers, and Phoebe Brady was compelled to take appropriate action. For this she enlisted the aid of a bland petty criminal by the name of Michael Harmsworth, a thirty-five-year-old with the strength of a bull. Four hundred pounds up front, another four hundred for delivering Willmot, bound and gagged, to the moors on the night of the winter solstice. And no, it was nothing illegal, more of a joke really, to teach the man a lesson.

Harmsworth coshed Willmot in an alley in the city, half dragged and half carried 'my drunken friend' out to the moors, took his money and ran. Phoebe and her daughter Verren, Assistant High Priestess, did the rest, carrying out with iron bars the sentence of the court of the sect, which had condemned the man to death for stealing the ring.

The court of law handed out a rather more lenient sentence, on 25 July 1980, of life imprisonment for all three defendants: Michael Harmsworth and the two Priestesses of the Devil Worshippers.

BRAKEL, Sylvia   To an untrained eye it would have looked just like a suicide; indeed, even the trained eyes of the Düsseldorf police had to do a retake before looking for more sinister motives. It was the morning of 31 May 1982, and officers had been sent in response to a report of a death 'in suspicious circumstances'. When they arrived at the broken-down flat in the notoriously scruffy Metzer Street district of the city they were confronted with the naked body of a man, sitting on a couch, his dead fingers still folded round the handle of a butcher's knife, the blade of which had pierced his chest and sunk deep into his heart. Blood had seeped through everywhere. According to the friend who found him and called the police, the dead man was a fellow Spanish immigrant called José Luis Mato Fernandez.

During a preliminary look around the faded apartment, the police found a book which appeared to be a sort of diary. Its cover was decorated with various signs and symbols of an occult nature – inverted crosses and that sort of thing – and on the inside of the cover a quaint curse warning of damnation for any who should read the contents. Like the hard-headed policemen produced by most major cities, the Düsseldorf team had been through worse than an adolescent curse, and plunged straight into the contents – damnation or no. Sprinkled at regular intervals were references to Lucifer, and other Satanic babbling – one page appeared to be a pact with the Devil, reading: 'O Lucifer, Prince of Darkness, I would sell you my soul.' The entries seemed harmless enough until detectives got to that for 30 April, Walpurgisnacht, one of the major witches' festivals: 'O Lucifer, Prince of Darkness, show me a sign. I want to be possessed by you totally. Come to me when Mato is sleeping.' 'Mato'. Mato Fernandez; now the police were interested.

Meanwhile, the police doctor had estimated time of death as a little over twenty-four hours before the body had been found; and it looked very much as though Mato Fernandez's 'suicide' had been faked.

A door-to-door inquiry around the apartment block revealed that since August 1981 the dead man had been living with twenty-two-year-old Sylvia Brakel. The relationship seemed to be a very open one, with regard to sex at least, and there appeared to be no disagreement about Fernandez entertaining a string of girlfriends as and when the fancy took him. Nor did it seem to cause any friction that Sylvia also lived part-time as husband and wife with her teenaged lesbian lover in another apartment. As she was known to have an obsessive interest in devil worship and witchcraft, it was clear that the diary found at Metzer Street had been kept by Sylvia Brakel. But how, if at all, was she connected with Mato Fernandez's death, and what did that message to the Prince of Darkness mean?

It happened that there was already a police file on Fraülein Brakel, dating from the time when she was charged with wounding a former boyfriend – with a knife. Social workers at the time learned that at the age of eight Sylvia had been sexually molested by her grandfather, and eight years later gang raped by nine youths. After spending a year in a juvenile offenders' institution, Sylvia Brakel teamed up with a baker's apprentice and during the three years they were together he introduced her to the pleasures of bi-sexuality and the excitement of Satanism. Then she spoiled it all by stabbing him.

And that, it was beginning to appear, was not the only time she had wielded a knife to bloody effect. By this time a number of Sylvia's devil-cult cronies had been brought in for questioning, among them a fellow Satanist to whom she had confessed to killing Fernandez within a couple of hours of his death. Apparently, Mato had incautiously accused Sylvia of being unfaithful – which she thought was a bit rich coming from him. There was an argument, and suddenly Mato Fernandez had a knife sticking out of his chest. After making it look like suicide, Sylvia had taken to her heels.

When Sylvia Brakel was brought into custody, she readily confessed to the killing, and, on 25 March 1983, following a four-day trial, was sentenced to life imprisonment.

BURY ST EDMUNDS WITCHES   The reign of terror that swept the eastern counties of England under the self-proclaimed Witchfinder-General, Matthew Hopkins, was responsible for some of the most notorious witch trials in the country, among them the trials at Bury St Edmunds.

At the Bury St Edmunds assizes of 1662, Rose Cullender and Amy Duny, two elderly widows of Lowestoft, were indicted before Mr Justice (later Lord Chief Justice) Hale with bewitching seven children aged between several months and eighteen years, one of whom died. In addition they were charged with various other acts of sorcery. Much of the evidence allowed was, at the very least, suspect – including the uncorroborated evidence of small children and the acceptance of 'spectral evidence'; that is to say, apparitions of the defendants which were said to frighten the children.

It all started when Mrs Dorothy Durent asked her neighbour Amy Duny to babysit her child William. Although warned against it by the mother, Amy Duny, in order to quieten the restless infant, gave it her nipple to suck on. When she admitted as much to Mrs Durent the woman became quite abusive, and in her own turn Mother Duny offered the mother a mild curse as she stamped out of the house. That evening baby William fell sick, and when he failed to recover from his 'strange fits of swounding' after some days, Mrs Durent called in a Dr Jacob of Yarmouth, celebrated in the county for 'helping children that were bewitched'. The good doctor advised Dorothy Durent to suspend the blanket in which little William slept in the chimney-corner by day, and to wrap the mite in it by night. However, if she were to find 'anything' in the blanket, Mrs Durent was immediately to throw it in the fire.

Sure enough that night, as she prepared to lay young William down, what should hop out of the blanket but a large toad. Fortunately, Mrs Durent's fright was eased by the presence of a neighbour's son – 'a young youth' – who she asked to catch the toad and burn it: 'Which the youth did accordingly, and held it there with the tongs; and as soon as it was in the fire made a great and horrid noise, and after a space there was a flashing in the fire like gunpowder, making a noise like the discharge of a pistol, and thereupon the toad was no more seen or heard.'

Next day Mrs Durent learned that Amy Duny was in 'a most lamentable condition', being burnt on the face, arms, legs and thighs. The implication was obvious, if rather silly.

Two years later, on 6 March, Mrs Durent's ten-year-old daughter Elizabeth was taken sick in much the same way as her brother William. This time the outcome was less happy, and despite careful ministrations the girl died: 'The cause of which [Mrs Durent] verily believeth was occasioned by the witchcraft of the said Amy Duny.'

Other children, more fortunate in that they survived their alleged 'bewitching', were paraded before the court at Bury 'and were in reasonable good condition. But the morning they came to the Hall to give instructions for the drawing of their Bills of

Indictment, the three persons (Dorothy Durent, Susan Chandler and Elizabeth Pacy) fell into strange and violent fits, screeking out in a most sad manner . . . and although they did after some certain space recover out of their fits, yet they were every one of them struck dumb . . .'

And so Mr Justice Hale, in his wisdom, ordered Amy Duny to approach the Pacy child and touch her; 'Whereupon the child without so much as seeing her, for her eyes were closed the while, suddenly leaped up and catched Amy Duny by the hand, and afterwards by the face; and with her nails scratched her till the blood came . . .'

Proof enough, thought the court, of Mother Duny's guilt!

Evidence brought against Rose Cullender did not include bewitching to death, but nevertheless emphasised the gross ignorance and superstition of the time as regards witches and enchantment. For example, in his testimony against Mother Cullender 'one John Soam of Lowestoft, yeoman, saith that not long since, in harvest time, he had three carts . . . And as they were going into the field to load, one of them wrenched the window of Rose Cullender's house, whereupon she came out in a great rage . . . And so they passed on into the fields and loaded all three carts. The other two carts returned safe home and back again twice loaded that day. But as to this cart that touched Rose Cullender's house, it was overturned twice or thrice that day.'

Later, Robert Sherringham gave evidence against Mother Cullender that 'about two years since he was much vexed with a great number of lice of an extraordinary bigness. And although he many times shifted himself [changed his clothes], would swarm again with them; so that in the end he was forced to burn all his clothes – being two suits of apparel – and then was clean from them . . .'

Thus did a rickety cart and an evidently unhygienic man help lead to the deaths of two old ladies whose only fault was a short temper. On the afternoon, of 13 March 1664, after a retirement of just thirty minutes, the jury returned a verdict of guilty on all thirteen counts, and three days later Amy Duny and Rose Cullender were hanged.

C

CANTERO, Jonathan Eric The question of what fuels the moment of insanity in which a person decides to kill has enjoyed considerable debate in the past decade, not least the link between fictional violence – as depicted on television and cinema screens – and violence in the home and on the street. This book has no space for a full forum on such matters, and besides, published volumes dealing with violent crimes have also been accused of exerting a corrupting influence. Certain types of music have likewise been blamed for inciting aggression, and it is true that some bands under the catch-all umbrella of 'heavy metal' do include overt displays of occult and aggressive imagery in their songs and performances. But board games?

Dungeons and Dragons is a popular fantasy role-play game in which the eternal battle between good and evil is played out in a make-believe world peopled with knights and trolls, wizards and kings, and any number of odd-looking residents of the under-world, not to mention damsels in distress. The game was invented by Gary Gygax in America in 1974, and since then has become internationally popular, particularly among teenagers. It was inevitable, perhaps, that in the desperate attempt to rationalise rising levels of crime and aggression, even the imagery of Dungeons and Dragons was subjected to scrutiny. In the United States strenuous efforts have been made to lay a number of suicides and homicides at the door of Dungeons and Dragons, and it is true that, on the face of it, a few D+D fanatics *have* taken their own and other people's lives. The reality is that it is not fantasy games but *people* who kill. What triggers a person's psychopathic inclination to take another's life is largely immaterial, it could be anything and it could happen at any time – after watching *Dirty Weekend*, reading *American Psycho*, listening to Megadeath or, it must be said, playing a game of Dungeons and Dragons.

Jonathan Cantero played Dungeons and Dragons; in fact, since he first got hooked on the game when he entered high school in Tampa, it had become something of an obsession. Whether or not it was the game's thread of ersatz magic that was to blame, Jonathan Cantero embarked on a 'study' of Satanism. It was probably a harmless enough phase that the boy would have worked through and grown out of, had his mother not been a mite impatient. It was understandable enough, she being an evangelical Christian, that Patricia Cantero should view her son's activities as the work of the devil. And it was not surprising that, in order to save his soul, she should first bombard her son with Biblical doctrine, and when this failed to have any impact, burn his collection of occult books and heavy metal recordings.

Still Jon Cantero went on with his 'studies', the sounds of ritual incantation from behind his bedroom door driving poor Patricia to distraction. In fact it drove her to slash her wrists in an attempt to escape the demon who was once her son. Mrs Cantero survived the suicide bid, and for a while at least things seemed to calm down. *Seemed* to calm down, because if Patricia Cantero had taken a look at the recent entries in Jon's 'Book of Shadows', his occult diary, she would have been even more terrified of her ungodly son. Jonathan was planning to kill her.

Already Cantero had written his list of necessary equipment; this included among other items: 'knife and sheath, vial for blood, plastic bag for left hand, handkerchief to cover mouth, Book of Shadows . . .' He had also written a script outline for the murder:

1. Go to school
2. Leave at 11.45
3. Pull up at Mom's house
4. Enter/greet Mom
5. Go to bathroom
6. Prepare knife and handkerchief
7. Go directly to Mom

8. When back is turned cover her mouth
9. Stab until dead
10. Cut off her left hand.

And that's more or less what happened. On 12 October 1988 Mrs Cantero's younger son discovered her bloody corpse lying in the hallway of her home. She had been stabbed forty times.

Jonathan Cantero was one of the first people interviewed by the team of homicide detectives and of course was horrified at the suggestion that he might know anything about the murder – kill his own mother, what sort of monster did they take him for? It was the bandage round Jon's hand that led the officers to realise just what sort of monster he was.

The bandage covered a cut; fell on a piece of broken glass, Cantero explained. Broken glass? said the doctor who examined him. That is a knife wound. Faced with his very obvious untruth, Jonathan Cantero confessed to killing his mother and led the police to the spot where he had buried his blood-stained clothing. There they also found Cantero's list of 'Equipment' and his itinerary; and there was something else, some gobbledegook addressed to the devil. Its author was about to explain. After cutting himself while killing his mother, Jonathan panicked and left before he had collected the vial of Patricia Cantero's blood and her left hand which he had intended to use in a black mass. However, he did allow himself the luxury of one insult to his mother's memory. Standing over her bleeding body he intoned a prayer: 'Lord Satan, I have stricken this woman from the earth, I have slain the womb from which I was born. I have ended her reign of desecration of my mind. She is no longer of me, yet only a simple serpent on a lower plane.'

Jonathan Cantero pleaded guilty to first-degree murder, and the Tampa, Florida, court sentenced him to life imprisonment. On 17 March 1989 he was led away to begin his minimum twenty-five-year stretch.

CARSON, James and Susan (aka Michael and Suzan Bear) Like many of their generation, James and Susan Carson were dropouts from respectable middle-class family backgrounds, who found the overt individual freedom that characterised the decades of the 1960s and 1970s irresistibly beguiling. The couple were first drawn together by a mutual obsession with mysticism and eastern religions, eventually being led by Susan's hallucinatory visions to change their names and declare themselves adherents to the Muslim faith.

So in 1981 they were Michael and Suzan Bear living in the hippy centre of the world, San Francisco, and melting comfortably into the sub-culture of drug dependency and drug dealing. One of their close acquaintances of the time – and a regular customer – was the one-time Hollywood actress Keryn Barnes. When Keryn went missing from the streets and bars, concerned friends asked her landlord if he knew where she had gone. He didn't; until he let himself into her apartment with his pass key and found Keryn's body slumped in the kitchen, her skull smashed and savage knife wounds in her face and neck. There was no evidence of a sexual motive and robbery was ruled out when Keryn Barnes' purse was found near the body with the money intact. When police found the name 'Suzan' scrawled around the flat they put out an alert for the Bears. But by that time the Bears had drifted on.

They had drifted to a pot farm in Humboldt County where Michael encountered Clark Stephens, a friend of a man who had earlier beaten him up. It was a loose connection, but proved motive enough for Bear to shoot him dead. The couple tried to burn Stephens' corpse, and like many before them discovered just how resistant the human body is to fire. Eventually they settled for covering it with rocks and chicken manure. But Clark Stephens was missed and therefore looked for, though by the time he was found in his makeshift cairn, the Bears had moved on once again, resuming a nomadic existence that was to take them into Oregon and then back to California.

In January 1983, the couple were picked up as hitch-hikers by thirty-year-old Jon Hillyar who drove them in his truck to just outside Santa Rosa. Unluckily for him, Suzan Bear had taken it into her drug-dazed head that Hillyar was a witch and must be killed. Suzan proved no match for the job of stabbing him to death and it fell to Michael's lot to deliver the *coup de grâce* with a bullet. But such activity cannot go unnoticed on a public roadside, and Michael and Suzan Bear were overtaken by the police, arrested and charged with murder.

Following their arrest the Bears insisted on holding a press conference from the California jail where they were being detained, and announced to the world that their instructions to kill had been personally given by Allah. Michael Bear admitted murdering Keryn Barnes, a witch who had put a spell on Suzan and was too dangerous to live. They both admitted complicity in the Stephens and Hillyar killings, but again as a benevolent gesture to rid the world of evil.

Tried in San Francisco first for the Barnes murder, Michael and Suzan Bear were convicted and sentenced to twenty-five years to life. Further trials for the other murders ended in convictions and similar sentences.

'CASTEL-A-MARE', The Haunting at   That ghosts and murders are frequently linked in the popular imagination comes as no surprise to serious psychical researchers. It is a long-held theory that the manifestations we label 'ghosts' can be simply explained if we use the 'tape-recorder' theory. One of the pioneers of this hypothesis was the celebrated English physicist Sir Oliver Lodge; in his *Man and the Universe*, Lodge explained that it was 'as if strong emotions could be unconsciously recorded in matter, so that the deposit shall thereafter affect a sufficiently sensitive organism and cause similar emotions to reproduce themselves in his subconscious, in a manner analogous to the customary conscious interpretation of photographic or phonographic records . . . Take for example a haunted house . . . wherein some one room is the scene of a ghostly representation of some long-past tragedy. On a psychometric hypothesis the original tragedy has been literally *photographed* on its material surroundings, nay, even on the ether itself, by reason of the intensity of emotion felt by those who enacted it . . . It is this theory that is made to account for the feeling one has on entering certain rooms, that there is an alien presence therein, though it is invisible and inaudible to mortal sense . . .'

This 'psychometric hypothesis' will also explain why, in the majority of cases, a ghost seems quite unaware of the presence of human beings – who clearly would not have been part of the 'recording'. Similarly, the fact that manifestations seem sometimes to 'just disappear', or to 'walk through a wall', indicates that when the image was transferred – when the ghost was 'created' – there was some obstruction, a partition, a wall, that would have kept it from view or, in the second case, that there was once a door, or opening, where that section of wall now is – the spirit is simply walking through it.

Most researchers will agree that the release of violent, often malevolent, energy that accompanies a brutal killing will more effectively imprint itself on to its surroundings; awaiting those conditions sympathetic to rendering it visible, audible and possibly destructive.

Because criminologists seldom concern themselves with such ethereal matters as the 'spirit world', hauntings that are associated with murders are rarely documented in any detail. Similarly, as it is frequently only the *fact* of a killing that interests the ghost-hunter, details of the crime itself are often scantily recorded.

The following case is of the latter kind, and is included here because what little we do know of the murder – which was never discovered in its own time – comes direct from the 'mouths' of those involved, via a spirit-medium.

'Castel-a-Mare' was an unimpressive, three-storey edifice 'standing on the left-hand side of Middle Warberry Road opposite "Edwinstowe", the back of the premises opening up to the road'.* The house was demolished in 1920 and the site now provides the garden for its former neighbour.

As far as can be determined, the crime took place around 1870; the participants in the drama seem to have been the master of the house, his maid and a mysterious doctor – possibly of 'foreign' extraction. The trouble with spirits is that they cannot always be relied upon to give the correct information in the correct narrative sequence. Consequently, we are by no means certain of the

* *Devon Mysteries*, Judy Chard, Bossiney Books, Bodmin, 1979.

course of events of that dreadful evening that were to etch themselves so indelibly into the fabric of 'Castel-a-Mare'. Our best analysis of the facts is that the guest – the foreign doctor – went berserk and first killed the master of the house and then strangled his maid. The fact that the murder remained undiscovered until the ghosts started talking may be due to the fact that the doctor could himself have issued a certificate stating that his victim's death had been due to natural causes; as for maids, they were being hired and fired all the time, prone to 'going off' with young grooms, or simply getting homesick and packing their bags.

We are fortunate in having a first-hand account of an investigation of this celebrated haunting recorded by Violet Tweedale* which, in an edited form, follows.

The Haunting of 'Castel-A-Mare'

In 1917 a friend rang me up and asked me if I would form one of a party of investigation at 'Castel-a-Mare'. The services of a medium had been secured and a soldier on leave, who was deeply immersed in psychic research, was in high hopes of getting some genuine results.

On reaching the house I found a small crowd assembled.

The medium, myself and four other women. The soldier, and an elderly and burly builder belonging to the neighbourhood, who was interested in psychic research. Eight persons in all.

As there was no chair or furniture of any description in the house, we carried in a small empty box from a rubbish heap outside and followed the medium through the rooms. She elected to remain in the large bedroom on the first floor, out of which opened the bathroom, and she sat down on the box and leaned her back against the wall, whilst we lounged about the room and awaited events. It was a sunny summer afternoon and the many broken panes of glass throughout the house admitted plenty of air.

After some minutes it was plain to see that the medium had fallen into a trance. Her eyes were closed and she lay back as if in

* *Ghosts I Have Seen*, Violet Tweedale, Herbert Jenkins Ltd, London.

sound sleep. Time passed, nothing happened, we were all rather silent, as I had warned the party that though we were in a room at the side of the house farthest from the road, our voices could plainly be heard by passers-by, and we wanted no interference.

Just as we were all beginning to feel rather bored and tired of standing, the medium sprang to her feet with surprising agility, pouring out a volley of violent language. Her voice had taken on the deep growling tones of an infuriated man, who advanced menacingly towards those of us who were nearest to him. In a harsh, threatening voice he demanded to know what right we had to intrude on his privacy.

There was a general scattering of the scared party before the unlooked-for attack and the soldier gave it as his opinion that the medium was now controlled by the spirit of a very violent male entity. I had no doubt upon the point.

The entity that controlled her possessed super-human strength. His voice was like the bellow of a bull, as he told us to be gone, or he would throw us out himself and his language was shocking.

The majority of our party were keeping at a safe distance, but suddenly the control rushed full tilt at the soldier, who had stood his ground, and attacking him with a tigerish fury drew blood at once. The big builder and I rushed forward to his aid. The rest of the party forsook us and fled, pell-mell out of the house and into the garden. Glancing through the window, near which we fought, I saw below a row of scared faces staring up in awed wonder.

The scene being enacted was really amazing. The frail little creature threw us off like feathers, and drove us foot by foot before her, always heading us off the bathroom. We tried to stand our ground and dodge her furious lunges, but she was too much for us. After a desperate scuffle, which lasted quite seven or eight minutes and resulted in much torn clothing, she drove us out of the room and on to the landing. Then suddenly, without warning, the entity seemed to evacuate the body he had controlled and the medium went down with a crash and lay at our feet, just a little crumpled, dishevelled heap.

For some considerable time I thought that she was dead.

After about ten minutes, she gradually regained her consciousness and seeming none the worse for her experience, she sat up and asked what had happened.

We did not give her the truth in its entirety, and contrived to account for the blood-stained soldier and the torn clothing without unduly shocking and distressing her. We then dispersed; the medium walking off as if nothing whatever had occurred to deplete her strength.

Some days after this the soldier begged for another experiment with the medium. He had no doubts as to her genuineness and he was sure that if we tried again we would get further developments. She was willing to try again, and so was the builder, but with one exception the rest of the party refused to have anything more to do with the unpleasant affair, and the one exception stipulated to remain in the garden.

After the medium had remained entranced for some minutes, the same male entity again controlled her. The same violence, the same attacks began once more, but this time we were better prepared to defend ourselves. The soldier and the stalwart builder warded off the attacks, and tried conciliatory expostulations, but all to no purpose. Then the soldier, who seemed to have considerable experience in such matters, tried a system of exorcising, sternly bidding the malignant entity depart. There ensued a very curious spiritual conflict between the exorcist and the entity, in which sometimes it seemed as if one, then the other, was about to triumph.

Those wavering moments were useful in giving us breathing space from the assaults, and at length, having failed, as we desired, to get into the bathroom, we drove him back against the wall at the far end of the room. Finally the exorcist triumphed, and the medium collapsed on the floor as the strength of the control left her.

For a few moments we allowed the crumpled-up little heap to remain where she lay, but quite suddenly a new development began.

She raised her head, and still crouching on the floor with closed eyes she began to cry bitterly. Wailing and moaning, and uttering inarticulate words, she had become the picture of absolute woe.

Thomas Allaway arriving
for his trial

The telegram that lured
Allaway's victim Irene
Wilkins to her death

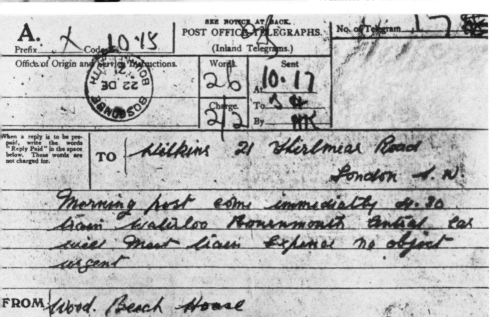

Above left: Kusor Bashir. Her parents believed that she had become inhabited by a *djinn* – an invisible spirit (*Quay Photographic Ltd*)

Above right: Mohammed Bashir (no relation), the 'holy man' whose violent efforts to exorcise the *djinn* from Kusor's body led to his conviction for her murder (*Quay Photographic Ltd*)

Mohammed Nurani, the local *pir*, who began the orgy of violence by placing Kusor inside a chalk circle and forcing her to inhale the fumes of burning mustard oil (*Quay Photographic Ltd*)

David Berkowitz, the 'Chubby Behemoth' who confessed to the Son of Sam killings (*Popperfoto*)

Just two of the victims of the notorious Son of Sam. Christine Freund (*left*) was shot dead on 30 January 1977; Judith Placido (*right*) was wounded on 26 June 1977 (*Popperfoto/UPI*)

¶ The Apprehenſion and confeſſion of three notorious Witches.

Arreigned and by Iuſtice condemned and executed at *Chelmeſ-forde,* in the Countye of Eſſex, *the 5. day of Iulye, laſt paſt.*

1 5 8 9.

¶ With the manner of their diueliſh practices and keeping of their ſpirits, whoſe fourmes are herein truelye proportioned.

A contemporary account of the trial of the Chelmsford Witches

The notorious Matthew Hopkins, Witchfinder-General of England, who was responsible for several hundred executions and many more imprisonments and tortures

Mark David Chapman (*Associated Press/Topham*)

John Lennon signs his autograph for the man who was to murder him, Mark Chapman (*Popperfoto*)

THEATRE, LINCOLN.

BY DESIRE OF

G. E. WELBY, Esq. M.P. & C. FURNOR, Esq.

THE STEWARDS OF THE STUFF BALL.

On WEDNESDAY Evening, OCTOBER 27th, 1830,

Will be presented, the celebrated drama of

Sweethearts and Wives.

Admiral Franklin, ... Mr. SHIELD.   Charles Franklin, ... Mr. SIMMS.
Sandford, ... Mr. CULLENFORD   Curtis, ... Mr. HODGSON.
Billy Lackaday, ... Mr. GURNER.
Mrs. Bell, ... Mrs. DANBY.   Susan, ... Mrs. GURNER.
Eugenia, ... Mrs. W. ROBERTSON.   Laura, ... Miss STEWART SMITH.

A COMIC SONG ...... by ...... Mr. HODGSON.

With (for the LAST TIME,) the new Tragic Melo Drama, in 4 Acts, founded on Fact, called the

RED BARN;

OR, THE PROPHETIC DREAM.

THE MUSIC SELECTED AND ARRANGED BY MR. STANNARD

WITH NEW SCENERY PAINTED FOR THE OCCASION BY MR. SIMMS.

Mr. ROBERTSON is induced to bring forward this piece, not only from the unprecedented success it has been received with at all the various Theatres in the Kingdom, but as a moral lesson, that
Murder, however for the time concealed, will speak with most miraculous organ. Every one must
be aware of the Incidents on which the Piece is founded, but the Dramatist has avoided the real
names of the parties, still blending all the principal Incidents, with an effect at once awful and in-
structive.

Cordel, a young Farmer, ... Mr. HAMILTON.
Mr. Delamere, a Magistrate, ... Mr. BRUNTON.
Wilton, a Gipsy Confederate of Cordel, ... Mr. TALBOT.
Marlin, a labouring Farmer in the vale of years, ... Mr. STYLES.
Robin, a Factotum to Chatteral, ... Mr. SIMMS.
Peter Christopher Chatteral, a Barber, Beadle, &c. .... Mr. GURNER.
Nell Hatfield, a Gipsy, .. Mrs. W. ROBERTSON, Anna Hatfield, her daughter, .. Mrs. GURNER.
Dame Marlin, ... Mrs. DANBY.   Mrs Cordel, ... Mrs. HAMILTON.
Maria Marlin, , ... Miss STEWART SMITH.

A Brief Sketch of the Incidents:
CORDEL for his numerous Crimes receives the CURSE of the GIPSY CHIEF.

CORDEL'S FIRST MEETING WITH MARIA MARLIN.

*His promise to marry her—The anguish of old Marlin and his Dame at parting with her—His proposition
to meet her at the RED BARN disguised in Man's Apparel—Her joy at the thoughts of Marriage.*

AWFUL MEETING AT THE RED BARN,
WHERE THE DEED IS PERPETRATED.

THE APPEARANCE OF MARIA TO HER MOTHER IN A DREAM.

The Interior of the Barn where the Body is discovered.

CORDEL's Marriage in London.—His living in splendour when the GIPSY's CURSE is fulfilled.

CORDEL'S APPREHENSION AND CONFESSION,

And the appearance of the Shade of Maria Marlin in Cordel's Dream, which produces the denouement.

*Among the minor Incidents to give effect to the serious part of the Melo-drama, some Comic Parts
are introduced which must set gravity at defiance.*

The psychic and sexual elements of the killing of Maria Marten by William Corder led the case to become one of Britain's most celebrated historic murders. The penny-dreadful treatment (*below*) and the poster for a melodrama (*left*) based on the 'Red Barn murder' demonstrate how great the public fascination for the case was

Dr Hawley Harvey Crippen

Hilldrop Crescent, north London, where Crippen's ghost is said to walk

Dubbed 'Satan's Laughing Hitman' by the press, Rodney Dale ran amok in the Burleigh Heads district of Australia's Gold Coast on 7 April 1990 (*Popperfoto*)

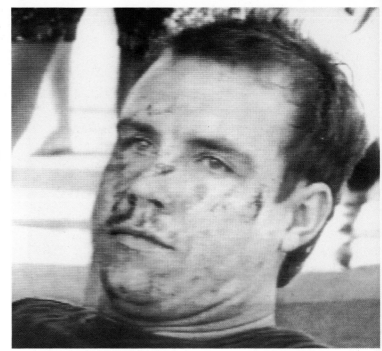

Gilles de Rais' search for the 'philosopher's stone' and his fascination with the Dark Powers led him to become one of Europe's worst child rapists and killers. He was executed by garrotte on 23 October 1440

'Another entity has got hold of her,' announced the soldier. It certainly appeared to be so.

All signs of violence had gone. The medium had become a heart-broken woman.

We raised her to her feet, her condition was pitiable, but her words became more coherent.

'Poor master! On the bed. Help him! Help him!' she moaned, and pointed to one side of the room. Again and again she indicated, by clenching her hands on her throat, that death by strangulation was the culmination of some terrible tragedy that had been enacted in that room.

She wandered, in a desolate manner, about the floor, wringing her hands, the tears pouring down her cheeks, whilst she pointed to the bed, then towards the bathroom with shuddering horror.

Suddenly we were startled out of our compassionate sympathy by a piercing scream.

The medium had turned at bay, and began a frantic encounter with some entity unseen by us. Wildly she wrestled and fought, as if for her life, whilst she emitted piercing shrieks for 'help'. We rushed to the rescue, dragging her away from her invisible assailant, but a disembodied fighter has a considerable pull over a fighter in the flesh, who possesses something tangible that can be seized. I placed the medium behind me, with her back to the wall, but though I pressed her close she continued to fight and I had to defend myself as well as defend her. Her assailant was undoubtedly the first terrible entity which had controlled her. At intervals she gasped out, 'Terrible doctor – will kill – he's killed master – help! help!'

Gradually she ceased to fight. The soldier was exorcising with all his force and was gaining power; finally he triumphed, inasmuch as he banished the 'terrible doctor'.

The medium was, however, still under the control of the broken-hearted entity and began again to wander about the room. We extracted from her further details. An approximate date of the tragedy. Her master's name, that he was mentally deficient when the murder took place. She was a maidservant in the house and after witnessing the crime she appeared to have shared her master's fate, though by what means we could not determine. The doctor was a resident physician of foreign origin.

At last we induced her to enter the bathroom, which she seemed to dread, and there she fell to lamenting over the dead body of her master, which had lain hidden there when the room was used as a large cupboard. It was a very painful scene, which was ended abruptly by her falling down insensible.

This was the last time I set foot in the haunted house, which is now being demolished.

The date and names the medium had given us were later on verified by means of a record of villa residents, which for many years had been kept in the town of Torquay.

If there is any truth in the story it falls under the category of undiscovered crimes. The murderer was able somehow to hide his iniquities and escape suspicion and punishment.

CATRILAF, Juana   I am indebted to Michael Newton's *Raising Hell*, an excellent encyclopedia of Satanic crime for this lead to the practices of the sorcerers of Chile's Mapuche indians.

When Juana Catrilaf was taken into custody in 1953 charged with the murder of her grandmother, she willingly confessed to killing the old woman, but insisted that her own increasing problems with epilepsy and the death of her child were directly attributable to the evil machinations of her grandmother, a *machi*. In her statement, Juana said that she battered the old woman to death, and then made a cut across her forehead and sucked blood from the gash; as she did so she felt enormous relief as what was described as 'a fiery devil' departed from her body – proof enough for any Mapuche that Juana Catrilaf had been bewitched.

The Mapuche tribe are almost obsessively concerned with the opposing concepts of good and evil, and there are very well regulated ways of dealing with them. Sickness and death, as well as misfortunes of a more mercenary nature are all the result of evil spirits. It stands to reason then, that given the frequency of life's little upsets, there is a great demand for the services of the *machi*, or shaman. The *machi* occupy a position of great respect and no little fear in the tribal hierarchy, having the capacity to deal directly with the forces of good in order to intervene against the forces of evil. Although the ceremony varies depending on the particular client's needs, that great authority on the Mapuche, L.C. Faron (*Hawks of the Sun*), describes the *machi*'s 'tool-kit': 'Her basic props consist of a *kultrun* (a shallow drum made from a wooden bowl covered with animal skin), a single drumstick (always decorated with symbols of special significance to the *machi*), bells and/or a gourd rattle, a *rewe* (a step-notched and carved pole outside her house which she climbs during certain ceremonies), considered to contain power transmitted by the *machi*'s familiars (*pillan*).' The line of *machi* does not descend through a family but relies on an experienced sorceress taking an 'apprentice' – girls, though very occasionally boys, who demonstrate 'special' capabilities such as magical dreaming and the ability to enter a spirit trance. The training of these children is paid for by parents and undertaken at the *machi*'s own home. As well as 'spiritual' training, the neophyte also learns the vast lore of folk-medicine which is the stock in trade of the *machi* – only when a sickness is too strong for herbal remedies will the *machi* perform a full ceremony and commune with the spirits, and when it is thought that a curse has been laid by a *kalku*.

The *kalku* is to the evil spirit what the *machi* is to the good. It is the *kalku* who is consulted, and whose services are purchased when malevolent work is afoot – an act of revenge, for example, the blighting of a neighbour's crop, sending sickness to his family or even death. Although *kalku* may inherit their powers from ancestors who were also in the business, it is more customary for them to receive training in the same manner as the *machi*. Sometimes young girls (for again, the majority of *kalku* are women) are taken against their will, and remain in the sorceresses' dens on pain of death. The fully trained *kalku* will then begin to acquire evil spirits to do her work, possibly the unprotected spirits of the dead which she will convert into *wekufe* which can take on hideous forms, called *witranalwe*, *piwichen*, *chonchon*, and so on.

Faron describes the process: 'The *kalku* operates most effectively from her *renu*, her haunt, which is described as a lugubrious den, the entrance to which is guarded by evil spirits in animal form. Witches foregather in the *renu*, where spirits of former *kalku* who have not entered living bodies reside. These unattached spirits of former *kalku* are the familiars of living witches. The assemblage of witches, corporeal and incorporeal, makes incantations over dead dogs, frogs, snakes, and the like against their human victims. Only *kalku* are able to enter the *reñu* with impunity. If a *machi* or anyone else stumbled upon the *reñu*, they would be captured and either put to death, so that their spirit could be converted into a familiar, or else pressed into the sisterhood as a corporeal witch and allowed to live as long as the *kalku*'s secrets were kept.'

Because she can also command the spirits of dead ancestors, the *kalku* is particularly feared by her own family, and there are many recorded instances of misfortune, sickness and death being visited upon a relative. This is particularly important in evaluating the case of Juana Catrilaf. It would, in the general run of things, be unthinkable that Juana's grandmother would inflict epilepsy on her and kill her child with magic if she were truly a *machi*. A *kalku*, yes; so it is possible that the finer details got lost in translation. There is another possibility. That the old woman had indeed been trained as a *machi*, but that her good spirits had been defeated by the forces of evil who forced her to act as a *kalku*.

So strong is the belief in supernatural possession among the Mapuche tribe, and so deeply ingrained in their culture, that the Chilean government was obliged to recognise a unique defence in such cases as that of Juana Catrilaf – that the accused was 'compelled by irresistible psychic force'. As a consequence Juana was acquitted.

A further example of the doctrine of 'irresistible psychic force' arose over the suspicious death in 1960 of five-year-old José Luis Painecur. It was later claimed that, in the wake of a terrible earthquake and tidal wave which had all but destroyed the Mapuche reservation at Lago Bundi, two men – Juan Panan and José Vargas – had thrown the boy into the sea at Cerro Mesa as a sacrifice to the water spirits. When they were arrested, Panan and Vargas insisted that they had been forced by one of the tribe's *machi* to carry out the sacrifice. Although they were initially convicted of murder and sentenced to terms of imprisonment, Panan and Vargas successfully invoked the unique law of 'irresistible force' and were released.

CHAPMAN, Mark David   In December 1980 everything was, at last, going right for John Lennon. He had been one of the world's favourite pop idols in the 1960s as the most charismatic member of the Beatles; had survived their break-up to pursue a not always brilliant solo career; had declined into a 'Lost Weekend' in the mid-1970s only to emerge a devoted father and successful businessman, under the influence of his devoted wife, the artist Yoko Ono. And now he was making his musical comeback with the release of a successful new album, 'Double Fantasy'. So the universal grief which greeted his murder outside the Dakota building in Manhattan on the night of 8 December 1980 was mixed with incredulity: why on earth would anyone want to shoot John Lennon?

The answer to that question is still clouded. The gunman, Mark Chapman, had enjoyed an unremarkable, but reasonably happy childhood in Georgia. As a teenager he became a mildly rebellious hippy, but at seventeen experienced a vision of Jesus, which prompted him to become a 'Jesus Freak' and a counsellor with the YMCA. In 1976 he enrolled at Convent College, Tennessee, but soon dropped out, ominously denouncing it as full of 'phoneys'.

Chapman's career became increasingly unsettled. He took employment as a security guard and learned to use a gun, but ditched the job for a six-month sabbatical in Hawaii. In 1977 he attempted to asphyxiate himself with the exhaust of his car. Mark Chapman was diagnosed as suffering from 'severe neurotic depressive reaction'.

But 1978 saw his return from six weeks in Tokyo a happier, more relaxed human being, with a Japanese Buddhist girlfriend, Gloria Abe. The couple married in June 1979 and settled in Honolulu. Suddenly Chapman's personality suffered another dramatic shift, characterised by occasional aggression and a general 'pushiness'; he had also become more than slightly careless with his wife's money. He resumed his job as a security guard, where a colleague described him, rather unkindly, as 'a creep – negative, cold and ugly'.

Mark Chapman's behaviour now became increasingly bizarre. In early 1980 he mounted a campaign of hate against the local branch of the Church of Scientology, making countless threatening telephone calls and marching up and down in front of the building muttering death threats. In October's issue of *Esquire* magazine he read an article revealing that John Lennon, far from being a working-class hero, was a prosperous businessman – *not a hero*, so he must be a phoney. Chapman next took to sitting naked in the yogic lotus position listening to Beatles records and chanting endlessly: 'John Lennon I'm going to kill you – you phoney bastard!'

On 23 October 1980, Mark Chapman signed off at work for the last time. Instead of his own signature he wrote 'John Lennon'; then he crossed it out. Had he already become his former idol? If he had, he knew there was no room for two John Lennons in the world. On 27 October he went shopping in downtown Honolulu, fitting himself up with a Charter Arms .38-calibre snub-nosed five-shot revolver, and a one-way ticket to Newark, New Jersey. He was unable to purchase ammunition in New York, so took a flying visit to Atlanta, Georgia, where an acquaintance supplied him with five vicious hollow-nosed dumdums.

Back in New York Chapman seemed to have a change of heart: he called Gloria to say that coming to the city had been 'a big mistake'. He had been planning to kill John Lennon, but now the episode was like a bad dream and he was coming home. 'I have won a great victory,' he said. But not for long. Chapman experienced two hallucinations in which the words 'Thou shalt not kill' appeared. And then, on Friday 5 December, he took off again for the metropolis. There were two items on his shopping list: a copy of the Double Fantasy album, and J.D. Salinger's novel *Catcher in the Rye*. The hero of the novel, Holden Caulfield, dismisses the objects of his dissatisfaction as phoneys. 'This is my statement,' Chapman wrote on the title page.

At 5 p.m. John Lennon was leaving the Dakota building when a copy of his new record was thrust into his hands by a plump young man. Lennon obligingly signed the album cover. He went on to the recording studio where he spoke of a premonition of death, and returned to the Dakota with Yoko at 10.50 p.m. Mark Chapman was still there. As Lennon passed, the youth drew his revolver and dropped into the combat position. 'Mr Lennon?', he called. The object of his obsession turned, and Chapman fired five bullets into his body. John Lennon was pronounced dead at New York's Roosevelt Hospital.

Was Mark David Chapman a psychotic, or was there more to it? Conspiracy theories have abounded, not least because of the close interest the FBI took in John Lennon. Where did Chapman, an ill-paid security guard, get the money for the flights, trips abroad and expensive hotels? How did his confused mind plot the scheme so perfectly? It has been suggested that he was brainwashed. The riddle remained unsolved at court, where Chapman's lawyer entered a very plausible plea of insanity. Chapman calmly and lucidly undermined his own defence by pleading guilty to murder, and on 24 August 1981 he was sentenced to between twenty years and life.

CHELMSFORD WITCHES   Although the case was not of itself of any great significance, the so-called 'first' trial of the 'Chelmsford Three' – Agnes and Joan Waterhouse and Elizabeth Francis – in July 1566 was important in legal terms. It was the first major witch-trial to be conducted after the passing of Elizabeth I's Witchcraft Act of 1563. It was also the first such trial to be published in popular form as a chapbook (the sole surviving copy of which is in Lambeth Palace Library, London). The trial was also significant in that the panel of judges included several of the highest appointed in the land, among them Sir Gilbert Gerard, the Attorney-General, and in the fact that the age at which children could give testimony (fourteen) was lowered for the purpose of trying the alleged witches.

The three women were charged with unrelated instances of causing sickness by witchcraft. Elizabeth Francis was sentenced to one year in gaol and four appearances in the pillory for bewitching the child of William Auger and others. In her confession, Elizabeth claimed that:

First she learned this art of witchcraft at the age of twelve years from her grandmother whose name was Mother Eve of Hatfield Peverell, deceased. Item, when she taught it her, she counselled her to renounce GOD and his word and to give of her blood to Satan (as she termed it) which she delivered her in the likeness of a white spotted Cat, and taught her to feed the said Cat with bread and milk, and she did so, also she [Mother Eve] taught her to call it by the name of Satan and to keep it in a basket.

When this Mother Eve had given her the Cat Satan, then this Elizabeth desired first of the said Cat (calling it Satan) that she might be rich and to have goods, and he promised her that she should – asking her what she would have, and she said sheep (for this Cat spoke to her as she confessed in a strange, hollow voice, but such as she understood by use) and this Cat forthwith brought sheep into her pasture to the number of eighteen, black and white, which continued with her for a time, but in the end did all wear away she knew not how.

Item, when she had got these sheep, she desired to have one Andrew Byles to her husband, which was a man of some wealth, and the Cat did promise she should, but that he said she must first consent that this Andrew should abuse her, and she so did.

And after, when this Andrew had thus abused her he would not marry her, wherefore she willed Satan to waste his goods, which he forthwith did, and with not being contented with this, she willed him to touch his body which he forthwith did whereof he died.

Item, that every time that he did anything for her, she said that he required a drop of blood, which she gave him by pricking herself, sometimes in one place and then in another, and where she pricked herself there remained a red spot which was still to be seen.

Item, when this Andrew was dead, she doubting herself with child, willed Satan to destroy it, and he bade her take a certain herb and drink it, which she did, and destroyed the child forthwith.

Item, when she desired another husband he promised her another, naming this Francis whom she knoweth, but said he is not so rich as the other, willing her to consent unto that Francis in fornication which she did, and thereof conceived a daughter that was born within a quarter of a year after they were married.

After they were married they lived not so quietly as she desired, being stirred (as she said) to much unquietness and moved to swearing and cursing, wherefore she willed Satan the Cat to kill the child, being about the age of half a year old, and he did so, and when she yet found not the quietness that she desired, she willed it to lay a lameness to the leg of this Francis her husband, and it did in this manner. It came in a morning to this Francis' shoe, lying in it like a toad, and when he perceived it putting on his shoe, and had touched it with his foot, he being suddenly amazed asked of her what it was, and she bade him kill it and he was forthwith taken with a lameness whereof he cannot be healed.

After all this when she had kept this Cat by the space of fifteen or sixteen years, and as some say (although untruly) being weary of it, she came to one Mother Waterhouse her neighbour (a poor woman) when she was going to the oven and desired her to give her a cake, and she would give her a thing that she should be the better for for as long as she lived, and this Mother Waterhouse gave her a cake, whereupon she brought her this Cat in her apron and taught her as she was instructed before by her grandmother Eve, telling her that she must call him Satan and give him her blood and bread and milk as before.

Also tried was sixty-three-year-old Agnes Waterhouse, like Elizabeth Francis hailing from Hatfield Peverell. Mother Waterhouse was charged with bewitching William Fynee, 'who languished until 1 November 1565 when he died'. It was Agnes who was given Elizabeth Francis' cat Satan, as she described in her confession:

First she received this Cat of this Francis wife in the order as is before said, who willed her to call him Satan, and told her that if she made much of him he would do for her what she would have him to do.

Then when she had received him she (to try him what he could do) willed him to kill a hog of her own, which he did, and she gave him for his labour a chicken, which he first required of her and a drop of her blood. And this she gave him at all times when he did anything for her, by pricking her hand or face and putting the blood to his mouth which he sucked, and forthwith would lie down in his pot again, wherein she kept him, the spots of all which pricks are still to be seen on her skin.

Also she said that another time being offended with one Father Kersie she took her Cat Satan in her lap and put him in the wood before her door, and willed him to kill three of this Father Kersie's hogs, which he did, and returning again told her so and she rewarded him as before, with a chicken and a drop of her blood, which chicken he ate up clean as he did all the rest, and she could find remaining neither bones nor feathers.

Also she confessed that falling out with one widow Gooday she willed Satan to drown her cow and he did so, and she rewarded him as before.

Also she falling out with another of her neighbours, he killed her three geese in the same manner.

Item, she confessed that because she could have no rest (which she required) she caused Satan to destroy the brewing at that time.

Also being denied butter of another, she caused her to lose the curds two or three days after.

Item, falling out with another of her neighbours and his wife, she willed Satan to kill him with a bloody flixe, whereof he died, and she rewarded him as before.

Likewise she confessed, that because she lived somewhat unquietly with her husband she caused Satan to kill him, and he did so about nine years past, since which time she hath lived a widow.

Also she said that when she would will him to do anything for her, she would say her Paternoster in Latin.

Item, this Mother Waterhouse confessed that she first turned this Cat into a toad by this means, she kept the Cat a great while in wool in a pot, and at length being moved by poverty to occupy the wool, she prayed in the name of the father and of the son, and of the holy ghost that it would turn into a toad, and forthwith it was turned into a toad, and so kept it in the pot without wool.

Also she said, that going to Brackstead a little before her apprehension, this Satan willed her to hurry home, for she should have great trouble and that she should be either hanged or burned shortly.

Agnes Waterhouse was found guilty and hanged two days later on 29 July 1566, when she 'yielded up her soul, trusting to be in joy with Christ her saviour which dearly had bought her with his most precious blood'.

The third defendant was eighteen-year-old Joan Waterhouse, daughter of Agnes, who was charged with causing the paralysis of twelve-year-old Agnes Brown's right arm and right leg by witchcraft. In her evidence, young Agnes Brown claimed she had been visited by the cat Satan which had taken on the form of a large black dog with a face like an ape and a pair of horns on his head.

Pleading her innocence, Joan told the court:

> First, that her mother this last winter would have learned her this art, but she learned it not, neither yet the name of the thing. She said she never saw it but once in her mother's hand, and that was in the likeness of a toad, and at that time coming in at a sudden when her mother called it out to work some things withal, she heard her to call it Satan, for she was not at any time truly taught it, nor did never exercise it before this time as followeth:
>
> Item, she confessed that when her mother was gone to Brackstead, in her absence lacking bread, she went to a girl, a neighbour's child, and desired her to give her a piece of bread and cheese, which when denied and gave her not, or at the least not so much as would satisfy her, she going home did as she had seen her mother do, calling Satan, which came to her (as she said) she thought out of her mother's shoe from under the bed in the likeness of a great dog, demanding what she would have, wherewithall she being afeared said she would have him to make such a girl afeared, naming this girl, then asked he her what she would give him, and she said a red cock, then said he no, but thou shalt give me thy body and soul, whereby she being sore afeared, and desirous to be rid of him, said she would: And herewith he went to this girl in the likeness of an evil favoured dog with horns on his head, and made her very much afeared, and does yet haunt her, now cannot these witches (as they say) call him in again, because they did not let him out. And more (saith she) she never did, but this her doing was the revealing of all the rest.

Joan Waterhouse was found not guilty by the court and released.

The second major witch-trial to be held at Chelmsford took place in 1579. Arraigned before John Southcote and Sir Thomas Gawdy, Justices of the Queen's Bench, were Elizabeth Francis (for the second time), Ellen Smith, Alice Nokes and Margery Stanton.

Elizabeth Francis was accused of bewitching to death Alice Poole, who died on 1 November 1578; Elizabeth was found guilty and hanged. Ellen Smith (whose mother had been hanged as a witch in 1574) was convicted of bewitching a child to death, and so was Alice Nokes; both met their end on the gallows. Margery

Stanton was accused of killing a horse and a cow by means of spells, but the court found there was insufficient evidence and she was released.

The third Chelmsford trial was held in 1589 when nine women and one man were indicted with various forms of witchcraft, in the main bewitching to death. Most of the evidence was given by young children, as the result of which four of the defendants were found guilty and three of them – Joan Cony, Joan Upney and Joan Prentice – were executed within two hours of their conviction. Alice Cony, whose own children had testified against her, was hanged later.

Biggest of the mass trials of witches at Chelmsford was that of July 1645, when most of the thirty-two women indicted had been 'discovered' by Matthew Hopkins, self-proclaimed Witchfinder-General of England. A failed lawyer of Manningtree in the county of Essex, Hopkins was to become the most feared man in the eastern counties of England. From the time he set up as arch inquisitor in March 1645, until he was forced to cease his excesses a year later, Hopkins was held to be responsible for several hundred executions and many more imprisonments and tortures. In the year of his death from tuberculosis, 1647, Matthew Hopkins published his notorious treatise *The Discovery of Witches*. Most of the alleged witches tried at Chelmsford had already confessed as the result of torture instigated by Hopkins, and in the end nineteen were hanged for murder by witchcraft.

'CHICAGO RIPPERS', *see* **SPREITZER, Edward,** *et al.*

CLAWSON, Eugene A.

> 6 April 1970
> Gentlemen,
> I have some information on the whereabouts of the bodies of the two missing West Virginia University coeds, Mared Malarik and Karen Ferrell. Follow the directions very carefully – to the nth degree and you cannot fail to find them.

Proceed twenty-five miles directly south from the southern line of Morgantown. This will bring you to a wooded forest land. Enter into the forest exactly one mile. There are the bodies. 25+1=26 miles total.

Will reveal myself when the bodies are located.

Sincerely

Δ

It was true enough, the nineteen-year-old coeds had been missing from Morgantown University campus since 18 January and despite a generous reward on offer and the enthusiastic assistance of the FBI, local police had failed to find even the smallest clue as to the girls' whereabouts. Bearing this in mind, it is strange that the police were so sluggardly in following up the information contained in the letter. Of course every lengthy murder enquiry attracts its clutch of crank letters and bogus telephone calls, but at least it was something. A few days later the press got hold of the letter and, characteristically, made a prominent feature of it. Still no official response.

On 12 April the Morgantown police received another letter, in the same hand, giving the same information, but this time adding a diagram of the site. For good measure the correspondent mentioned that the bodies were covered with twigs and leaves and had been partially devoured by nature's scavengers.

This time there was action, and on 16 April a team of National Guard searchers found two headless corpses, lightly covered with brush and bearing the marks of feasting by woodland creatures. Despite a painstaking search, the heads could not be found.

On 21 April another anonymous letter arrived on the desk of Morgantown's sheriff:

Gentlemen,

I have delayed writing another letter in the hope that you would conclude more information by this time, concerning finding the bodies. Since this has not substantially happened, I will send along another clue while your men are in the area.

The heads can be found from the position of the bodies by striking out 10 degrees south-west for the first head and approximately 10 degrees south-east for the second, roughly one mile. You are already seven-tenths of that mile. They are within the mine entrance – if you can call it an entrance considering its condition. They are buried not over 1 ft in depth.

The ones responsible for the murders scattered some of the girls' personal effects over the general area creating a pattern of confusion making it difficult for you to pinpoint any exact location. My first two letters triggered your intensive search. Don't give up now!

Sincerely

Δ

The heads were not, in fact, located at this spot, and have never been found. But the publication of this latest epistle did prompt the author to reveal himself, or rather themselves; and the story they told the Morgantown police was as bizarre as any that those professionally cynical men had ever heard.

Not long after the police enquiry into the disappearance of Karen Ferrell and Mared Malarik had come to a dead end, a resident of La Vale, Maryland, some eighty-odd miles from Morgantown, decided to intervene on the supernatural plane. The man's name was Fred Schanning, and he had a friend and psychic counsellor named Rev. R. Warren Hoover. Hoover in turn had a spirit guide who called himself 'Dr Spencer' and claimed to be a nineteenth-century London physician. The result of this spiritual collaboration was that Rev. Hoover went into a trance and spoke with the voice of Dr Spencer while Schanning recorded the message on tape.

The bare bones of this 'conversation' were conveyed to the police in the letters of 6 and 12 April, and subsequently on the 21st further directions concerning the decapitated heads. In the meantime, the obliging spirit from beyond the grave had described the manner in which the two young women had been sacrificed by two men as part of an initiation ceremony into a devil cult: 'One was black, five feet seven inches tall, and from West Virginia. The other was white and has blond hair, cold, steel blue eyes, and an expressionless face.' In the presence of this unconventional detective work, the bewildered Morgantown police did what came naturally – they arrested Schanning and Hoover on suspicion of murder. It is only fair to add, however, that both men were quickly set free and, on 24 July, a press release stated that there was no shadow of suspicion attaching to them.

Nothing more was added to the open file on the murdered coeds until January 1976, when police in Morgantown received a thirty-five-page confession to the Ferrell/Malarik killings. The document had been compiled by a prison inmate called Eugene A. Clawson. In their joy at closing the file at last, detectives tended to ignore a number of warning bells which might otherwise have aroused their suspicions. For a start Clawson had a history of mental illness and was known to have confessed on a number of occasions to crimes he could not possibly have committed. The details given in the Ferrell/Malarik confession were in places so wildly inaccurate that they flew in the face of both post-mortem evidence and common sense; nor were the two missing heads where Clawson said they were.

By the time Eugene Clawson was brought to trial in October 1976 on a double murder charge, he had retracted his confession, explaining that the few accurate details contained in the document had been culled from an account of the case he had seen in a magazine. Nevertheless, Clawson was convicted on his uncorroborated, inaccurate, retracted confession and sent back to jail with a life sentence.

Everybody, it seems, was happy with the result and yet another vicious crime could be successfully tied up. Or *almost* everybody was happy; clearly Eugene Clawson was none too pleased, and nor was the Rev. Hooper, who has lost no opportunity to express his dissatisfaction at the conclusion of the investigation and to press for a search for the two Satanists so clearly described by Dr Spencer.

COCK LANE GHOST In the first two months of the year 1762, number 33 Cock Lane was the location of one of London's most celebrated hoaxes – the Cock Lane Ghost – itself a story of murder and mystery.

Following the death of his wife in 1757, a stockbroker named William Kent and his sister-in-law Fanny took lodgings in the house of Thomas Parsons, clerk of St Sepulchre's, at 33 Cock

Lane [now demolished]. In 1759 Kent lent his landlord a sum of money which he had to resort to law to try to get back. Predictably, a great animosity arose between the two men.

Meanwhile, Fanny was taken ill, and for reasons unknown, Parsons' twelve-year-old daughter Elizabeth shared her bed on several nights, during which they were kept awake by mysterious banging and scratching sounds. Fanny was convinced that it was an omen of her impending death, while others were openly suggesting that the noises emanated from the restless spirit of her sister, William Kent's wife, admonishing Fanny for cohabiting with him.

The couple later moved to new rooms in Bartlet Court, Camberwell, where after making a will in William's favour, Fanny died – according to the death certificate, of smallpox. She was interred in the vault beneath St John's Church, Clerkenwell.

Coincidental with Fanny's death, the mysterious noises returned to 33 Cock Lane, centred on the bed in which young Elizabeth Parsons slept; what was more, the girl was complaining of seeing a ghostly figure, shrouded in white, with no hands. Failing to discover any natural explanation for the phenomena, the Parsons' servant, Mary Frazer, convinced that a spirit was trying to communicate, set about the task of interrogating the ghost – taking one rap for 'yes', and two raps for 'no'. By this uncertain means, a hocus-pocus story was concocted that the spirit was indeed that of Fanny, and she claimed that William Kent had poisoned her with red arsenic administered in a cup of warm ale. She had returned to the world of the living, she said, to ensure that her murderer was hanged.

Cock Lane had by now become a place of pilgrimage for sensation-seekers from the whole of London and miles around, blocking the narrow lanes and alleys around Newgate and Smithfield, day and night, in the hope of hearing the now-famous ghost. William Hogarth incorporated the scene into his engraving 'Credulity, Superstition, and Fanaticism', and Oliver Goldsmith was just one of many celebrated visitors.

Emboldened by her recent success, Mary Frazer announced that the spirit would rap on her own coffin in St John's church, whither sped a great assembly of eminent men, including Dr

Samuel Johnson (who later wrote the essay *Account of the Detection of the Imposture in Cock Lane*). The shade, however, did not manifest itself, setting up the first stirrings of cynicism and doubt. The authorities now, in their wisdom, decided to intervene and investigate this troublesome business; it was discovered that when Elizabeth Parsons' hands were held, the noises stopped. An examination of her clothing disclosed a small board concealed between her stays, by the manipulation of which the wicked girl had been producing the tapping and creaking noises. The secret was out! The Cock Lane ghost had been laid!

But this is not the end of the story. The only person who had not been enjoying the excitement was William Kent, whose reputation as a wife-slayer was spreading the length and breadth of the City. He now prosecuted Parsons, his wife and daughter, Mary Frazer, a clergyman, and several tradesmen, who were subsequently convicted of conspiring against Kent's life and good name.

Thomas Parsons was put in the pillory at the corner of Cock Lane and then imprisoned for two years, his wife was put away for a year, and the servant Mary Frazer for six months. Of Elizabeth's fate there is no accurate record though it is unlikely that a child would suffer severe punishment. The sentence on the clergyman and the tradesmen was that they should make reparation to William Kent to the tune of several hundred pounds.

In 1845, Fanny's coffin was opened and revealed a corpse that showed no sign of putrefaction or even discoloration – which is one of the characteristics of arsenic poisoning.

In 1941, St John's, Clerkenwell, was reduced to rubble by German bombs, and Fanny's coffin could no longer be identified. Thus the mystery of her death has long outlived the mystery of the Cock Lane ghost.

COLLEY, Thomas As a means of determining innocence or guilt, 'swimming' has a pedigree dating back to the third millennium before Christ, when the Babylonian king Hammurabi decreed that if a man accused his fellow of sorcery, then the accused must jump into a river to prove, by floating, that he was innocent. However, if the man drowned, he was guilty and his goods fell forfeit to his accuser. On the other hand, if the accusation proved false then the accuser forfeited not only his property, but his life.

In the eleventh century, Edward the Confessor established *Iudicum aquae* – trial by water – as a test for all crimes, but reversed the judgement so that a suspect who *sank* was considered innocent. Although it was officially abolished in the reign of Henry III, 'swimming' persisted in common use until the late nineteenth century, mainly as a trial by ordeal for those suspected of witchcraft.

Not surprisingly, this brutal treatment frequently resulted in injury and sometimes even death. On Saturday, 24 August 1751, at the exotically named Gubblecut Cross, Thomas Colley was executed for causing just such a death.

It was not uncommon in those superstitious years of the seventeenth and eighteenth centuries to find a mob hammering on the door of some hapless old woman who somebody, with more spite than common sense, had accused of sorcery. Indeed, such occasions took on an almost festive atmosphere, with much drinking and merry-making. The finale would not infrequently be to drag the supposed witch to the village pond, or river, and apply the ludicrous test of trial by 'swimming'.

Such was the scene that took place in the month of August 1751 on Marlston Green in the parish of Tring, Hertfordshire. The victims were an old couple named John and Ruth Osborne, and they were accused of being, respectively, a wizard and a witch, though with no good reason. The rumour was that old Osborne and his wife had bewitched a local farmer named Butterfield, the result of which was that his cattle began to die. He also claimed that a spell cast by Ruth caused him sometimes to bark like a dog, sometimes to mew like a cat. It was not considered at the time that Butterfield's other occupation – landlord of the Black Horse alehouse – might have something to do with his peculiar behaviour.

The mob was led by three ruffians named Thomas Colley, William Humbles and Charles Young, called 'Red Beard'. When the unfortunate Osbornes had been dragged from the safety of their home, they were stripped naked and forced into a sitting position on the ground with their arms and legs crossed and their thumbs tied to their big toes. In this way they were rendered helpless and unable to spoil the fun to come. While the rabble carried their victims to Marlston Mere, Humbles and Young stood either side of the pond, a rope stretched between them. One end was threaded through the crossed arms and legs of John Osborne, and he was pushed into the mere by Colley, who waded after him and ducked and dragged the wretched fellow through the muddy water. When they had enjoyed their sport with Osborne, the half-drowned man was hauled out of the pond to be replaced by his wife. Again Colley was in there, forcing the helpless woman's head under the water till she could not breathe. But this time the self-appointed witchfinder had gone too far and Ruth Osborne choked to death on mud and water.

When Thomas Colley appeared before the Hertford Summer Assizes he stood charged with murder – a charge of which he was justly convicted and was sentenced to death by the Right Honourable Sir Thomas Lee, the Lord Chief Justice.

On the day of execution, Colley was taken to the gallows at Tring, hanged, and then hung in chains from a gibbet, a stern warning to any who might feel inclined to emulate his crime.

COLLINS, John Norman The first victim in what were later called the 'Michigan Murders' was Eastern Michigan University student Mary Fleszar on 10 July 1967. On 7 August, her body was found two miles north of Ypsilanti, badly decomposed and without hands or feet; she had been stabbed to death. As nineteen-year-old Mary's remains lay in the funeral parlour, a young man arrived, told the receptionist he was a close friend of the Fleszar family and made a bizarre request to take a snapshot of the corpse 'for the family'; the outraged morticians rightly refused. Besides, he was not carrying a camera.

It was almost a year later, on 6 July 1968, that twenty-year-old student Joan Schell's body was found with forty-seven stab wounds on a construction site at Ann Arbor; she had last been seen by a college friend five days earlier getting into a two-tone red car containing three young men. She had also, according to fellow students, been in the company of twenty-one-year-old university student Norman Collins. Collins, however, claimed that he had been with his mother in Detroit at the time, and there seemed no reason to pursue what was probably a case of mistaken identity.

On 21 March 1969, a third Eastern Michigan student, twenty-three-year-old Jane Louise Mixer, was found dead beside the cemetery gates at Denton Township. She had been shot and strangled, and close to the body a gift-wrapped package was found, addressed to 'Jane'. It was known that she had been offered a lift, possibly by a fellow student, to her mother's home at Muskegon. Four days later, on Tuesday 25 March, the body of a sixteen-year-old, Maralynn Skelton, known by the police to be a drug user and dealer, was found after she had gone missing while hitch-hiking. She had been sexually abused, extensively beaten, probably with a large-buckled belt, and her head had been bludgeoned. Three weeks after Maralynn Skelton's body was found, schoolgirl Dawn Basom, who had disappeared the previous evening, was discovered, strangled and dumped by the side of a country road; she was just thirteen years old. University graduate Alison Kalom was the Michigan murderer's sixth victim. She was found by three teenage boys at the edge of a field in Northfield Township; her body had been stabbed all over and her throat cut; cause of death had been the gunshot wound in her head.

Six corpses, all within the space of two years; six young women, one only just into teenage, molested and savagely murdered within a couple of miles of town – and still there were no suspects. In June 1969, Ann Arbor's citizens' committee and the press took over and invited the successful Dutch-born psychic detective Peter Hurkos, then living in Hollywood, to visit Ypsilanti. The profile Hurkos gave was of a man, under twenty-five years old and slightly built, with a moustache; a description that could have fitted a fair proportion of Eastern Michigan's male student population. Hurkos added that the youth was effeminate, liked dressing in women's clothing, and was fond of dolls and stuffed toys. This was not to be a conspicuous success for the psychic; indeed he was correct in only one major point of his profile – the killer rode a motor-cycle.

Peter Hurkos was absolutely right about another thing, though – that the killer would strike again. The last of the co-ed slayer's victims was eighteen-year-old student Karen Sue Bieneman, missing from campus since 23 July and found strangled, beaten and sexually abused three days later. This time the police had a break. On the day she disappeared Karen had visited Joan Goshe's wig-shop in town, and the manageress had seen her companion waiting outside on a motor-cycle; from her excellent description the young man was identified as Norman Collins.

Taken into custody, Collins denied having anything to do with the murder and refused to take a lie-detector test. But now that they had a suspect, the police could start investigating from a position of strength. Collins, it turned out, was an habitual thief, and a number of girl students had complained of being pestered by him. He had also, according to some of his dates, made scary references to the recent murders. Norman Collins was positively identified by the shop owner who had seen him with Karen Bieneman; and more damning still were the clippings of hair that had become attached to the last victim's underwear, and which were a perfect match with hair clippings found by forensic experts on 30 July in the basement of his uncle David Leik's house. Collins had been feeding Leik's dog while the family were on holiday, and must have brought the girl back to the house and killed her. Spots of blood on the basement floor which matched Karen's group added to an already strong case.

In a unanimous jury decision John Norman Collins was convicted of murder on 19 August 1970, and sentenced to life imprisonment with hard labour.

CONSTANZO, Adolfo de Jesus, et al.   Mark Kilroy, a twenty-one-year-old student at the University of Texas, was on spring vacation with three classmates when they decided to take in the Mexican town of Matamoros. They arrived on 14 March 1987, and during a tour of the town's bars, Mark disappeared. Investigations instigated by the Kilroy family seemed to have reached a dead end when in April 1989 Mexican drug squad officers informed the parents that during a recent raid on the remote Rancho Santa Elena, twenty miles outside of Matamoros, they had detained several men, one of whom claimed that he had seen a 'blond gringo' bound and gagged in the back of a van parked at the ranch.

As the search of the Santa Elena progressed, large quantities of marijuana and cocaine were found in a shed, as well as a formidable arsenal of weapons and a dozen brand-new cars fitted with two-way radios. The shed itself was dominated by a makeshift breeze-block altar, and around the building were an alarming number of bloodstains, scraps of human hair, and a substance only later identified as human brain pulp. In view of this, the least of the horrors was a prominently displayed severed goat's head.

Those detained in the drug raid claimed allegiance to the sinister cult of Palo Mayombe, loosely based on Santeria, and said that Mark Kilroy had been kidnapped and later 'sacrificed' on the orders of the cult's leaders – a Cuban they referred to reverentially as El Padrino (The Godfather), born Adolfo de Jesus Constanzo, and Sara Maria Aldrete, the cult's High Priestess. The primary object of the slaughter appears to have been to appease Satan in return for inviolability from police arrest and so that they would not be harmed by bullets in the event of a shoot-out. Whenever a major drug deal was about to take place, a human sacrifice was offered and the victim's heart and brains ripped out to be boiled up along with other unsavoury ingredients in a cauldron, or *nganga*, as a 'cannibal feast'.

Later, the detainees led officers to the graves of fifteen men and boys, including Mark Kilroy. Many of the bodies had been decapitated and all of them had been extensively mutilated.

Needless to say, by this time Constanzo and Aldrete were on the run.

On 5 May 1989, neighbours called the police complaining of a violent quarrel going on in the next-door apartment of a block in Mexico City. When officers arrived on the scene, Constanzo leapt to the window of the apartment and opened fire with a Uzi semi-automatic, provoking a siege which lasted forty-five minutes. During this time Constanzo burned $3,000 in banknotes and threw handfuls more out into the street. Following the gun battle, Sara Aldrete fled the building screaming: 'He's dead! He's dead!' Police entering the apartment found three of the cult's members alive, but Constanzo and his homosexual bodyguard-cum-lover, Martin Quintana, had been shot dead, locked in a final embrace in a walk-in wardrobe; they had been killed on their own orders, rather than be taken into custody. Sara Aldrete, not surprisingly, denied any involvement in the killings, but was indicted along with the other survivors of the cult on multiple charges including murder and drug offences.

On 8 May 1989 one of the most bizarre press conferences in Mexican police history took place. Before the assembled media representatives cult members under arrest were presented by senior police officers behind a table decorated with lighted candles, swords, black robes, skulls and other voodoo paraphernalia.

Among the 'celebrities' at the conference was Alvaro de Leon Valdez, a professional gangster also known as 'El Dubi'. It was El Dubi who had been ordered by Constanzo to kill him and Quintana. According to his statement, the gunman was not enthusiastic: 'He told me to kill him, but I didn't want to. Then he said I was going to suffer in hell if I didn't. Then he hugged Martin, and I just stood in front of them and shot them with a machine gun.' De Leon also told horrified reporters that Mark Kilroy had been kept bound for twelve hours before being killed by a machete blow to the head; then his back was opened up and his vertebrae pulled out to make a 'magic' necklace.

On a more mundane note, US Customs Agent Oran Neck announced that, under cover of all the mumbo-jumbo, Constanzo's gang were smuggling as much as 900 kilogrammes of marijuana a week from Mexico into the United States.

In August 1990 Sara Maria Aldrete was acquitted of Constanzo's murder, but sentenced to six years' imprisonment for criminal association; she awaits trial on charges arising out of the ranch murders. Constanzo's killer, Alvaro de Leon Valdez, was sentenced to thirty years for double murder, and the two other men taken in the Mexico City apartment, Juan Fragosa and Jorge Montes, were tried for the ranch murders and an assortment of drugs and firearms offences and sentenced to thirty-five years each. Another cult member, Omar Orea, was convicted of the same crimes but died of Aids before he could be sentenced.

CORDER, William The murder for which this most diabolical criminal underwent condign punishment was as foul and dark a crime as ever stained the annals of public justice. Maria Marten was born in July 1801, and was brought up by her father, a mole-catcher of Polstead in Suffolk. Possessed of more than ordinary personal advantages – a pretty face and a fine form and figure – it is little to be wondered at that she was beset by admirers. Thus an unfortunate step ruined the character of the young woman, and a mishap with a gentleman of fortune, residing in the neighbourhood of her father's house, left her with a child. About the year 1826 she formed another liaison, with the man who became her murderer, William Corder.

Corder was the son of a wealthy farmer at Polstead. Having become acquainted with the girl Marten, the consequence of an illicit intercourse which took place between them was a child. From that time he became much attached to her, and was a frequent visitor at her father's house. The child died a short while after its birth, and from the circumstances of its having died suddenly, and of Corder having taken it away at night and disposed of the body, an idea was entertained that it had come unfairly by its death. However, it does not appear that any real evidence was ever produced to support this impression; but the unhappy girl made use of the circumstance to induce the father of the child to fulfil a promise to make her his wife. On 18 May 1827, Corder called at the Marten house, and said that no time should be lost, and that the marriage might be as private as possible. The next day was appointed for the wedding, and he persuaded Maria to dress herself in a suit of his own clothes, so as to ensure the greatest secrecy, and then to accompany him to a part of his farm called the Red Barn, where she could exchange them for her own, and from whence he would convey her in a gig to a church at Ipswich. The girl consented to this singular proposition, and Corder immediately left the house, and was followed soon after by his hapless victim, who carried with her such of her own clothes as would be needed to appear with in church.

Within a few minutes of quitting the house Corder was seen by Maria's brother to walk in the direction of the Red Barn with a pickaxe over his shoulder, but from that time nothing was ever heard of the unfortunate girl, except through the fictitious communications received from Corder who still remained at his mother's house in Polstead. The return of Maria Marten had been expected within a day or two; but as she occasionally exhibited considerable irregularity in the duration of her visits to Corder, and as also there was an understanding that the latter should procure her a temporary lodging, little anxiety or alarm was at first felt at her prolonged absence. A fortnight elapsed, however, and then her mother questioned Corder upon the subject, when he declared that she was quite safe and well, and that he had found lodgings for her some distance away. Thus from time to time he put off such enquiries; but in the month of September he declared that he was in ill-health, and left Suffolk with the avowed object of proceeding to the Continent. Before he left Polstead Corder expressed great anxiety that the Red Barn should be filled high with stock – a desire which he personally oversaw. He took with him about four hundred pounds in money; and several letters were subsequently received by the Martens, in which he stated he was living with Maria on the Isle of Wight. It was remarked that, although he represented his residence to be in the Isle of Wight, his letters always bore the London postmark. At length strange suspicions began to be expressed, there having been no personal communication received from his supposed wife. The parents of the unhappy girl became more and more disturbed; and the circumstances which eventually led to the discovery of the most atrocious crime are of so extraordinary a nature as almost to manifest the special intervention of Providence.

In the course of the month of March 1828, Mrs Marten dreamed on three successive nights that her daughter had been murdered and buried in the Red Barn. Terrified at the repetition of the vision, an undefined suspicion which she had always entertained that her daughter had been unfairly dealt with appeared fully confirmed in her own mind; and so strong were her feelings, and so convinced was she of the truth of the augury, that on Saturday 19 April she persuaded her husband to apply for permission to examine the Red Barn, with the professed object of looking for their daughter's clothes. The stock of grain which had been deposited in the barn had by this time been removed and, permission having been obtained, the wretched father applied himself to the spot pointed out to his wife in her dream as the place in which her daughter's remains were deposited; and there, upon digging, he turned up a piece of the shawl which he knew his daughter had worn at the time of her leaving her home. Alarmed at the discovery, he searched still further, and when he had dug to the depth of eighteen inches, with his rake he dragged out a part of a human body; horror-struck he staggered from the spot. Subsequent examination proved that his suspicions were well founded, and that it was indeed his murdered daughter, whose earthly resting place had been so remarkably pointed out. The body, as may be supposed, was in an advanced state of decomposition; but the dress, which was perfect, and certain marks in the teeth of the deceased, afforded sufficient proofs of her identity.

By the time a coroner's jury had assembled, a medical examination of the body had taken place. Mr John Lawden, a surgeon, testified that there were appearances sufficient to indicate the deceased had come to her death by violent means. He said that there was a visible appearance of blood on the face and on the clothes of the deceased, and also on a handkerchief which was round the neck; that the handkerchief appeared to have been tied extremely tight, and beneath the folds a wound was visible in the throat, which had evidently been inflicted by some sharp instrument. There was also a wound in the orbit of the right eye; and it seemed as if something had been thrust in which had fractured the small bones and penetrated the brain. When the body was found it was partly enveloped in a sack, and was clothed only in a shift, flannel petticoat, stays, stockings and shoes.

No sooner had the body been discovered than all eyes turned to Corder as the murderer. Information having been despatched to London, officer Lea, of Lambeth Street police station, was sent in pursuit of the supposed offender. He traced Corder from place to place, until at length he found him residing at Grove House, Ealing Lane, near Brentford, where, in conjunction with his wife, whom he had married only about five months before, and to whom he had introduced himself through the medium of a matrimonial advertisement, he was carrying on a school for young ladies. It was necessary to employ a degree of stratagem to obtain admission to the house; but at length Lea claimed he had a daughter that he wished to put to school. He was shown into a parlour, where he found the object of his search sitting at breakfast with four ladies. Corder was in his dressing-gown, and had his watch in front of him, with which he was minuting the boiling of some eggs. The officer called him on one side, and informed him that he had a serious charge against him; he also enquired whether he was acquainted with a person named Maria Marten, at Polstead. Corder denied that he had any knowledge of such a person even by name. He was then arrested. Upon his house being searched, a pair of pistols, a powder-flask and some balls were found in a velvet bag, which, on its being subsequently seen by Mrs Marten, was identified by her as having been carried by her daughter when she left the house for the last time. A sharp-pointed dagger was also found, and this was identified by a person named Offord, a cutler, as being one which he had ground for William Corder a few days before the murder was committed. Corder was immediately escorted to Polstead, where he underwent an examination before the coroner. On his appearance before the coroner the prisoner was dreadfully agitated; and the circumstances which we have described having been testified to under oath by various witnesses, a verdict of wilful murder was returned against William Corder.

Thursday 7 August 1828 was set for the trial of this malefactor before the Lord Chief Baron Alexander. He left the jail at a quarter before nine o'clock, having previously attired himself with much care in a new suit of black, and combed his hair over his forehead, which he had previously worn brushed up in front. On account of the number of challenges made by the prisoner, it was some time before a jury was empanelled. At length, however, the prisoner was arraigned upon the indictment preferred against him, and he pleaded not guilty. The evidence for the prosecution differed but slightly from the circumstances we have detailed. Proof was given that at the time of the discovery of the body, marks were distinctly visible which showed that she had received a pistol-shot or gun-shot wound; and it was proved, by the brother of the deceased girl, that the prisoner, at the time of his quitting the house of old Marten on the day of the murder, carried a loaded gun.

The prisoner, when called upon to make his defence, read a manuscript paper in a low and tremulous tone of voice. He declared that when he and the girl reached the barn, harsh words were spoken, and Maria flew into a passion.

> I was highly irritated, and asked her, if she was to go on in this way before marriage, what was I to expect after. She again upbraided me and, being in a passion, I told her I would not marry her, and turned from the barn; but I had scarcely reached the gate when the report of a pistol reached my ear. I returned to the barn, and with horror beheld the unfortunate girl extended on the floor, apparently dead. I was for a short time stupefied with horror, and knew not what to do. It struck me to run for a surgeon – and better would it have been for me had I done so – but I raised the unfortunate girl, in order, if possible, to afford her some assistance, and found her altogether lifeless; also, to my horror, I discovered that the dreadful act had been committed by one of my own pistols, and that I was the only person alive who could tell how the fatal act had taken place. The sudden alarm which seized me suspended my faculties, and it was some time before I could perceive the awful situation in which I was placed, and the suspicions which must naturally arise from my having delayed to make the tragedy instantly known. I at length thought that concealment was the only means by which I could rescue myself from the horrid imputation, and I resolved to bury the body as well as I was able.

The Lord Chief Baron summed up, and a verdict of guilty being returned, he sentenced the prisoner to death:

> William Corder, it now becomes my most painful but necessary duty to announce to you the near approach of your mortal career. You have been accused of murder, which is the highest offence that can be found in the long annals of crime. You denied your guilt and put yourself upon your deliverance to your country. After a long, patient and an impartial trial, a jury of that country has decided against you, and that decision is most just. You stand convicted of an aggravated breach of the great prohibition of the Supreme Being – the Almighty Creator of mankind – 'Thou shalt do no Murder.'

Nothing remains now for me to do, but to pass upon you the awful sentence of the law and that sentence is – that you be taken back to the prison from whence you came and that you be taken from thence, on Monday next, to a place of Execution and that you there be Hanged by the Neck until you are Dead; and that your body shall afterwards be dissected and anatomised; and may the Lord God Almighty, of His infinite goodness, have mercy on your soul.

On his return to the jail, Corder exclaimed 'I am a guilty man', and immediately made a written confession:

Bury Gaol, Aug. 10, 1828. Condemned Cell.
Sunday evening, half-past 11.
I acknowledge being guilty of the death of poor Maria Marten, by shooting her with a pistol. The particulars are as follows: When we left her father's house, we began quarrelling about the burial of the child, she apprehending that the place wherein it was deposited would be found out. The quarrel continued for about three-quarters of an hour upon this and about other subjects. A scuffle ensued, and during the scuffle, and at the time I think she had hold of me, I took the pistol from the side pocket of my velvetoon jacket and fired. She fell, and died in an instant. I never saw even a struggle. I was overwhelmed with agitation and dismay – the body fell near the front doors, on the floor of the barn. A vast quantity of blood issued from the wound and ran on to the floor and through the crevices. Having determined to bury the body in the barn, about two hours after she was dead, I went and borrowed the spade of Mrs Stowe; but before I went there, I dragged the body from the barn into the chaff-house, and locked up the barn. I returned again to the barn and began to dig the hole; but the spade being a bad one, and the earth firm and hard, I was obliged to go home for a pick-axe and a better spade, with which I dug the hole, and then buried the body. I think I dragged the body by the handkerchief that was round her neck – it was dark when I finished covering up the body. I went the next day, and washed the blood from off the barn floor. I declare to Almighty God, I had no sharp instrument about me, and that no other wound but the one made by the pistol was inflicted by me. I have been guilty of great idleness, and at times led a dissolute life, but I hope through the mercy of God to be forgiven.

W. Corder.
Witness to the signing by the said William Corder,
John Orridge (Governor of Bury Gaol)

He subsequently appeared much easier in his mind, and just before he was turned off the gallows he said in a feeble tone: 'I am justly sentenced, and may God forgive me.'

After the execution a spirited bidding took place for the rope which was used by the hangman; and as much as a guinea an inch was obtained for it. Large sums were offered for the pistols and dagger which were used in the murder, but they became the property of the sheriff of the county, who very properly refused to put them up to public competition. A piece of the skin of the wretched malefactor, which had been tanned, was exhibited for a long time afterwards at the shop of a leather-seller in Oxford Street.*

[This account of the crime derives from one of the many contemporary records of what must be Britain's most celebrated historic murder. So great was the interest in the Red Barn incident at the time – not least because of its sexual and psychic ingredients – that it inspired all manner of by-products, from Broadsheets to Porcelain Figures, from Songs to Sermons.]

Postscript
And so what are we to make of the apparent intervention of 'providence' in pointing out Maria's last resting place? It all depends, in the end, on whether or not one believes such a thing possible. Colin Wilson, in his admirable study of *Psychic Detectives*, presents one explanation: that as Maria suffered both shot and stab wounds she did not die instantaneously, and Anne Marten was able to pick up a telepathic message from her fatally wounded daughter which remained in her unconscious mind until it was unlocked in sleep and manifested as a recurring dream.

On the other hand, Donald McCormick, in his *Red Barn*

* These relics are now on public display in the Moyse's Hall Museum, Cornhill, Bury St Edmunds.

Mystery, suggests a wholly more rational and more sinister explanation. An article published in the magazine *John Bull* six days after Corder's execution revealed that already local people were beginning to suspect that the 'dream' was rather too convenient to be true and that Mrs Marten knew rather more about events than she was telling. It was also learned later that among the few books found in the Marten household was one entitled *The Old English Baron*; it related the story of a father who, acting on instructions given in his wife's dream, discovered the place where their daughter was buried. Coincidence? McCormick offers the possibility that Anne Marten suspected that Maria had been murdered and that the Red Barn was the most likely place Corder would have buried her (remember his filling the building with grain shortly afterwards?). The dream would then have been invented in order to persuade her husband to search the barn.

Whichever of the explanations comes nearest, one thing is certain, we are unlikely ever to know the truth.

CRIPPEN, Dr Hawley Harvey The story of one of the United States' most notorious criminal exports is almost too well known to need repeating at length. However, there is one twist in the tale that many reporters have ignored.

Hawley Harvey Crippen, an American citizen with a medical degree, arrived in England in 1900. His marriage to an unsuccessful music-hall singer called Belle Ellmore soon fell into ruin and Crippen took himself a mistress – a typist called Ethel Le Neve.

Mrs Crippen disappeared, last being seen alive on the evening of 31 January 1910, and in reply to subsequent police enquiry, Crippen claimed that she had returned to the United States and there had died of pneumonia. The police, however, were dissatisfied with the explanation and instituted an investigation, the fear of which prompted Crippen and Ethel Le Neve (disguised as a boy) to board on ocean liner bound for America.

Meanwhile, the police had uncovered human remains from the cellar of the Crippen house, 39 Hilldrop Crescent, which were identified as Mrs Crippen from an abdominal scar on the body. As a result a message was sent to the ship on which Crippen travelled, by means of the newly invented wireless telegraphy system. The two fugitives were arrested as the ship neared Quebec.

The cause of his wife's death was traced to a large dose of the poisonous drug Hyoscine – of which Crippen was proved to have purchased five grammes. Despite overwhelming evidence against him at his trial, Crippen maintained his innocence to the end.

Hawley Harvey Crippen was convicted of murdering his wife, and was hanged at Pentonville Prison on 23 November 1910. There was considerable sympathy for Crippen as a result of the clear evidence of the miserable life that Belle had given her husband, and it was even said that the surprise was not that he had killed her but that he had not done it sooner.

Ethel Le Neve, who was tried as an accessory to the murder, was acquitted.

The Ghost of Hilldrop Crescent
The Hilldrop Crescent of this story has undergone significant changes at the hands of the developers since the Crippens' time, and the war-damaged site of Number 39 (along with its immediate neighbours) was rebuilt as Margaret Bondfield House, a block of flats. But if Hilldrop Crescent lost a house or two, then it would appear that it has gained a ghost: for some say that the shade of Hawley Harvey Crippen walks still, on the night of 31 January, replaying the night of Belle's death.

The first sighting of the ghost was recorded by Peter Underwood, President of The Ghost Club, in his *Haunted London*. On the night after Crippen's execution a man stood vigil on a piece of waste ground close to the house, a patch where the late doctor was accustomed to walk – perhaps to clear his head . . . perhaps to plan . . .

It was just before midnight that the already chilly air developed an icier touch . . . and from the shadow of a high wall a form began to take shape . . . a shortish man with a drooping moustache . . . and gold-rimmed spectacles. As the figure moved out of sight it was seen to be carrying a parcel. When it returned some minutes later, it was empty-handed . . . and quickly evaporated into the night.

What was wrapped in the parcel is anybody's guess . . . But what would a man who has just killed and decapitated his wife be likely to dispose of at the dead of night?

D

DALE, Rodney 'Satan's Laughing Hitman', that's what the press called him. And it is true that he did have cut on the palms of his hands the number 666 – the signature of the Beast of the Apocalypse. It is also true that as he ran amok in the Burleigh Heads district of Australia's Gold Coast he was laughing; he 'hit' eight people in a thirty-minute reign of terror, one of whom died. Other, more prosaic reports simply referred to a 'crazed sniper'; he was that too.

The madness began on the afternoon of Saturday 7 April 1990. At 4.00 p.m., officers at the Broadbeach police station were alerted to the fact that a lone gunman, dressed in black and wearing a balaclava, was firing shots with a .233-calibre rifle and a pump-action shotgun from the balcony of a flat in Tweed Street into the crowded street below. Within minutes seven police cars had been dispatched to the scene of the incident, though by the time they arrived, the man had moved to a position outside the CES (social security) office, leaving behind him his first victim lying badly wounded on the Gold Coast highway. As the gunman continued firing wildly at anything that moved, five ambulances and further police units were arriving from Coolangatta and Burleigh.

One of the things that moved was a trio of vehicles taking a bride and her family to her wedding. As Robyn Porter and her father sat in their chauffeur-driven limousine behind the two cars carrying the bridesmaids the mad sniper opened fire with his automatic rifle, showering the vehicles in a hail of bullets. The driver of the limousine was hit in the left arm and shoulder and the right hand, but bravely drove on until he was out of firing range. Speaking of his ordeal after emergency surgery, Raymond

Davis recalled: 'At first I thought he was acting the mick. He was firing like hell; I thought he must have had rubber bullets. I said, "What's that fool doing?", then I heard the deafening sound and sped up a bit. If I hadn't sped up I may have been shot in the head – then I realised I had been hit. I thought he was going to wipe us all out. He looked like something out of *Rambo* – it was like a movie, I still have that in my mind.' In the car immediately in front the chief bridesmaid, Mandy Winter, was wounded in the leg as bullets ripped through the door panel. The wedding did go ahead at the Merrimac Catholic church, and after the ceremony, with courageous understatement, the new Mrs Robyn Kelly said: 'The wedding went well, but the shooting put a damper on it.'

Meanwhile, the first of the ambulances, with a heavy police escort, was ferrying victims to the Gold Coast Hospital, and the gunman was still shooting randomly at a nearby hotel complex. At this point a hero enters in the person of Sergeant Robert Baker, a thirty-eight-year-old officer attached to Burleigh police station. Deciding that it was time for positive action, Bob Baker, armed with a Magnum revolver, walked straight across the Gold Coast highway towards the gunman. What followed was more like a Wild West shoot-out than a scene in the sunshine strip of Australia's popular holiday resort.

As Sergeant Baker approached his target he called out to the man to drop his weapon; instantly the gunman's weapon was trained on him, loosing off a spatter of bullets which, miraculously, failed to hit the officer who had also opened fire. It was the fourth slug from Bob Baker's Magnum that ended the afternoon's bloodshed as the gunman dropped his weapon after receiving a shot to the arm. In the second piece of remarkable understatement of the day, officer Baker told the press: 'I thought I was going to get killed, but it was something that had to be done. It was really tragic for the people involved. I feel really sorry for the victims – it was pretty lousy.'

With one man and seven women shot, one so badly that she would later die in hospital, everyone wanted to know one thing – who was the maniac gunman?

By the following morning the newspapers were already telling us. He was twenty-six-year-old Rodney John Dale, who lived in the block of units from the balcony of which he began his murderous spree. Neighbours spoke of him as being 'a very nice, friendly guy . . . he was always pleasant and always very happy'. He was also, according to other sources, involved with a Satanic cult – which may explain why he had carved the number 666 in the palm of each hand before, as he put it in a note left for his girlfriend, 'Going out hunting . . .'

Quite how significant Rodney Dale's peripheral involvement with the 'black arts' was in relation to his shooting spree only psychiatrists will be able to elucidate. However, there was no shortage of word space given to the opinions of the 'opposition'. Mrs Jan Groenveld, director of the organisation Freedom in Christ and one who has dealt extensively with dabblers in the occult, claimed that people who were already psychologically disturbed were liable to be strongly influenced by occult activity: 'A person who was fascinated by Satan worship and listened to [heavy-metal] music groups like AC/DC, Black Sabbath and Metallica could be pushed into violent behaviour.' She added, quite correctly, that in the United States there were people waiting on Death Row because of occult-influenced crimes.

That Rodney Dale is psychologically disturbed is denied by nobody. Indeed, his own defence lawyer, Mr Bill Potts, suggested that his client might be suffering from some form of psychosis and urged that he be psychiatrically examined in prison and, if necessary, treated. It was so ordered by the Southport magistrates and Rodney Dale, on the latest information, is undergoing psychiatric evaluation.

DANIEL, St Clair On Wednesday 2 March 1988 the tropical sun was bathing the Caribbean island of St Thomas as it did every morning; that is why it receives so many visitors. However, on this particular morning two of those tourists were not enjoying themselves at all, and Police Captain Hyndman was feeling anything but sunny. At shortly after 7.00 a.m., the local station had received a report that a man had been seen down on the beach chopping up a body with a machete.

It was true. When officers dispatched to the site arrived at Vessup Bay they found the decapitated and savagely mutilated remains of a woman later identified as fifty-three-year-old Genevieve Lewis. Mrs Lewis was normally resident on the island of Saint-Pierre et Miquelon, off the Newfoundland coast, but she had recently undergone a serious operation and was recuperating in the sun with her husband. Earlier that morning, it was learned, she had taken their small dog by car to the beach where they were accustomed to take a leisurely walk. The dog had also been hacked to death. At about the time Mrs Lewis and pet were taking their constitutional, twenty-nine-year-old Steven Cornish was also walking along the sand at Vessup Bay. Cornish was originally from Lansing, Michigan, but was staying on the island filling in his time with a bit of gardening – and as if to prove it to the world, he was carrying a pair of grass-shears. His was the second body found by the police, about one hundred yards from that of Mrs Lewis; he, too, had been separated from his head.

Unused as they were to such brutal goings-on on St Thomas, the local police swiftly mounted an extensive murder enquiry. One of the early clues in the investigation came from a neighbour of Genevieve Lewis who had been on the beach even earlier than either of the victims, and had come face to face with a wild-looking man waving a machete; wisely, she fled. From this eye-witness description it was hoped to identify the killer quickly before he escaped from the area – if he had not already done so.

Meanwhile, the police had begun to find other witnesses to the murders. Several had seen a man with a machete at about the same time in the same place, and a fisherman on one of the boats in the bay had actually witnessed the killer dismembering and disembowelling Mrs Lewis – he had even taken photographs of it. Another woman was greatly shocked to see the killer emerge naked from the sea after abandoning his clothes and washing the blood from his body; she also saw him attack Steve Cornish with a machete. It was surprising when all the information-gathering had been done quite how many witnesses there were to this double tragedy; better still, their descriptions of the protagonist were remarkably consistent. He was a black man in his early thirties, average height and build, but with distinctive short dreadlocks, a straggly goatee beard and with two upper front teeth missing.

Once the description had been pieced together and circulated, identification was a simple matter. In fact a man closely fitting that description had been arrested a number of times in the past, mainly for drug offences. Just a fortnight earlier he had been taken into custody after indecently exposing himself in a shopping mall while high on PCP; his name was St Clair Daniel. It only remained to track him down, and with half the island's police drafted in to do the job, and with a rather conspicuous naked, bloodstained fugitive, this proved no difficult task. Within the hour Daniel had been surrounded by heavily armed officers, captured and taken to police headquarters for questioning. Just ten hours after his appalling crimes, St Clair Daniel was arraigned before Magistrate Geoffrey Barnard. He was charged with two counts of first-degree murder, two counts of mayhem and one count of carrying a dangerous weapon. However, the trial was not destined to be plain sailing by any means.

It opened on 12 January 1989, when, via his counsel, Daniel entered a plea of not guilty by reason of insanity. Although he had made a confession while in custody, it was one without much mitigation. Daniel claimed that he thought Mrs Lewis's dog was going to attack him, so he killed it. Then he feared Mrs Lewis might shoot him, so he killed her too. Because Steve Cornish was in the area and might have seen the murder and attacked him for it, Daniel dispatched him too. But why, the court wanted to know, did he butcher his victims so completely?

On the answer to that question St Clair Daniel's insanity plea would pivot. According to his defence, Daniel had dismembered his victims because he feared that their spirits (called 'jumbies' in voodoo) would return and haunt him. One of the psychiatrists speaking in Daniel's defence explained to the court that voodoo was a 'beautiful and strict' religion to be found throughout the Caribbean area, and it was particularly active on St Kitts, which is where Daniel originated from. Indeed, his family (who, incidentally, thought he might be Satan) were still living. Adherents to the voodoo cult, the doctor said, were terrified of becoming zombies – living dead. One of the ways in which a person could be 'zombified' is when somebody dies an unnatural death. It is believed that their *petit von ange*, or 'little angel', hovers around the body for a week, during which time it can create zombies. The only way to prevent this is to cut off or destroy the head.

Of course, the prosecution was not about to accept this as proof of insanity, and attorney Mark Bonner insisted that what he called 'a cultural belief' did not amount to proof of insanity. The jury, though, were clearly confused, and as a result split their decision. On 19 January they announced a verdict of first-degree murder in the matter of Genevieve Lewis, but found Daniel insane in his murderous attack on Steve Cornish. They seem to have been swayed in part by the possibility that Daniel had mistaken the gardener's shears for a weapon. It didn't really matter much – a single count of 'murder one' was enough to keep St Clair Daniel in prison for the rest of his life without the possibility of parole.

DAVIS, Sergeant Arthur, Murder of It is difficult today to conceive of the barbarous wickedness to which the native Scots were subjected after the crushing of the Jacobite risings of 1715, '19 and '45. Following their defeat at Culloden in 1746, the land and property belonging to those clans who had opposed the Hanoverian government were seized by Act of Parliament, and 'factors' appointed to manage them; the men (frequently Scots) given this authority as rewards for their loyalty in the recent conflict were *per se* fiercely anti-Jacobite. Their spite against the defeated clans was often more vicious even than that of most English officers.

One of the comparatively more benign of those factors was Sergeant Arthur Davis (or Davies), attached to General Guise's Regiment of Foot. The following account of Davis's murder and the alleged return of his ghost derives from a text printed for the Bannatyne Club at the instigation of Sir Walter Scott, who wrote the Introduction.

INTRODUCTION

It was about three years after the battle of Culloden that Sergeant Arthur Davis was quartered with a small party of eight men in an uncommonly wild part of the Highlands, near Inverey in the country of the Farquharsons. A more waste tract of mountain and bog, rocks and ravines, without habitations of any kind is scarce to be met with in Scotland. A more fit locality for murder could hardly be imagined, nor one which would tend more to induce superstitious feelings. Davis was attracted to the country where he had his residence, by the great opportunity for sport which it afforded, and, when dispatched upon duty across these mountains, he usually went ahead some distance from his men, following his game without regard to the warnings about danger from the local people. To this he was exposed, not only from his being entrusted with the odious office of depriving these people of their arms and national dress, but still more from his usually carrying about with him a stock of money and valuables, enough of itself to be a temptation to murder.

On the 28th day of September [1749], the Sergeant set forth, along with his party, which was to communicate with another group of English soldiers at Glenshee; but when his men came to the place of rendezvous, Davis was not with them, and the privates could only say that they had heard the report of his gun after he had separated from them to hunt. In short, Sergeant Davis was seen no more in this life, and his remains were long sought for in vain. At length a native of the country, named Alexander M'Pherson, made it known to his master Donald Farquharson that the spirit of the unfortunate huntsman had appeared to him, and told him he had been murdered by two local Highlanders named Duncan Terig (alias Clerk) and Alexander Bane Macdonald. When Farquharson followed M'Pherson to the spot, there lying on the peat moss was the scattered skeleton of Sergeant Davis, identifiable from his tattered uniform.

A witness was found to testify that lying in concealment upon the Hill of Christie, the spot where poor Davis was killed, he and another man saw the crime committed with their own eyes; and a girl whom Clerk afterwards married, was at the same time seen in possession of two valuable rings which the Sergeant used to have about his person. Notwithstanding all these suspicious circumstances, the defendants were ultimately acquitted by the jury at their trial at the Edinburgh High Court of Justiciary in January 1754.

This was chiefly owing to the ridicule thrown upon the story by the incident of the ghost, enhanced by M'Pherson's claim that the spirit spoke as good Gaelic as he had ever heard in Lochaber.

'Pretty well,' countered defender M'Intosh, 'for the ghost of an English sergeant!'

This was indeed no sound jest, for there was nothing more ridiculous in a ghost speaking a language which he did not understand when in the body, than there was in his appearing at all. But still the counsel had a right to seize upon whatever could benefit his clients, and there is no doubt that this observation rendered the evidence of the spectre yet more ridiculous.

The most rational explanation seems to be that knowledge of the crime had come to M'Pherson by ordinary means, and he had simply invented the ghost, whose commands, according to Highland belief, were not to be disobeyed.

However that may be, the reader may be intrigued to scan the original description of M'Pherson's spectre taken from the Bannatyne Club publication:

When he [M'Pherson] was in bed, a vision appeared to him as of a man clad in blue, who told him: 'I am Sergeant Davies', but that before he told him so, M'Pherson had taken the said vision at first appearance to be a real living man, a brother of Donald Farquharson's: That he rose from his bed, and followed the vision to the door, and then it was, as has been told, that he said he was Serjeant Davies who had been murdered in the Hill of Christie, about near a year before, and desired the deponent [M'Pherson] to go to the place he pointed at, where he would find his bones, and that he might go to Donald Farquharson, and take his assistance to the burying of him: That upon giving Donald Farquharson this information, Donald went along with him, and finding the bones as he informed Donald, and having then buried it with the help of a spade which M'Pherson had alongst with him: And for putting what is above testified upon out of doubt, that the above vision was the occasion of his going by himself to see the dead body, and which he did before he spoke to anybody. And further, that while he was in bed another night after he had first seen the body, but had not buried it, the vision again appeared naked, and minded him to bury the body; and after that he spoke to other folks, and at last complied and buried the bones. That upon the vision's first appearance to the deponent in his bed, and after going out the door, and being told by it he was Serjeant Davies, the deponent asked him who it was that had murdered him, to which it made this answer, that if the deponent had not asked him, he might have told him, but as he had asked him, he said he either could not or would not, but which of these two expressions the deponent cannot say; but at the second time the vision made its appearance to him, the

deponent renewed the same question, and then the vision answered,
that it was the two men now in the dock that had murdered him.

DeFEO, Ronald 'Butch'   Greguski was the first officer on the
scene. The call had come through to the Amityville Village police
department at 6.35 that evening of 13 November 1974: 'Hey,
kid's just run into the bar. Says everyone in his family's been
killed.' So in the autumnal gloom patrolman Kenneth Greguski
was dispatched to Ocean Avenue where a small crowd was
beginning to assemble. The centre of attraction seemed to be the
young man crouched down sobbing that they had got his mom
and dad. It turned out that 'they' had got a lot more than that.
When Greguski worked his way through the house he made the
body count six; they were later identified as Ronald DeFeo
Senior, a wealthy motor trader, his wife Louise, their daughters
Dawn and Allison, aged eighteen and thirteen respectively, and
sons Mark, twelve years old, and John, seven. Still weeping on
the porch was Ronald junior, twenty-three years old and the sole
survivor of the DeFeo family massacre.

   When he was finally settled in at the Amityville police station,
Ronald 'call me Butch' DeFeo had a strange tale to tell. As the
detectives listened, 'Butch' told them that his father had been
involved with the Mafia, and in particular had crossed swords
with one of the mob's hit-men named Louis Falini. A fortnight
earlier there had been an armed hold-up when money was being
transported from the DeFeo car showroom to the bank, during
which Ronald junior had been obliged to part with the company's
takings. According to his present narrative, Butch's father had
accused him of inventing the robbery story and stealing the
money for himself.

   On the morning of the murders Ronald junior had got up early
and driven to the showroom; several times during the morning he
had tried to phone home but there had been no reply. At noon
Ronald returned to Amityville where he spent the afternoon
drinking with friends. Early evening he left the bar for home,
throwing over his shoulder the casual remark that he had
forgotten his keys and would have to break in through a window.
While this interview was going on, other officers were checking

out Butch's friends, and learned that he was a gun fanatic. What's more, the DeFeos had all been shot with a Marlin .35-calibre rifle – and there was a cardboard box which had contained a Marlin 35 in Butch's wardrobe. Understandably Ronald DeFeo found himself spending longer in police custody than he had bargained for. He whiled away the time inventing ever more preposterous accounts of the killings until at last he was detained on a holding charge of the second-degree murder of his brother Mark.

It was nearly a year later that DeFeo stood trial, and he had made good use of this time feigning insanity; truth to tell, he had made a pretty good job of it – at least, defence psychiatrist Dr Daniel Schwartz was prepared to give expert testimony that at the time he killed his family Butch was suffering from mental disease – 'paranoid delusions' the doctor said, a belief that if he did not kill them they would kill him. As if to add weight to his insanity plea, when Ronald was shown a photograph of his mother lying dead on her bed, he claimed: 'I have never seen this person before.' But Butch didn't have it all his own way. Dr Harold Zola for the prosecution gave his opinion that the defendant was not a psychopath but a sociopath, who had so devalued human life that even his parents were expendable in Butch's drive to assert his superiority. And the jury obviously agreed, because they found Ronald DeFeo junior guilty on all six counts of murder. DeFeo was sentenced to twenty-five years to life on each count and confined to the Dannemora Correctional Facility, New York. As the six slayings are legally considered to form part of a single act, the sentences are being served concurrently.

And so a dreadful crime might have been forgotten. But that is to reckon without the power exerted when the supernatural meets Hollywood. The DeFeo home in Amityville, ironically called 'High Hopes', was subsequently sold to a family who, after only a year, fled the house following a series of disturbances by what they called 'evil forces'. This phenomenon was first re-created as a best-selling book and then not one but several films in the 'Amityville Horror' sequence. It is just as well the media cashed in when they did – the present owners of 'High Hopes' find the place a very quiet and pleasant home.

DE RAIS, Gilles At the pinnacle of his power in the mid-fifteenth century, Gilles de Laval, Baron de Rais, Marshal of France, champion of the Maid of Orleans, was the wealthiest man in Europe. Surrounded by a bodyguard comprising the two hundred knights who had fought alongside him in the army of Joan of Arc against the English, Gilles lived more lavishly than an emperor, perhaps even than Charles VII of France himself.

To increase his wealth still further, and to replace that frittered away on a profligate lifestyle, Gilles embarked upon an alchemical search for the elusive 'philosopher's stone', which was believed to transmute base metals into gold. As he became increasingly bewitched by the Dark Powers, so Gilles began to sacrifice in the time-honoured way, to his new gods and demons, building on an already notorious reputation.

And still the Baron might have remained free to continue a career of child sacrifice and sexual sadism, but for a small error of judgement, that of insulting a brother of the powerful Treasurer of Brittany, Geoffroi de Ferron, by beating and imprisoning him. Unfortunately, Jean de Ferron was also a priest and, in a civil suit, Gilles was brought before the Bishop of Nantes and the Inquisitor General of France, in September 1440, charged as a heretic. Of course, there was considerably more to the charge than met the eye – after all, Gilles de Rais had been living an heretical life for many years without interference. But here, with the watertight case of the maltreatment of a priest, was an opportunity to secure a conviction and in doing so allow all those concerned in the prosecution of the case to enjoy a share in the confiscation of Gilles de Rais' not inconsiderable wealth.

There were forty-seven charges made against Gilles de Rais arising from three categories of heresy: first, 'abuse of clerical privilege' (attacking de Ferron); second, 'the conjuration of demons'; and third, sexual perversions against children. For example, charge number fifteen read:

> . . . according to the lamentable outcries, tears and wailings, and denunciations coming from many people of both sexes, crying out and complaining of the loss and death of children, the aforesaid Gilles de Rais has taken innocent boys and girls, and inhumanely butchered,

killed, dismembered, burned and otherwise tortured them, and the said Gilles has immolated the bodies of the said innocents to the devils, invoked and sacrificed to evil spirits, and has foully committed the sin of sodomy with young boys and in other ways lusted against nature after young girls . . . while the innocent boys and girls were alive, or sometimes dead, or sometimes even during their death throes.

After six sittings hearing one hundred and ten witnesses, the court put Gilles de Rais and his servants to the torture to extract yet further incriminating evidence. One servant, Etienne Corillait, testified that:

> . . . to practise his debauches with the said boys and girls, against the dictation of nature, he first took his rod in his left or right hand and rubbed it so it became erect and sticking out; then placed it between the limbs of the boys and girls, not bothering with the natural female receptacle, and rubbed the rod or virile member on the belly of the said boys and girls with much libidinous excitement until he emitted sperm on their stomachs . . .
>
> . . . after having had an orgasm . . . he had considerable pleasure in watching the heads of the children separated from their bodies. Sometimes he made an incision below the neck to make them die slowly, at which he became very excited, and while they were bleeding to death he would sometimes masturbate on them, and sometimes he would do this after they had died and their bodies were still warm . . .
>
> In order to stifle the cries of the children when he wished to have relations with them, he would first put a rope around their neck and hang them three feet off the floor, and just before they were dead would cause them to be taken down, telling them not to utter a word. Then he would excite his member and afterwards have an emission on their stomachs. When he had done this, he had their throats cut and their heads separated from their bodies. Sometimes he would ask, when they were dead, which of them had the most beautiful head.

Of course, even by the standards of the often ludicrous procedures of the Inquisition, the trial of Gilles de Rais was a farce. Most of the incriminating evidence was either elicited under torture or was given out of spite or self-interest. Eventually even

Gilles de Rais himself succumbed to torture on 21 October 1440, and was prepared to admit whatever the court told him to admit. Two days later, at Nantes, Gilles was executed by garrotte and thrown on to a bonfire. As little could be served by this last indignity, his friends and family were allowed to remove his body from the pyre before it was lit.

Such truth as ever emerged from the trial of Gilles de Rais has in any case been embellished and distorted by time and fashionable prejudice. It is certain that Gilles was one of Europe's worst child rapists and killers; whether his death toll ever reached the often quoted 500 to 800 is doubtful. There have always been doubts about the motives for accusing de Rais of such a preposterous number of killings, and this must necessarily be seen as the fatal consequence of popular mythology embellishing the depravities of its favourite *bêtes noires*; not least because de Rais' 'confession' was coerced by threats of excommunication.

DE SALVO, Albert   A reign of terror haunted the city of Boston between June 1962 and January 1964, leaving thirteen women dead, and provided the state capital with a modern legend.

The killing ended on 4 January 1964 with the discovery of the body of nineteen-year-old Mary Sullivan. Like all the other victims of the killer who had become known as the 'Boston Strangler', she was found in her own apartment. She had been stripped and bound, raped and strangled; and in a final sadistic gesture, Mary's killer had left a New Year's greeting card wedged between the toes of her left foot.

This maniac's first murder was back on 14 June 1962, when a fifty-five-year-old divorcée named Anna Slesers was found by her son, naked, raped and strangled with the belt of her own blue housecoat. The killer's method remained unvarying. After targeting his victim, the Strangler gained admission to her home by posing as a workman. All his victims were women, all were sexually assaulted and all were strangled – usually with an item of their own clothing, often a pair of stockings or tights which he tied with a bow under the chin. In some cases strangulation had been accompanied by biting, bludgeoning and even stabbing.

Despite the customary false confessions, and a blanket police response to the city's mounting panic, the Boston Strangler remained an enigmatic object of terror.

After the murder of sixty-eight-year-old Helen Blake on 30 June 1962, the police enlisted the expertise of forensic psychiatrists in order to help build a profile of the killer. In the opinion of the experts he was a youngish man, eighteen to forty, suffering delusions of persecution and with a hatred of his mother (so far only elderly women had been attacked). This 'word portrait' was run alongside police records of known sex offenders, and although a number of suspects emerged from the files and were interviewed, the Strangler remained free to kill seventy-five-year-old Mrs Ida Irga on 19 August.

On 5 December 1962, the psychological profile of a 'mother-hater' collapsed when Sophie Clark was murdered; she was twenty years old, just three years younger than two of his next three victims. Just over a year later, after the death of Mary Sullivan, the 'father' of American psychological profiling, Dr James Brussel, provided a new 'psychofit' of a thirty-year-old man, strongly built, of average height, clean shaven with thick dark hair; possibly of Spanish or Italian origin – and a paranoid schizophrenic. It was to prove remarkably accurate. Meanwhile, another specialist used to working in the dark, Dutch psychometrist and psychic detective Peter Hurkos, had entered the investigation.

In the end it was for the Strangler to make himself known. On 27 October 1964 he entered, as he had done before, a young woman's apartment posing as a detective. The intruder tied his victim to the bed, sexually assaulted her, and then inexplicably left, saying as he went, 'I'm sorry.' The woman's description of her assailant led to the identification of Albert De Salvo, and the publication of his photograph resulted in scores of women coming forward to identify him as the man who had sexually assaulted them.

But De Salvo was still not suspected of being the Boston Strangler. It was only in 1965, while he was being held on a rape charge and confined to the Boston State Hospital, that De Salvo confessed in detail to the Strangler's crimes. His knowledge of the murders was such that at the time no doubt could be entertained as to the truth of his confession. Nevertheless, there was not one single scrap of direct evidence to support these claims, and in a remarkable piece of plea-bargaining, De Salvo's attorney agreed that his client should stand trial only for a number of earlier crimes unconnected with the stranglings. Albert De Salvo never stood trial for the crimes of the Boston Strangler, but was instead convicted of robbery and sexual offences and sent to prison for life.

On 26 November 1973, Albert De Salvo was found dead in his cell, stabbed through the heart; he was forty-two years old.

That, then, is the generally accepted narrative of the serial killings of the man known as the Boston Strangler. However, there is a strange and not often related twist to the case involving the psychic, Peter Hurkos.

It has never been revealed who financed Peter Hurkos' involvement in the Strangler case – Gerold Frank, in his definitive study *The Boston Strangler*, claims that it was an industrialist who wanted to remain anonymous. However, it apparently met with the approval of Attorney General Edward W. Brooke Junior, and his Assistant, John S. Bottomly.

Hurkos arrived on the scene on 29 January 1964, and spent the first couple of days subjecting to psychometry the contents of two boxes filled with such evidence as the scarves and stockings left behind by the Strangler. He also made similar tests on hundreds of photographs taken at the scenes of the murders. In the days that followed, Peter Hurkos went through all the mugshots of suspects hoping to identify the Boston Strangler; he claims he found two rapists and a murderer, but not the right one. He refused to discuss these cases for fear of 'cluttering his mind'.

One impressive piece of work was when Hurkos traced lines across the back of a map of Boston with a hair comb belonging to one of the victims. He stopped suddenly over an area where Boston College, a Jesuit institution, the home of Cardinal Cushing and St John's Seminary stand. With great excitement, he announced: 'Here you will find the killer. He looks like a priest . . . he gets thrown out by the monks. He speaks French, I hear a French accent.' Hurkos also suggested that the suspect was a homosexual. The following day things hotted up; a police officer handed a note to the clairvoyant, who immediately insisted that it had been sent by the murderer. The name at the bottom of the letter was the one changed by Gerold Frank to 'Thomas P. O'Brien', for the purposes of his book – for obvious reasons, because 'O'Brien' was never charged. The address from which the letter had been sent was Boston College, where Peter Hurkos had stopped the comb on the map.

Now the psychic began to describe the killer's physical characteristics: 'About five foot seven or eight inches, high hairline, a mark on his left arm and something wrong with his thumb. He has a French accent, is a homosexual and hates women. He has something to do with a hospital. He is taking blood and washing his hands in the blood . . . He does not do normal work, he is not normal himself. He has blue-grey eyes, killer's eyes, and a sharp, pointed nose and large Adam's apple'. Then he drew a picture of the man.

Peter Hurkos also started to have dreams, all of which were diligently recorded – they were like films of the murderer at work playing in his head. It was always the same man. It was always 'Thomas P. O'Brien'. And when the police began checking on the background of 'O'Brien' it was discovered that Hurkos' predictions had been uncannily accurate in almost every descriptive aspect. In fact for a long time 'O'Brien' was a leading police suspect and was interviewed at length in the mental hospital in which he had been lodged. Hurkos visited 'O'Brien' in the hospital, and left even more convinced than ever that he was the Boston Strangler.

When the police eventually picked up Albert De Salvo and he confessed to the Strangler's crimes, Hurkos remained convinced they were holding the wrong man. Till his death in 1988 Peter Hurkos stubbornly insisted that he was right and the police were wrong. As to De Salvo's ability to tell police details of the Strangler's murders, Hurkos had a simple explanation – De Salvo had been held in the same mental hospital as 'O'Brien', and they had spent much time together.

As Albert De Salvo was never tried for the murders, we will never know what verdict a jury would have given. However, in the years since the case was big news, doubts have increasingly been expressed over the safety of accepting De Salvo's confession.

DESHAYES, Catherine, *see* **LA VOISIN**

DE VITO, Tony, Murder of The case of the disappearing gangster was to prove one of the most successful investigations undertaken by the Dutch psychic (or 'paragnost', as he was sometimes described) Gerard Croiset.

It all began on the evening of Sunday 27 September 1953. Twenty-four-year-old gangster Tony De Vito left his home in Brunson Street, St Paul, Minnesota, waving a cheery 'I'll be back later tonight' to his mother. She never saw him again. It was claimed that De Vito had been planning to marry the following week and, as a gesture to his future bride, had promised to give up being a hood and get a proper job.

It was not until March 1958 that the true story of Tony De Vito's vanishing trick came to light. On that fatal night in 1953, De Vito had been lured to Alary's restaurant on Wabash Avenue and afterwards kidnapped and killed by four gangsters named Rocky Lupino, John Azzone, Sam Cimin and Alex De Goode. The body was interred without ceremony in East St Paul, though the grave was sprinkled with lye and red pepper to deter predatory dogs – a final grudging gesture of respect for the dead, perhaps.

At any rate that was the story according to Alex De Goode, who was spilling the beans in the St Paul police headquarters. The problem was that a painstaking search of the area pinpointed by De Goode had failed to reveal De Vito's body. Which was a pity, because without it the case against his killers was somewhat slim.

Enter Minneapolis broadcasting station KSTP, who were looking for a good mystery for radio and television programmes. William E. McGivern, head of news at KSTP, had heard of the strange powers possessed by Gerard Croiset and immediately contacted him via the Parapsychology Institute in Utrecht, where Croiset worked under Professor Tenhaeff. The psychic agreed to help, and in early February 1960, he received an envelope containing two photographs of Tony De Vito and a map of St

Paul and Washington County. Croiset examined the documents and started off by providing some remarkably detailed personal information about De Vito himself. Then the clairvoyant moved on to the murder. It was correct, he confirmed, that four men were responsible. Croiset described the kidnapping as taking place outside a large country house close to six smaller buildings and near to a plot of open ground, such as a park. There was a railway near the house, and a road crossing the railway. So far this corroborated what the police already knew of the kidnapping. Gerard Croiset then proceeded to plot the route the gangsters took, right down to the details of the road numbers. De Vito had been taken out of the car and led to a plot of ground with a hole in it. This coincided with the version told by Alex De Goode, who claimed they strangled De Vito with a rope and buried him in a five-foot hole.

Passing on to details of the main participants in the plot, Croiset accurately described the last meal that De Vito ate at the Alary restaurant, the man who lured him there, Tony Legato, and Legato's girlfriend – right down to the clothes she had on and the jewellery she wore. This is his word-portrait of one of the gangsters: 'About 1.68 metres tall, between forty-eight and fifty-two years of age, weighs about 180 pounds. He has a fat neck with a roll of flesh under his chin, and carries his head very backwards. He has a light-blue signet ring on his right hand. When he speaks he lisps. He seems to be a man who does not do any work, but who gambles and is the boss of a night-club.' This is an almost perfect physical description of the murderers' alleged ringleader, Rocky Lupino – even down to the signet ring with a blue stone. The only point that could not immediately be confirmed was whether Lupino lisped; but one fact is known – his wife does.

So astonished and delighted were the bosses of KSTP with their postal experiment that they descended, uninvited and unannounced, on the Parapsychology Institute. There they filmed and recorded Gerard Croiset at work. It resulted in a television programme and a radio series. However, at this point there was a rather sad breakdown of goodwill. Professor Tenhaeff felt betrayed by having the work of the Institute and of his friend and colleague exploited so extravagantly, and refused any further cooperation with KSTP.

Despite the fact that the station tried several times to lure Gerard Croiset to the United States, he has declined, emphasising that although he is sure he could locate Tony De Vito's last resting place he is no longer interested in the case.

DOMINGUEZ, Julian   In February 1982, twenty-six-year-old Julian Dominguez told the San Antonio, Texas, court: 'I was convinced he was the Devil. I rushed out of the building, frightened because I thought I had just killed Satan . . . I was drenched in blood . . .'

And well he might have been, because on 3 November 1978, Dominguez had just stabbed to death his fifty-two-year-old father Lino, driving the ten-inch blade into his body thirty-four times.

The following day he repeated the awful crime on his cousin Mary Ledesma.

Dominguez explained to the jury that he had been told by 'voices' that he was the true Christ, and that his relatives were incarnations of the Devil; so he butchered them. It may have seemed the obvious thing to do for one as unhinged as Julian Dominguez, but it hardly represented a justification to the tough Texan jury, who convicted him of murder.

DRINAN, Michael   As this book demonstrates, the assistance given to police enquiry teams by clairvoyants and mediums can sometimes lead to dramatic developments in a case. Most of these practitioners use some form of intermediary object to communicate with the unseen power which gives them knowledge. A great number employ 'psychometry', which involves physical contact with an item – often of clothing – which has been closely associated with the object of the search. Others may 'dowse' with rods or pendulums over ground or maps, or receive messages from 'spirits' or 'contacts'. Very few use that traditional implement of divination, the ouija board (so called from the French and German words for 'yes' – 'oui' + 'ja'); one of its most remarkable successes was achieved not through a professional psychic, but through a dabbler.

Towards the end of December 1971, forty-nine-year-old night-club chef Michael Drinan reported his wife Laura's disappearance from their Swansea home. Not long afterwards – on New Year's Eve to be precise – Drinan could be found in the club, weeping into his drink and complaining how much he missed his dear Laura. For twenty-two-year-old Eileen Gagnon it was all a bit too much. Eileen worked at the same local night-club as Drinan, and was not at all keen on him; but there was more to it than that. Given his previous demeanour, the whole act seemed false. Then, a few days later, on 5 January, Drinan came in for his shift at the club carrying a large suitcase. Still the girl kept her suspicions to herself – after all it was a police enquiry now, and besides it was well known that Mrs Drinan had a lover and everybody thought she had run off with him.

However, when several months had passed and the police still had not traced the missing Laura Drinan, Miss Gagnon decided to enlist the help of the occult. In short, she went out and bought a ouija board. It was the month of May now and while most other people were forgetting the Drinan case, Eileen and her cousin Pearl Radlett were crouched over the ouija board, their fingertips lightly touching the top of the planchette. 'Is Mrs Drinan still alive?' asked Eileen warily. As though the wooden marker was itself alive, it transported their fingers smoothly across the board until it came to rest at 'NO'. With a knowing look at her cousin, Pearl asked: 'Was she murdered?' The response was immediate and the planchette glided across the board to 'YES'. 'Who by?' the marker going from letter to letter now, 'D-R-I-N-A-N'. 'Michael Drinan,' the girls said together. Eileen Gagnon had just one more question: 'Was the suitcase connected with the murder?' No hesitation: 'YES'.

It was a rather bewildered and very sceptical Chief Superintendent Pat Molloy who sat in his office at mid-Wales CID and was told not only that he had a murder on his hands, but that the young woman sitting in front of him had solved it, with a bit of occult help. But anyway, since his own officers were getting nowhere with the enquiry, what was there to lose?

When Molloy confronted the suspect with his special knowledge, Drinan did not take long to crack. He claimed that he had arrived home from work on 29 December and found his wife lying dead on the bed; he thought she might have committed suicide. In a panic because he thought he would be blamed for her death, Drinan decided to dispose of the body and report his wife missing. That is where the suitcase came in. The suitcase and the flame-gun which was normally used for torching weeds and which Drinan had hired on 4 January. Having transported Laura's body to an isolated quarry Drinan set about reducing it to a pile of ashes which he dumped into the sea. Officers visiting the quarry later found burn marks on the ground and fragments of charred human bone.

In the end, the police did not believe Michael Drinan's story that his wife was already dead when he found her. It seemed more likely that he had killed Laura during an argument, perhaps over her rather adventurous extra-marital activities, and he was charged with murder.

The jury at Newport Crown Court chose a middle path and found Drinan guilty of manslaughter. He was jailed for six years.

Following the hearing, Detective Chief Superintendent Pat Molloy expressed his gratitude for Eileen Gagnon's somewhat unorthodox detective work when he told reporters: 'Without the help of Miss Gagnon and her ouija board, Drinan would probably have got away with it. They managed to do what five months of intensive investigation failed to do.' Praise indeed.

DYER, Ernest When they left the Service at the end of the First World War, the two young Army officers remained close friends – like many whose relationships had been cemented by the mutual hardships of active service in a war notable for its privations. It was to prove a great irony that one of these young men was to achieve what the Kaiser's Army could not – the shooting of his friend.

For twenty-five-year-old Eric Gordon-Tombe and Ernest Dyer the world made free by the blood of their comrades was their oyster. Tombe had a healthy bank balance, and Dyer knew some ways to manipulate it. Their first business partnership – a motoring venture in Harlesden – quickly ran into difficulties, as did a second attempt to make a fortune from the new mode of transport. Clearly having learned from their mistakes, Messrs Tombe and Dyer exchanged four-wheeled vehicles for four-legged ones, and in 1920 Eric's money bought them a racing stable and stud farm at Kenley, in Surrey. The farmhouse had been called 'The Welcomes', a name Ernest Dyer took to heart when he moved in with his wife and children, leaving Eric Tombe to reside either at his London apartment or in a hotel room in Dorking, not a great distance from the farm.

The proposition was no great success, in a large part due to Dyer's preference for backing horses rather than breeding them; and it was no doubt this financial instability that was responsible for the mysterious fire which damaged 'The Welcomes' in April 1921. Dyer's claim for £12,000 on the insurance was instantly rejected by the insurers, and he prudently let the matter drop. But it could be no curb to Ernest's passion for spending money – he had already been borrowing heavily from Tombe, and now began to forge the young man's signature on cheques. Not unreasonably, Eric saw this as a decidedly unfriendly gesture, if not treacherous, and consequently harsh words were exchanged. They may well have been the last words the unlucky Eric Tombe ever uttered; certainly it was the last time anyone remembered having seen him alive.

Although they could not be called an intimate family, the Tombes had always enjoyed each other's company and confidence. Tombe senior was a retired clergyman, and both he and Eric's mother were of those advancing years when the presence of a son can be a great comfort. The sort of parents to fret when filial duty was not felt to be done. And when Eric seemed to have disappeared out of their – and everybody else's – life without leaving any word of explanation, the family was rightly worried. The weeks dragged on into months, and still there was no word from the errant son. A man of action, however eccentric, the Reverend George Gordon-Tombe began to insert a series of advertisements into the personal columns of newspapers – 'Anyone knowing the whereabouts . . .' etc. When these did not produce the result so anxiously awaited by the distressed parents, sixty-year-old George Gordon-Tombe went himself to London and scoured the West End haunts so familiar to Eric and Ernest, the two young men-about-town; but with no conspicuous success. Then George Tombe recalled a letter from his son in which he mentioned his hairdresser, a Mr Richards who operated an establishment in London's fashionable Haymarket. Yes, the barber remembered Eric's pal – Dwyer was it, Eric called him? Lived somewhere down in Surrey – 'The Welcomes'.

Dyer was not at home when the old clergyman called, but his wife was able to shed some light on the disappearance of his son. Mrs Dyer remembered her husband saying he had received a telegram from Eric, excusing his absence: 'Sorry to disappoint. Have been called overseas.'

The Rev. Mr Tombe next thought he might benefit from an interview with young Eric's bank manager, and that gentleman received him with courtesy, and sympathy for the old fellow's evident anxiety. Anxiety which, the manager told him, he could rid himself of that very instant. Eric Tombe had been in regular contact with the bank by correspondence, and a letter had only recently been received instructing them to allow power of attorney to his partner Ernest Dyer. It was dated 22 July 1922. The old man's relief lasted no longer than it took to reach the bottom of the page; 'But this is not my son's signature, this is a forgery.' And the bank's file on the Tombe account revealed a whole series of such forgeries – one, for example, had transferred £1,000 to a Paris bank 'for the use of Ernest Dyer'. Indeed, the man Dyer seemed to have quite cleaned out the account – and more besides. That he had fleeced his son was bad enough, but it began to occur to the tenacious old clergyman that Dyer might also be privy to his son's disappearance. But where *was* Ernest Dyer? He seemed to have vanished as completely as Eric Tombe.

It was not until many months later, in November 1922, that the question was answered; and then only by the intervention of chance. A man calling himself James Fitzsimmons had been advertising in the local Scarborough newspaper, up in Yorkshire. It was one of the oldest confidence tricks in the book – 'Contact advertiser for employment with outstanding prospects; small financial investment asked' – and the district police force had tracked Fitzsimmons to the Old Bar Hotel, Scarborough.

On 16 November, Detective Inspector Abbott entered the hotel and asked to see Mr Fitzsimmons; as the man in question was escorting the policeman up to the room he occupied on an upper floor he made a movement which looked very like, in the words so beloved of the motion picture, 'going for his gun'. Abbott lunged at him, there was a struggle, the gun went off and, true to the movie scenario, Fitzsimmons went limp . . .

But he was not Fitzsimmons after all. He was Dyer; and a search of the room revealed a treasure trove of incriminating evidence; not least among which were a pile of cheques with the forged signature E. Tombe, and a suitcase bearing the initials E.T.

And what of Eric Tombe? We might suppose that the one key to his whereabouts was now beneath six feet of earth. But that would be to reckon without the supernatural: to ignore those powers which are neither explicable nor controllable, the unknown secrets of the mind. Mrs Tombe, until now but a sad and silent bystander in this family tragedy, began to dream.

She dreamed such nightmares as to wake her shouting and shivering with fear. The dream was always the same, always she saw the dead body of her son lying at the bottom of a well.

It was some days before the persistence of George Tombe succeeded in persuading the hard-headed Francis Carlin of Scotland Yard's Murder Squad to take the dreams seriously. But after he and his handful of diggers arrived at 'The Welcomes', they had to take them very seriously indeed; at the bottom of a well, beneath stones and rubble, was the body of Eric Tombe, the back of his head removed by the blast of a shotgun.

As a postscript to this curious narrative, Jonathan Goodman in one of his excellent thematic compilations (*The Supernatural Murders*, Piatkus, 1992) has appended William Henry's astrological confirmation of the Dyer murder. For those of us only semi-literate in the reading of astrological charts it is quite heavy going in places, but of William Henry's personal convictions there can be no doubt: 'No matter how carefully a killer may try to cover his tracks, there is always a piece of evidence he can never destroy: namely, the positions of the planets at the time of his crime.' Accepting that everything (even events) can be described in a combination of planets (called a 'signature'), then these can be cross-checked. In the present case, Henry asks, can we discover a murder signature in Ernest Dyer's astrological chart for the time at which Eric Tombe died? Fortunately for the theory we can. More impressive still: 'Tombe was killed precisely during that one brief period in his life when the position of his progressed Sun would complete the Mars–Saturn–Uranus–Hades "murder patterns" in Dyer's horoscope.' And if it can be believed that murders can be revealed by dreams, why then should they not be written in the planets?

F

FARNARIO, Norah Emily I have not been to the Isle of Iona for many years now – too many years; for what the Holy Island lacks in size (it is barely five square miles) it compensates in beauty and mystery. Even the seemingly endless tread of visitors' feet cannot spoil the majesty of the graves of the Scottish kings, nor the clicking of their cameras disturb the serenity of the Abbey, founded 1,500 years ago by the Irish monk Columba, who brought Christianity to the pagan Picts of the north.

But there is a more recent mystery commemorated there in the quiet Reilig Odhrain burial ground. I am told the stone still remains, its simple message cut into the white marble: 'N.E.F. died 19 November 1929. Aged 33 years.'

Sixty-five years ago. Before MacBrayne's ferries ran their Three-Island pleasure tours from Oban, round Mull, to Staffa and Iona; before electricity; before telephones and running water. In those days few but the hardy islanders would journey along the thirty-odd miles of rough track, through Glen More, along the shoreline above Loch Scridain, and across the weather-beaten Ross of Mull to the Fionnphort ferry, there to cross the mile-and-a-half of water that is the Sound of Iona.

Norah Emily Farnario was what in London would have been called a 'bohemian', a 'free spirit' – much given to wearing colourful folk-weaves and exotic jewellery. Like most of her type, Norah was passionately interested in folk-lore and 'earth mysteries'; which would have been very cosy had it not led to a somewhat more dangerous fascination with a study of the occult. Miss Farnario spent what some may think an unhealthy amount of her time trying to contact the spirits of the dead; in this pursuit she was greatly encouraged by Mrs Moina Mathers, a gifted spirit-medium and clairvoyant, and wife of the magician Samuel Liddell Mathers (see 'A blasphemous sect' below). The Mathers also encouraged Norah Farnario to experiment with telepathy and faith-healing, and she had become a member of the Order of Alpha and Omega, one of the many occult groups inspired by the Mathers' Hermetic Order of the Golden Dawn.

For Norah the hardships on the journey to Iona were seen through the eyes of the enlightened, and when she arrived in the autumn of 1929 it was as though she had come to a spiritual home. She took lodgings at an island croft, and even if the local people found her habits a little alien, a little 'weird', she was left alone to pursue her poetry and her lonely treks across the barren, windswept moors; nocturnal journeys during which, she later claimed, she communicated with the spirits of the island.

Whose these spirits were we can only guess – the long-dead islanders of those pagan times before St Columba replaced their ancient rituals; or the shades of the monks whose lives were savagely taken by the Norse pirates?

In the course of time, the state of Norah Farnario's mind appears to have become unbalanced, and she turned restless and anxious, sometimes rambling incoherently about contact with 'the world beyond'. Then quite suddenly she seemed to be gripped by a great panic, accompanied by an urge to leave the island immediately. Whether things would have turned out differently if it had not been a Sunday, or if the Fionnphort ferry had operated on the Sabbath, it is difficult to say; probably by this time it was too late. Norah, her bags packed and waiting, was marooned on the island for at least another night – and at this point she almost certainly knew that she would never again cross the Sound of Iona.

The following morning, Norah's landlady found her room empty, her bed unslept in, and her clothes neatly folded beside it. When Norah had not returned by early afternoon, a search party was raised among the crofters to search for her; a search which failed to find any trace of the strange woman who roamed the moors at night.

The following day the searchers were successful – two islanders found Norah Farnario's body. Not, as was earlier expected, at the foot of the craggy shoreline, but spreadeagled on the bleak heather moor, naked but for the magical robe of her Order and a tarnished silver chain round her neck. Her face was frozen in a grimace of stark horror, and the soles of her feet cut to ribbons in her desperate flight from who knows what? One hand still gripped tightly a long-bladed knife – almost certainly her ritual athame, a weapon of magical power; and when her body was moved it was seen that she had used it as a last bid for protection, for with the sacred instrument of Art she had cut a crude cross in the rough turf on which she lay. Her last act of invocation had been in vain.

And there, officially, the case of Norah Farnario ended. The local doctor, as bewildered as everybody else by the mystery, simply wrote 'heart failure' on her death certificate; and Norah hopefully found peace in her small plot in God's little acre.

But there were many in the occult world who were not as easily satisfied as the island police – they *knew* how Norah Farnario had met her death: she had been the victim of a vicious psychic murder. Some (among them the celebrated occultist Dion Fortune) were prepared to go as far as to name a suspect, a person with a history of involvement in psychic attacks – Mrs Moina Mathers.

Had Norah offended her one-time mentor? Had she broken some vow connected with the Alpha and Omega? Was she engaged in some rivalry with an Adept more powerful than herself? One thing is sure; whatever attacked Norah Farnario on that freezing November night, it was no earthly thing, nor any heavenly phenomenon – poor Norah had looked straight into the jaws of hell.

'A blasphemous sect . . .'
It is difficult to understand the implications of Norah Farnario's mysterious death without some appreciation of the risky nature of the occult studies in which she was clearly immersed, and the people with whom she was involved in London.

Norah had for many years been a friend and associate of Mrs Moina Mathers, a gifted clairvoyant and occultist. Mrs Mathers' husband, Samuel Liddell Mathers, was to a very great extent responsible for the introduction to Britain of the occult practices current in nineteenth-century mainland Europe – particularly

France and Germany. This revival of interest in magic – generally known as the 'Western Esoteric Tradition' and based broadly on the Qabalah – had been generated by the French mage Eliphas Levi (Alphonse Louis Constant), and popularised by such contemporary novelists as Honoré de Balzac and Bulwer-Lytton.

In 1884, a clergyman by the name of Dr William Woodman purchased an esoteric manuscript from a bookstall in London's Farringdon Road and showed it to the then London Coroner, William Wynne Westcott, an authority on the Qabalah and member of the group known as the Rosicrucians (which had been formed in Paris by Levi's chief disciple, the Marquis Stanislas de Guaita). Westcott in turn recruited the aid of Liddell Mathers (also a Rosicrucian) and, with his wife's help, Mathers translated the manuscript which dealt in the main with a Qabalistic interpretation of the Tarot. This became the basic working document of a whole new 'tradition' of occult study, and the foundation of the Hermetic Order of the Golden Dawn. According to Moina Mathers, the Order 'studied the intellectual forces behind Nature, the constitution of man and his relation to God'; in reality it became the theatre of war for a psychic battle between the immense egocentricities of its leading members. Within a short time, Mathers who, convinced that he was descended from the clan McGregor, had taken to calling himself 'McGregor Mathers' and 'Comte McGregor de Glenstrae', had forced out the founders and taken over total control of the Golden Dawn and its lodges in Edinburgh, Paris, London, Bradford and Weston-super-Mare.

In 1898, a young man named Aleister Crowley joined the Order, and attempted to unseat Mathers from its leadership. Space does not allow a discussion of the remarkable personality and magical career of the man called 'The Beast', but suffice it to say that when Crowley sought power it was a fight without rules. In *The Great Beast*, his biography of Crowley, John Symonds describes the psychic war that resulted from Crowley's attempt to wrest the Golden Dawn from Mathers.

Mathers, his pride wounded by such temerity, conjured up a vampire to smite down his enemy; Crowley combated the she-devil and finally overcame it 'with her own current of evil'. The

following is a first-hand account of the struggle by author J.F.C.
Fuller:

> At once recognising the power of her sorcery, and knowing that if he
> even so much as contemplated her Gorgon head, all the power of his
> Magick [sic] would be petrified, and that he would become but a
> puppet in her hands, but a toy to be played with and when broken cast
> aside, he quietly rose as if nothing unusual had occurred; and placing
> the bust on the mantelpiece turned towards her and commenced with
> a magical conversation; that is to say a conversation which outwardly
> had but the appearance of the politest small talk, but which inwardly
> lacerated her evil heart, and burnt into her black bowels as if each
> word had been a drop of some corrosive acid.
>
> She writhed back from him, and then again approached him, even
> more beautiful than she had been before. She was battling for her life
> now, and no longer for the blood of another victim. If she lost, hell
> yawned before her, the hell that every once-beautiful woman who is
> approaching middle-age sees before her; the hell of lost beauty, of
> decrepitude, of wrinkles and fat. The odour of man seemed to fill her
> whole subtle form with a feline agility, with a beauty irresistible. One
> step nearer and then she sprang at Frater P. [Crowley] and with an
> obscene word sought to press her scarlet lips to his.
>
> As she did so Frater P. seemed to play around the head of the
> vampire, and then the flaxen hair turned the colour of muddy snow,
> and the fair skin wrinkled, and those eyes that had turned so many
> happy lives to stone, dulled and became as pewter dappled with the
> dregs of wine. The girl of twenty had gone; before him stood a hag of
> sixty, bent, decrepit, debauched. With dribbling curses she hobbled
> from the room.
>
> As Frater P. left the house, for some time he turned over in his
> mind these strange happenings and was not long in coming to the
> opinion that Mrs M[athers] was not working alone, and that behind
> her probably were far greater forces than she.

Crowley then responded by setting a pack of psychic blood-
hounds on the Mathers. After mortal combat, Mathers created a
spell which struck dead the whole baying pack with one blow; and
for good measure he put a curse on the Crowley servant who went
mad and tried to kill Mrs Crowley. Incensed, Crowley summoned
up from hell the demon Beelzebub and forty-nine of his cohort of

devils and dispatched them to Paris to torment the Mathers.

Expelled from the Golden Dawn, Aleister Crowley later founded the society called A A (*Argentium Astrum* – Silver Star).* Ironically, perhaps, it was in the year of Norah Farnario's death, 1929, that Crowley published his masterpiece *Magick in Theory and Practice*, arguably the best single volume written on the subject.

Before leaving the subject of Crowley, it is interesting in the context to note that in seeking a secluded place in order to pursue his study of the Magical System of Abra-Melin the Mage, he chose Boleskine House, near the village of Foyers, just above Loch Ness:

> On first arriving at Boleskine [August 1899], I innocently frightened some excellent people by my habit of taking long walks over the moors. One morning I found a large stone jar at my front door. It was not an infernal machine; it was illicit whisky – a mute, yet eloquent appeal not to give away illicit stills that I might happen to stumble across in my rambles. I needed no bribe. I am a free trader in every sense of the word.

> *The Confessions of Aleister Crowley*

FLANAGAN, Dale, *et al.* It was just coming up to midnight on 5 November 1984, and like many other ordinary couples who had settled on the outskirts of Las Vegas, fifty-eight-year-old Carl Gordon and his wife Colleen were getting ready for bed. Suddenly, there was a violent crashing of glass as intruders burst into the Gordons' home and ruthlessly murdered them. Colleen was dragged up to the bedroom, thrown on to the bed and shot twice through the head; Carl, rushing to her rescue, stopped no fewer than seven slugs.

Carl and Colleen had both been born and raised in California, and it was in the Sunshine State that they had married and brought up their own family. When the children had grown up and left home, the Gordons had headed for Nevada and in 1979

---

* Described in the magazine *The Looking Glass* as 'a blasphemous sect whose proceedings conceivably lend themselves to immorality of the most revolting character . . .'

had settled in a comfortable house on Washburn Road outside Las Vegas. Not long before their untimely death, Carl and Colleen had invited their nineteen-year-old grandson Dale Flanagan to park his caravan at the back of their property.

Not unnaturally, Dale was top of the list of suspects wanted for questioning in connection with the brutal crimes. By 10 December Flanagan was being held in custody charged with murder. A week later, five of his friends were also answering questions – Michael Walsh and Johnny Luckett, both seventeen years old, and Thomas Akers, Roy McDowell and Randy Moore, all eighteen. Despite their disarmingly normal, civilised appearance, it was being claimed that all six youths were committed to the worship of Satan and to carrying out his works. One of the most pressing 'works' was the assassination of Carl and Colleen Gordon in order that their worthless grandson might inherit their not inconsiderable estate. It had been Flanagan himself who suggested the plan at one of their coven meetings the month before the murders.

It is surprising how a few weeks in custody facing murder charges in a state employing the death penalty will loosen even tongues bound by Satanic vows of silence. Thomas Akers turned state's evidence in exchange for a suspended sentence on a guilty plea to voluntary manslaughter. Michael Walsh picked up four life terms for pleading guilty to two charges of murder with a deadly weapon. The remaining four defendants entered not guilty pleas, and following a ten-day trial, were convicted by the jury as charged. Dale Flanagan and Randy Moore, who had fired the fatal shots, were both sentenced to death, Johnny Luckett was given life without the possibility of parole and Roy McDowell received a life sentence.

FLOWER, Margaret and Philippa A pamphlet was published in London in 1619 (*The Wonderful Discovery of the Witchcrafts of Margaret and Philip* [sic] *Flower*) detailing the arraignment of the two sisters before Sir Henry Hobart and Sir Edward Bromley at the Lincoln Assize in March 1618.

Daughters of a notorious witch and 'monstrous malicious woman' Mother Joan Flower, Margaret and Philippa had been dismissed from service at Rutland Castle, and had, according to their confession, concentrated the full power of their witchcraft in 'the destruction of Henry, Lord Rosse, and the children of the Right Honourable Francis, Earl of Rutland'.

Philippa's admission describes the manner in which she secreted from the castle Lord Rosse's right-hand glove and handed it over to her mother. Mother Flower called upon her 'spirit' or 'familiar'. in the form of a cat, named Rutterkin, and rubbed the glove on the creature's back. The glove was then plunged into boiling water, and 'afterwards she pricked it often and buried it in the yard, wishing that Lord Rosse might never thrive'.

As a result of similar sorcery it was claimed that Rutland's eldest son also died, for which Margaret and Philippa Flower were publicly executed.

G

GAMBLE, Phillip   It was fashionable around the 1970s and 80s for teenagers in America to dabble in the peripheral activities of the occult, and few high-school campuses failed to produce at least one Satanic cult group. With notable exceptions, these excursions into the black arts were no more than an excuse for drink, drugs, sex and heavy-metal music, and the sort of adolescent need to belong to a 'secret society' that is familiar to any parent or teacher of teenagers. Most of these junior cultists grow out of it as they leave school and discover close relationships and the pressures of employment.

Phillip Gamble was one of these kids, and at fifteen he was a member of the coven at Airport High School, in Monroe County, Michigan. In fact if truth be told, he was the only one of the group who really took it seriously.

Like most adolescent Americans (and a few mature adults too) who claimed to be Satanists, Phillip Gamble acknowledged Anton LaVey's *Satanic Bible* as his textbook and final authority. That is where he learned that 2 February is the occult festival of Candlemas, a time for greeting the spring with sacrifices.

On 2 February 1986, Phillip's seventeen-year-old brother Lloyd became one of those sacrifices. According to Phillip Gamble's subsequent statement, he walked in on Lloyd as he slept and blew his head away with a shotgun – a gift to Satan. Phillip was eventually placed in a young persons' institution.

GARNIER, Gilles   To all those who believe that bestial mass murder is a phenomenon of the late twentieth century, Gilles Garnier is a sharp reminder that serial killers have always been with us. In the case of Gilles, superstition gave him another, no less fearsome, name – werewolf.

By the year 1573 savage assaults on young children had reached alarming levels around the town of Dôle, in the Franche-Comté region of France. Worse still, such witnesses as there were told of the infants being carried off by a werewolf. All this was sufficient for the local *parlement* to issue a proclamation that:

> . . .in the territories of Espagny, Salvange, Courchapon and the neighbourhood a werewolf has often been seen, who, it is said, has already carried off several small children so that they have not been seen since. And as he has attacked and injured also some horsemen, this court, wishing to prevent further danger, permits those who live in these said places, notwithstanding all edicts concerning the chase, to assemble with pikes, halberds, arquebuses and sticks, to pursue the werewolf in every place they might find him, to bind and to kill, without incurring any penalties.

Two months later, on 9 November, a group of peasants rescued a young girl from the jaws of a huge wolf in a field called La Poupée, near Authune. The child had already been savaged by the creature's fangs, and her rescuers were certain they recognised in the wolf the features of Gilles Garnier.

Garnier, an impoverished recluse from Lyon, lived in a squalid hovel with his wife Appoline, near Armanges; he was known locally as 'the hermit of Saint Bonnot'. Like most eccentrics, Garnier was viewed with mistrust and fear, and when, just two weeks later, a ten-year-old boy went missing and was later found minus most of his flesh, Monsieur and Madame Garnier were arrested and charged with lycanthropy (the medical and legal term for being a werewolf).

While he was in custody Gilles made a series of confessions. In one he detailed the murder of a twelve-year-old boy in August 1573 at a pear orchard near the village of Perrouze. 'Despite the fact that it was Friday', Garnier felt the need to eat the child's flesh, but had been disturbed by the approach of a group of men; on this occasion he had been in human rather than lupine form. Two months later, according to his admission, Garnier had been in the shape of a wolf when he attacked a ten-year-old girl in a vineyard near a wood named La Serre. This time he was not interrupted, and after killing the child with tooth and claw, Garnier stripped her naked and ate her flesh; indeed he found it so toothsome that he kept some of the tenderest cuts back for Madame Garnier.

Gilles Garnier was tried at Dôle, and on the basis of his confessions, convicted of murder and lycanthropy. According to custom he was sentenced to be burned at the stake, and this awful penalty was carried out on 18 January 1574. It is worth mentioning that Garnier's crimes were considered so heinous that the traditional mercy accorded to those who confessed – strangulation before the pyre was torched – was refused in Garnier's case and he was burned alive.

GREEN, Howard, and **MARRON, Carol**   Although it is rather unsatisfactory as regards its lack of detail and conclusion, this as-yet unsolved double murder deserves mention simply for the grotesque way in which the victims' bodies were treated.

Howard Green, a fifty-three-year-old taxi-driver and amateur artist, and thirty-three-year-old secretary and part-time fashion designer Carol Marron shared an apartment in New York's DeKalb Avenue. On the evening of Sunday, 16 December 1979, a motorist driving along Route 80 at West Paterson, New Jersey, saw the bodies of a man and a woman on the grass verge; they were later identified as Green and Marron.

The manner in which the couple had been killed left no doubt in the minds of experienced police officers that this was a ritual murder. Both victims had been bludgeoned on the left side of the skull and had been stabbed through the right eye; most fantastic of all was that their bodies had been totally emptied of blood, probably with the use of the sort of large syringe employed by vets. The occult theme was reinforced when detectives searching the DeKalb Avenue apartment found a number of pieces of occult paraphernalia.

A curious footnote to the case was added by the arrival of an anonymous letter addressed to the newspaper reporter Maury Terry (who investigated the Satanist connections in the 'Son of

Sam' murders – see page 34). The brief note mentions that Carol Marron had been asking people about the Ordo Templi Orientis, and begs Terry to look into the case. Although the OTO is a magic society mostly associated with the name of Master Occultist Aleister Crowley, there are branches all over modern-day America, and its headquarters is said to be in New York City.

GREENACRE, James On 28 December 1836, a bricklayer passing some new building works in London's Kilburn district noticed a package wrapped up in sacking hidden behind a paving stone which had been leaned up against the wall. When he removed the stone for a closer look, the labourer was appalled to see that the package rested in a pool of frozen blood. After the superintendent of works and other witnesses had been assembled together, the bundle was opened to reveal the trunk of a woman later estimated to have been about fifty years of age. Of the head and limbs there was no trace.

On 6 January of the following year Matthias Rolfe, a lock-keeper at Stepney, was closing one of the canal gates when he fished out a human head. The flesh, it has been recorded, was 'quite perfect, but the jawbone was broken and protruded through the skin, and one of the eyes seemed to have been knocked out by means of a blunt instrument. One ear was split, and an ear-ring hole was pierced above it. The ears had the appearance of the ear-rings being torn out. The skull had been fractured by a heavy blow, and the surgeon estimated that the grisly relic had been in the water four or five days.' The head belonged to the dismembered trunk.

It was 2 February before the legs came to light, being the unwelcome find of a man cutting osiers in Coal Harbour Lane. The very decomposed limbs were matched with the exhumed torso and found to correspond perfectly.

A sordid and distasteful crime, but one which might have passed unnoticed among the many such murders in a brutal age. But there is one feature that lifts it out of the ordinary. A quite incorrect assertion was subsequently made that the head had been found after its whereabouts had been revealed in a dream. The claim appears in Emily Henderson's biography of her father, the eminent barrister and historian John Adolphus, and was based on Adolphus's own diaries:

> I remember my father's uneasiness when the suspect was brought before the magistrate day after day and he could not go on towards committal, the head of the wretched victim not having been found. Circumstances were strongly against the prisoner, but the law would not permit a trial unless the body could be identified. Then a most wonderful circumstance occurred at last and settled the matter. The victim had lodged some months before at a little shop in Goodge-street, and the very night of her murder she called to take leave of the people there, saying she was going to be married the next day. Soon after they heard of her murder. The woman of the shop said one morning to her husband: 'I have now dreamt for four nights of a place where I know we shall find that head, and if you still refuse to go with me, I am determined to hire a man to dig there, and I shall find it.' At last she prevailed upon her husband and took him a long way off (I think in the Bayswater direction), where they were laying foundations for houses, a large open space. 'Dig there,' she said. He did so, and found the head buried in a sack . . . The head was quite perfect, and the features had not been mangled in the least.

This wild flight of fancy on the part of a man who, perhaps, should have known better, is not corroborated by any other contemporary account of the case.

After the finding of the head (in the canal lock-gate) a man who had reported his sister missing viewed the body and identified it as Hannah Brown. As Brown knew of his sister's relationship with one James Greenacre, it was not long before that individual found himself under arrest. He had in his possession pawn tickets from Hannah Brown's silk dresses and shoes, and his lodgings revealed the four locked trunks which testified to his imminent departure for America. In an adjoining room there were remnants of bloodstained cloth of the same type that was found near the sack containing the body. Although he attempted suicide, Greenacre recovered to stand his trial, be convicted of Hannah Brown's murder and sentenced to death. He was executed at Newgate on 2 May 1837.

GREENWOOD, Vaughn Orrin It was one of those unique patterns, so bizarre that nobody on the investigation team could doubt that they had a single serial killer on their hands. And a weird one at that.

Over two months beginning in early December 1974, Skid Row vagrants were being found dead in doorways and alleys dotted around Los Angeles. But these winos and deadbeats were not the usual victims of malnutrition and the winter cold; each had his throat meticulously cut open before the killer scattered salt around his body. Then he removed the victim's shoes and left them pointed at his feet. Ritual killings. There was no chance that any of the deaths could have been copy-cat murders because details of the 'Skid Row Slasher's' *modus operandi* had not been released to the press. The problem was that winos do not have the best of memories, and interviews with dozens of them had the effect of providing dozens of different descriptions of a possible suspect. In the end a composite picture was built up of a strongly built young white man with long fair hair.

Which was a waste of time, because they should have been looking for a black man. He was thirty-one-year-old Vaughn Greenwood, and he was picked up on 3 February 1975 – three days after the ninth victim was found – after an axe attack on two men in Hollywood.

When the 'Skid Row Slasher' appeared in court he stood charged on eleven counts – the nine recent Skid Row jobs and two murders committed in 1964. On 29 December 1976 Greenwood was convicted of nine of the murders, the two earlier ones being declared by the judge to have been mistried. Just over a year later he was sentenced to life imprisonment.

GRIERSON, Isobel It is often difficult in these times of comparative enlightenment and freedom from superstition to imagine the extent of bigotry which resulted in the deaths of scores of British men and women during the witch hunts of the sixteenth and seventeenth centuries. By no means as widespread as the witch mania that spread through mainland Europe like a pestilence, the Scottish experience was, nevertheless, significant in its sheer ruthlessness. One of the most outrageous of the Caledonian trials for witchcraft took place in the Supreme Criminal Tribunal in Edinburgh in 1607.

The subject of this process was Isobel Grierson, the wife of John Bull, a labourer of Prestonpans. On 10 March 1607, Grierson stood accused on six charges. First, that having taken against one Adam Clark, she did, around the hour of midnight during November 1606 'in the likeness of her own cat, accompanied with a great number of other cats, in a devilish manner, enter within their house where they made a great and tearful noise and trouble; whereby the said Adam, then lying in bed with his wife, and servants that were then in the house, apprehended such a great fear that they were likely to go mad'.*

Secondly, Isobel was charged with engineering the death of William Burnet and the terrorising of his wife, Margaret Miller. According to the charge she left a piece of raw flesh on the Burnet threshold causing a demon, in the mortal form of a naked child, to haunt the house upwards of six months. As if this were not enough, Grierson herself was said to appear as a spirit and 'in a most ungodly and filthy manner, to piss over Margaret Miller and various other parts of their house'. Such was the shock to Burnet's sensibility that 'in great dolour and pain' he died.

Isobel Grierson was thirdly charged with casting a spell on Robert Peddan in October 1598, whereby he fell sick. Peddan, lucky fellow, remembered in time that he owed Mrs Grierson a debt of nine shillings odd. After begging her forgiveness for his tardiness in making good this debt, Robert Peddan recovered his health. However, he was clearly not off the hook entirely, for he claimed that, in June 1606, Isobel Grierson passed the open window of his house and put her hand in to stroke the cat sitting on the sill. At the time Peddan was brewing beer which 'immediately turned rotten and black, thick like dirt in the gutters, with a filthy and pestilent odour, so that no one could drink or even smell thereof'. This was the substance of the fourth charge.

The fifth charge levelled at Isobel Grierson also concerned the unfortunate Peddan family; this time it was Robert's wife,

---

* Quotations are taken directly from the records of the trial proceedings, called the *Books of Adjournal*.

Margaret McDonald. Margaret, it was said, took sick and, fearing Isobel Grierson was the cause, tried to appease her. Margaret recovered but Grierson, smarting at being accused of witchcraft, threatened Mrs Peddan in no uncertain terms. Her exact words were: 'The faggot of hell light on thee, and in hell's cauldron may you seeth.' Margaret did. But clearly not for long enough, because she recovered to receive yet another of mistress Grierson's curses. This one went: 'Awa' thief, I shall have your heart for spreading false rumours about me.' Poor Margaret fell sick again and perished.

The final charge laid to the account of Isobel Grierson in that dark time was that she was 'a common sorcerer and a witch, an abuser of people by laying on and taking off sickness and disease, and using all manner of devilish and ungodly means to earn a livelihood . . . a user of charms and other wicked practices'.

It is possibly unnecessary to say that Isobel Grierson was found guilty by the jury 'and convicted of all and sundry heads and points of the indictment'. She was, according to the practice of the time, executed by burning at the stake, in her case on Castlehill, just outside Edinburgh. She was accorded the mercy of strangulation by the executioner before being reduced to ashes.

H

HAGLEY WOOD CORPSE It was late on the afternoon of
Sunday 18 April 1943, when the three lads approached a venerable wych elm which had stood in the Hagley Wood for as long as
anybody could remember. The boys had been bird-nesting on the
grounds of Lord Cobham's Hagley Hall, and it occurred to their
experienced eye that the multitude of tangled, spiny branches
looking for all the world like a land-bound sea anemone, would
provide an ideal nesting place. The most agile of the hunters
scrambled up between the twisted growth until he reached a point
where a deep cavity eroded by time and decay stretched down
inside the trunk. To his horror, when the lad looked into the hole
he saw a skull grinning back at him.

When they had recovered their breath after the fastest run
home any of them had ever made, and with all thoughts of birds
and their eggs long pushed out of their minds, the shaken trio
blurted out their amazing story to incredulous parents.

It was Sergeant Skerratt who was given the task of opening the
investigation, and having posted a constable to stand guard
overnight, he waited for daylight before exploring the interior of
the tree – a few more hours were not going to make much
difference to the elm's occupant.

On that bright Monday morning a team of detectives from the
Worcestershire force cautiously examined the cavity in the main
trunk of the tree. From the top it dropped several feet, but was
only about two feet across at its widest, which, with the hazard of
the almost impenetrable branches, made it a very unlikely place
to choose to hide a corpse. Or part of a corpse, as it turned out.
The body had been mutilated at some stage, though a painstaking
search of the ground around the wych elm managed to turn up a

shin bone, some finger bones and some pieces of fabric which were presumed to be remains of the victim's clothing.

The man who was entrusted to make some physical sense of this bizarre discovery was Professor J.M. Webster. As Dr Webster he had launched the country's first forensic laboratory in 1929 in Sheffield; less than a decade later he had established one of England's most prestigious forensic establishments – the West Midlands laboratory at Birmingham. Nor was he any stranger to problematic murder cases – he had been involved in the Nodder case in 1937 (see page 177); he would also, two years after the present case, be part of the medical team attached to the investigation into the death of Charles Walton (see page 218). The Hagley Wood remains could not have been in better hands.

Despite the unpromising material with which he had to work, Professor Webster was not only able to build up an almost complete skeleton, but was also able to tell detectives that the victim had been a woman about five feet tall, around thirty-five years old, with irregular teeth in her lower jaw, and brown hair; she had been dead for approximately a year and a half. More remarkable still perhaps was the Professor's reconstruction of the woman's clothes based on the fragments found around the tree. She had been dressed in a blue and yellow striped woollen cardigan and an ochre-coloured skirt with a peach taffeta underskirt and a light-blue belt; on her feet the woman had been wearing blue crêpe-soled shoes and on her wedding-ring finger a cheap ring ('value 2/6d'). Cause of death proved more problematic because there was no physical evidence of injury or disease; however, because a ball of clothing had been forced into the mouth of the skull it was possible that this had been done before death, resulting in asphyxia. Professor Webster offered one more informed guess: it was his opinion that, due to the difficulty of wedging the body into its resting place, it had been put there before the onset of rigor mortis.

In all, it was a tremendous piece of forensic detective work. Ironically, not a single one of the clues proved capable of getting the police team any nearer to identifying the Hagley Wood corpse. Missing person files could produce nobody of the victim's description, and a trawl of dentists failed to jog a memory of those irregular front teeth.

Having eliminated the normal avenues of level-headed crime investigation, the police were reluctantly obliged to look at the less rational explanations for the murder. Local folk-lore held that Hagley Wood had once been a place of witches – but that was long, long ago. And it is true that in Druidical tradition spirits dwell in trees – in fact a later belief was that the spirit of a witch could be 'bound' by a hollow tree. But this was all getting a bit *too* supernatural for the good men of the Worcestershire CID. One puzzle that could not be so easily dismissed was the severed hand. Why had one hand been buried separately if not as part of a ritual disposal?

Then the messages started appearing, painted on walls around the area – 'Who put Bella down the wych elm – Hagley Wood?' Sometimes Luebella was substituted as a name but whether this revealed a special knowledge of the victim or the crime, or was simply a flight of fancy was never discovered, and the author or authors of the graffiti never identified. Later, that indefatigable authority on folk-lore and witchcraft, Margaret Murray, was to state her opinion that the Hagley Wood body was the victim of Satanists.

Although the case continued to enjoy periodic revivals, no useful progress was made, and the official part of the enquiry was laid to rest. The case remains officially 'unsolved'.

HAIGH, John George   To the residents of the Onslow Court Hotel, Kensington, where he lived during 1949, Haigh could do no wrong; he was polite, attentive and charming. Little wonder then, that he had no difficulty in gaining the confidence of a wealthy sixty-nine-year-old widow, Mrs Olive Durand-Deacon.

Mrs Durand-Deacon was looking for an active way of investing her not inconsiderable fortune, and turned to Haigh for advice on a scheme she had to manufacture and market false fingernails. Haigh invited her to visit his engineering factory (in reality no more than a storeroom) at Crawley in Sussex where they could further investigate Mrs Durand-Deacon's investment.

On 18 February 1949 the two of them drove to Crawley. Only Haigh returned, for during the visit he had shot the unfortunate woman through the neck, stripped her of her jewellery and fur coat and dumped her into an empty oil drum; this he filled with sulphuric acid which he had ordered just two days earlier. For the sake of effect, Haigh went with a fellow resident of the hotel to report Mrs Durand-Deacon's disappearance. The police thought that Haigh was perhaps just a little too smooth. And besides he already had a criminal record. To be on the safe side they paid a visit to the Crawley 'factory' and found – as well as the barrel of sludge that was Olive Durand-Deacon, traces of blood and a recently fired revolver.

And it was at this point that Haigh made a big mistake. He was under the misapprehension that murder cannot be proved without a body and told the police: 'Mrs Durand-Deacon no longer exists. I've destroyed her with acid.' He also claimed to have killed and similarly disposed of eight other people – three members of the McSwan family, Dr and Mrs Henderson, and three unknowns who were more than likely figments of Haigh's imagination. Further, the contents of the oil drum also contained a plastic denture, unaffected by the action of the acid, which was identified by her dentist as having been made for Mrs Durand-Deacon.

Haigh's defence at the Lewes Assizes in July 1949 was one of insanity, but despite the improbable claim that he had drunk his victims' blood, he was judged quite sane enough to be found guilty of murder and hanged at Wandsworth Prison on 10 August 1949.

This insistence by his defence counsel, the celebrated Sir David Maxwell Fyfe KC MP, on establishing Haigh as a psychopathic vampire, had the effect of making both his client and the only – for Haigh did not speak on his own behalf – defence witness, Dr Henry Yellowlees, appear, respectively, untruthful and incompetent. Certainly the transcript of this part of the court proceedings shows how irritated and antagonistic the judge, Mr Justice Humphreys, became with the medical evidence.

Although for reasons best known to himself, Sir David did not present it as evidence, Haigh had already laid the foundations for his vampire act as early as 28 February 1949 when, in his statement to the police concerning the murder of Mrs Durand-Deacon, Haigh claimed *inter alia*: 'Then I went out to the car and fetched a drinking glass and made an incision, I think with a penknife, in the side of the throat, and collected a glass of blood, which I then drank.'

When John George arrived at Lewes Prison after his committal on 2 March 1949, he elaborated this fantasy to the Reception Officer: 'This is the result of doing six people,' he boasted, 'but not for personal gain. It was not their money but their blood that I was after. The thing I am really conscious of is the cup of blood which is constantly before me. I shot some of my victims, but I couldn't say if I shot them in the head, if the hole was not there to show afterwards. But I can say I made a small cut, usually in the right side of the neck, and drank the blood for three to five minutes, and that afterwards I felt better. Before each of the killings I have detailed in my confession, I had my series of dreams, and another common factor was that the dream cycle started early in the week and culminated on a Friday.'

It was Haigh's dreams that were the pivotal point of Dr Yellowlees' belief that Haigh was, albeit insanely, *driven* to commit murder. In the light of what was to follow, and in particular of the judge's scurrilous attitude towards him, it might be as well to repeat Sir David Maxwell Fyfe's introduction to the witness: 'He is a medical gentleman who, apart from an ordinary degree in medicine, is a Fellow of the Royal College of Physicians in Edinburgh and London and the corresponding body in Glasgow, and in his military experience he has been Consulting Psychiatrist to the British Expeditionary Force in France in 1939 and 1940; amongst his other appointments he has been physician and psychological lecturer at St Thomas's Hospital and examiner in those subjects at the University of London.' Sir David might also have added that Dr Yellowlees was also the Physician Superintendent at the famous York Retreat hospital, and a consultant with a thriving Harley Street practice.

In the present context, it was Dr Yellowlees who examined John George Haigh during his remand in Brixton Prison, London, with the help of Brixton's Medical Officer, Dr Matheson.

Which is why, on the second day of Haigh's trial at the Lewes Assizes, Tuesday 19 July 1949, he was telling the jury about Haigh's background – that his mother 'was greatly given to studying dreams, in a fortune-telling or future-telling sense, and believed that the future could be told by them, and books upon those subjects were readily available to him . . .'

Much was also made of the intensely religious upbringing that Haigh was given by his father, a member of the strict order of Plymouth Brethren. Between the ages of ten and sixteen Haigh was a scholar (and chorister) at Wakefield, and it was during this period that, according to Dr Yellowlees' testimony, Haigh 'experienced a constantly recurring dream which he called the dream of the Bleeding Christ. In this dream, he said, he could see either the head or sometimes the whole body of Christ on the Cross with blood pouring from his wounds.'

Then, around 1944 there were the 'tree dreams'. Dr Yellowlees explained:

The dream he describes is that he goes out into a forest and sees before him an entire forest of crucifixes. These gradually turn into trees, and the trees, which have branches stretching out at right angles, appear to be dripping with dew or with rain. As he gets nearer he sees that it is blood that is dripping from the trees, and not water. One of the trees then gradually assumes the shape of a man who holds a bowl or a cup beneath one of the dripping trees, and collects the blood which comes from it. As this happens he sees the tree getting paler in colour, and he himself feels that he is losing strength. Then the man in the dream, when the cup is full, approaches him, offers it to him, and invites him to drink it. He says that at first he is unable to move towards the man, the man recedes, and he cannot get to him, and the dream ends. He then tells me that this dream may be repeated for some nights in succession, and then again he said four or five nights. During the time when the dream is recurring he is uneasy, distrait, able to do his daily functions all right, but not really at ease. He says that after this his killings occur, and after them – I think he said after one or two of them, but I am not sure – he dreams again the same dream, but this time the man does not recede from him, and he is able to drink the blood.

Mr Justice Humphreys wanted to make quite sure: 'You have said that after the killing he had a dream of satisfaction, so to speak, where he got the blood?'

DR YELLOWLEES: Yes.

MR JUSTICE HUMPHREYS: Did he tell you whether this series of recurring dreams occurred before each of the killings or not?

YELLOWLEES: He said so, yes.

HUMPHREYS: Did he say what effect they had on him, how they affected his mind and relief?

YELLOWLEES: I have just said that, after the dream, he was distrait and ill at ease. They confirm his views that he was divinely guided; he gave that as evidence of some mystic spirit arranging things for him.

So Haigh, far from being the greedy, callous killer who would pawn the victim's jewellery, was now a victim himself – of a mystic spirit! To be more precise: 'He says that he is just an instrument of outside power . . . in one case he said he did not know until a minute or two before he was going to kill the victim . . .'

Mr Justice Humphreys, confused as well he might be, tried to get the flow of questioning more on course: 'But does he really think he will not be punished? Does he think that if he's caught stealing or killing he will not be punished?'

YELLOWLEES: I asked him, and he said: 'I am awaiting the trial with complete equanimity; I am in the position of Jesus Christ before Pontius Pilate, and the only thing I have to say, if I was going to say anything, would be: "He can have no power against me, unless it be given to him from above." '

HUMPHREYS: That may well be.

Even so, Sir David Maxwell Fyfe seemed intent on returning to the 'vampire' theme:

SIR DAVID MAXWELL FYFE: The other point to which my learned friend the Attorney-General referred in opening was the question of the drinking of the blood. In the statement he made he has given a history, which we have heard, that in each case, as he put it, he tapped the victim and drank some blood. What do you feel about the truth or otherwise of that statement?

YELLOWLEES: I think it is pretty certain that he tasted it; I do not know whether he drank it or not. From a medical point of view, I do not think it is important, for the reason that this question of blood runs through all his fantasies from childhood like a *motif* and is the core of the paranoid structure that I believe he has created, and it does not matter very much to a paranoiac whether he does things in fancy or in fact. That is what I feel medically about it.

It was all becoming rather laboured, a gallant but misdirected attempt to find some sort of medical excuse for the actions of a man whom the judge and jury clearly saw as a callous scoundrel who made a living through killing people and plundering their possessions. The jury retired to consider their verdict at 4.23 p.m. and returned to court at 4.40 p.m. There were two possible verdicts – guilty of the murder of Mrs Durand-Deacon or guilty but insane; the jury predictably opted for the former.

HARRIS, Ian Twenty-five-year-old Territorial Army soldier Ian Harris was convicted in 1989 of one of the most horrific killings in recent British legal history. Harris had enjoyed a four-year-long relationship with twenty-one-year-old Mandy Jackson when things began to sour between them. Mandy had received well-deserved praise for her success in the dental equipment business, and her greatest treasure was a signed certificate given personally by the Prince of Wales during an award ceremony in Birmingham. It was just the encouragement she needed – Miss Jackson was a young woman who was going somewhere in life. Not so Ian Harris; he was going nowhere. Which would not have been so bad had he not bitterly resented Mandy's success. After a particularly acrimonious row she told him: 'I'm a different person now . . . we are finished.' A bad loser with a wide streak of viciousness, Harris tracked his former girlfriend down to a night-club, and when she left, skulked along behind her to her new home in Uplands, Swansea.

Shortly afterwards, Harris was on the doorstep, and Mandy Jackson, with more kindness than good sense, invited him in. Realising that Mandy was serious about the continuing separation, Ian Harris at first became quarrelsome and then, being a long-time dabbler on the fringe of the occult, drew out a tarot pack and dealt her two cards – The Devil and Death. It was what he later described as a message for her 'before I taught her a lesson'. What followed can only be described as grotesque.

While Mandy Jackson was making them a cup of tea, Harris soaked her with petrol and lit it with a match. Then he stood watching as the terrified girl, a human torch by now, tried to put out the flames with a fire extinguisher. When she failed, she tried desperately to crawl to the tap in the kitchen sink, leaving behind a trail of burnt flesh and clothing. Mercifully her agony was short-lived; but as Mandy died, Harris was already on his way out, having not lifted a finger to help her.

At his trial at Swansea Crown Court in July 1989, Ian Harris denied murder but admitted manslaughter. The jury, however, after a retirement of three hours returned a verdict of guilty of murder. Describing the killing as 'a wicked crime', Mr Justice Judge sentenced Harris to life imprisonment.

Although on the face of it, the literal depictions of Death and The Devil on the tarot cards could not have been more appropriate in this case, Harris was clearly unaware of the occult interpretation of these two most forceful images of the major arcana. Death, in fact, is one of the least ominous of all the cards, signifying as it does an end to worldly preoccupations in favour of a spiritual rebirth – a sign of change for the better on a psychic level – a renewal. The Devil is a warning *against* evil – a reminder that man, like Lucifer, has fallen from Light. But it is also a reminder that Lucifer is the *bringer* of Light. As Frank Lind wrote in his *How to Understand the Tarot*: 'There can be no progress without error, and so even the Devil has his purpose in the scheme of things. Each of us has to learn wisdom by our sins.'

HEDIN, Tore One of the most remarkable feats of psychic detection was achieved by the Swedish clairvoyant Olof Jonsson, in the case of Tore Hedin.

Jonsson, who had been born in Malmö, was later apprenticed to an engineer. After service in the Swedish merchant marine during the Second World War, he became aware of certain latent psychic powers. Jonsson was tested in several parapsychology departments in his native country before emigrating to America, where he settled in Chicago and took up an appointment with an engineering company. He also collaborated on a number of psychic experiments, notably with Professor J.B. Rhine.

In March 1952, Jonsson was telephoned by another expatriate Swede, a journalist named Leif Sunde, who had reported on a number of parapsychological tests carried out by Jonsson. This time the psychic was being asked to embark on quite a different kind of experiment. There was a multiple killer on the loose in the area around Tjornarp, Sweden. Almost as soon as Sunde had uttered those words, Jonsson blurted out: 'It is definitely a man, and the motive is robbery.'

This was believed by the local police to be true, for on the night of 27 November 1951 a fire had broken out in an old mill and its neighbouring house at Tjornarp. The buildings were occupied by the miller Folke Nilsson. Firefighters were unable to save either of the buildings, and when it came to a search of the smouldering rubble they found Nilsson's charred remains. A post-mortem examination established the fact that he had been killed before the fire was started. A broken-open cash box was also found in the ruins, and it was learned that a local farmer had paid Nilsson almost fifteen hundred kroner the day before his death; robbery, then, seemed the most likely motive. It was just one of a number of mysterious fires in the district which turned out to be murder.

As he sat in the comfort of his Chicago home, cradling the telephone in his hand, Olof Jonsson's head was suddenly filled with a dreadful vision – a woman lying in a room clutching at a bloody wound in her stomach; the building was on fire, and as she struggled to escape, the flames slowly reached the dying woman, setting her clothes alight. Then the woman's screams dispelled the vision.

With no more hesitation, Olof Jonsson and Leif Sunde left America for Sweden, where they were met by the police officer who was to escort them around the sites of the arson attacks. Constable Tore Hedin, who had been called out to the Nilsson fire, was considered a good, loyal policeman. He now found himself attached in the capacity of liaison officer to the murder squad investigating the killings; and to be truthful, it involved quite a lot of extra work. Hedin's mother and girlfriend noticed that he seemed to be under great strain, but put it down to the additional duties.

On the third day of Jonsson's visit, officer Hedin handed him the charred remains of a rifle which, he thought, might help the 'psychic investigation'. He could not have been more right. That afternoon, Olof Jonsson lay on the bed in his hotel room and let his mind receive whatever pictures came into it. Nothing could have been more horrifying; each of the murders was re-enacted in his head like a ghastly film. The only difference was that Jonsson could smell the choking fumes of the fires and feel the victims' pain as, every time, they were felled with a shot from the gun officer Hedin had placed in his hands. When his ordeal was over, Olof Jonsson felt strangely calm. He had solved the case. In each of the scenes of his dreadful nightmare he had seen the killer's face; the same face. The face of Tore Hedin.

Jonsson and Sunde immediately telephoned the police station only to be told that Constable Hedin had gone missing since he left the two men at their hotel. A warrant was issued for his arrest, and a few days later searchers found Hedin's car concealed on the shore of Lake Bosarpasjon, about fifty miles from Hurva. In the vehicle was a detailed statement written by Hedin, confessing to the murders and signed 'Tore Hedin, Murderer'. In their search of the lake, police divers eventually found Tore Hedin's body roped to two stone blocks.

According to his biographer Brad Steiger (*The Psychic Feats of Olof Jonsson*), the clairvoyant believed that Hedin had entered the world of crime because entertaining his girlfriend was costing far more than his modest salary could stretch to; killing was to avoid detection of the robberies, arson to avoid detection of the killings.

HENRY, Colin It was a story made for the more flamboyant of the tabloid press – 'Why I Killed Kinky Knix Council Chief' roared one. The 'I' of the story which followed this banner headline was Colin Henry; the 'Kinky Knix' referred to a black PVC basque, which was being worn by 'Council Chief' Christopher Rogers when he was stabbed to death in what the papers referred to as a 'bizarre row over witchcraft'.

The reason the public was being given this glimpse of a world many didn't even know exists was because thirty-seven-year-old joiner Colin Henry was standing his trial at Nottingham Crown Court for the murder of Councillor Rogers, the forty-year-old deputy chairman of Manchester City Council's education committee.

Mr Peter Joyce QC, opening for the Crown on 7 February 1994, said the killing took place the previous February, when Christopher Rogers visited the home at Catton, Nottingham, where Colin Henry lived with his homosexual lover who was also a friend of Rogers. Chris Rogers and the friend had a meal together and then returned to Henry's house and the three of them settled down to an evening's entertainment – which in their case was the watching of pornographic sado-masochist videos and dressing up in women's underwear. And some might say, why not? The problem arose when the consumption of alcohol caused tempers to fray, and an argument – really about nothing – ended in murder.

It emerged in evidence that while Christopher Rogers was an enthusiastic supporter of Satanism, Colin Henry's preference was for witchcraft. The pair began to squabble over the relative merits of their different passions, the result of which was that Councillor Rogers made the mistake of calling Henry 'stupid', a suggestion which Colin Henry resented and which cost Rogers his life. A little later that night, Henry, still smarting from the insult, stabbed his guest twice in the chest with a six-inch-bladed sheath knife, shouting: 'You'll never call me stupid again.' About that he was absolutely right, though he denied committing murder. In his own testimony, Colin Henry said that he could remember little of the argument, save that Christopher Rogers was trying to convert him from witchcraft (of which he was apparently a bonded high priest) to the worship of Satan.

However, juicy meat for the tabloids as this was, it had nothing on the revelations contained in the expert testimony of pathologist Professor Stephen Jones. Professor Jones told the court that he had found many small injuries to the victim's body indicating that he was at least as enthusiastic a masochist as he was a Satanist. There were descriptions of floral design scratch marks around Rogers' nipples and arms, and other scratches and scars on the buttocks.

In Colin Henry's defence, psychiatrist Dr David Gill said that Henry genuinely believed the boasts he claimed Rogers made of being involved in the kidnapping, torture and death of as many as five young men. The psychiatrist said that Henry was convinced that his victim 'had mental powers to manipulate him'. None of which swayed the jury, who convicted Colin Henry of murder, and he was sentenced to life imprisonment.

HOWARD, William   In 1908, when we first encounter William Howard, he was in his mid-twenties; at the time he was serving as a private in the US Army, stationed at Fort Rodman in New Bedford. Despite having been described as 'unprepossessing, with a sullen face and ugly, turned-down lips', Howard was a huge success with the girls who, it seems, he attracted like a magnet. Whatever *it* was, Will Howard had lots of it.

One particular sweetheart who played an important part in Howard's life was nineteen-year-old Grace Sturtevant, who was said to be rather plain of feature, but well educated and with aspirations both to write and paint pictures. Certainly she was a far superior companion to those that Will had become accustomed to. It was during their courtship that the tragedy occurred which might be said to have served as the beginning of Mr Howard's downfall.

Will and Grace were sitting in Hazelwood Park one evening, getting up to the sort of things that young lovers usually get up to, when a passing lout named Dewhurst happened to make an insulting remark. So Will Howard hit him; and the unfortunate Dewhurst breathed his last. It was all a bit of a mess – but as Grace was the only witness, and as she was avowedly in love with him, Howard felt safe – for the time being.

But William Howard clearly liked taking chances – at least where women were concerned. When his term of enlistment ended, Will said *au revoir* to Miss Sturtevant and made a trip back to his native Tennessee; where he met Ida Williams. Meanwhile, Gloria Sturtevant kept in touch by means of a series of increasingly passionate letters. This sort of thing:

> My Sweetheart Will,
> I have been so very lonesome and sad tonight that I can only rest my mind in writing to you. No truer heart ever beat for you than mine. I do love you with my whole heart . . . Oh, Will, if only you knew how dearly I love you, you would not stay away from me so long. This letter is written amidst tears – Do you realise how long you have been gone? Good night, love, and God bless you. That you may come back is my only prayer. From your true and faithful sweetheart . . .
>
> Grace

Well, Will did go back. But when he returned to New Bedford to re-enlist, William Howard was accompanied by Mrs Ida Howard; his only gesture to caution was to refer to her as his sister, and find her lodgings in town while he remained at the camp.

However, the marriage was clearly not one made in heaven, and soon Mr and Mrs Howard fell to quarrelling. Which led to Ida turning Will in to the police for the Dewhurst killing. It could have been curtains for William Howard had not the ever-loyal Grace gone into the witness box and testified that he had acted entirely in self-defence. Having lost this round, Ida Howard next took her husband to court for not supporting her (they were still living apart). The result was that she was awarded a regular sum from his pay. One-all. The final straw was Ida falling pregnant – more demands on William's time and money.

One summer evening, William Howard left camp telling his sergeant that he was going fishing, and taking a boat. At the same time Ida Howard was visiting Madame Isherwood, a clairvoyant, and telling her that she was on her way to meet Will so that they could look at a house in Pandanarum, on the bay, which he had promised to rent for them.

The following morning Will Howard and his boat were back at camp, and Ida's body was floating face down in the bay. An accident? Not a bit of it, insisted the doctors, Mrs Howard had been strangled before she was put in the water.

And that is how Private Howard came to be standing before a judge and jury, indicted with the murder of his wife. One of the most controversial of the prosecution witnesses was the psychic, Madame Isherwood, who was called to testify about the conversation she had with Mrs Howard the night she died. When it came his turn to cross-examine, Howard's counsel, Mr Morton, decided that it was better to attack than defend; attack the credibility of the medium. He asked Madame Isherwood why she had not come forward with her information earlier. The answer was one that nobody in the court could have predicted: because it was only recently that the spirit of the late Ida Howard had appeared to her and told her to reveal the details of their conversation. Like the jury, Morton was momentarily stunned. Then he seized his opportunity, launching into a string of facetious questions: 'What kind of spirit was it? Was it a plump spirit more than five feet high? Did she have spirit clothes on? Did she carry a harp? Or have a halo?' At the end of this tirade defender Morton asked: 'Did this spirit appear to you frequently?' 'Every night,' replied Madame, eliciting from the attorney this riposte: 'Don't you take a glass of whisky every night before going to bed?'

One witness for the defence was a diminutive girlfriend of Howard's named Lena Watson – 'Bug' to her friends. Loyally, if rather unwisely, she was in court to tell the jury that Howard spent the night of the murder in her company. The jury clearly did not believe a word of it, but had now become so bewildered by psychics and perjurers that they opted for the easy verdict. When they returned to court after their deliberations the foreman announced that they found William Howard guilty of murder, but only of second-degree (non-capital) murder. He was sentenced to life imprisonment.

J

JACK THE RIPPER During the months between the end of August and the beginning of November 1888, the Whitechapel area of the East End of London was witness to a series of vicious, and still unsolved murders. The killings were characterised by an unparalleled savagery; each of the five victims – all prostitutes – had been attacked from behind and their throats cut. The bodies were afterwards subjected to varying degrees of mutilation and dissection, the nature of which led to the inevitable conclusion that there was a perverted sexual motive.

This is a contemporary description of the injuries suffered by the last of Jack's victims, Mary Jane Kelly:

> The throat had been cut right across with a knife, nearly severing the head from the body. The abdomen had been partially ripped open, and both the breasts had been cut from the body; the left arm, like the head, hung to the body by the skin only. The nose had been cut off, the forehead skinned, and the thighs, down to the feet, stripped of the flesh. The abdomen had been slashed with a knife across and downwards, and the liver and entrails wrenched away. The entrails and other portions of the frame were missing, but the liver, etc., it is said, were found placed between the feet of this poor victim. The flesh from the thighs and legs, together with the breasts and nose, had been placed by the murderer on the table, and one of the hands had been pushed into her stomach.

The Ripper murders are arguably the most famous set of serial killings in the history of the world crime, and need no more discussion here. The Ripper literature has encompassed theories of Jack's identity which range from the outrageous to the improbable to the barely possible; so it would be odd if there were no 'solution' that had an 'occult' connection.

Robert Donston Stephenson, who changed his name to Dr Roslyn D'Onston (presumably because it sounded more impressive), studied various occult subjects under Bulwer Lytton, and later contributed articles on the Whitechapel Murders to the *Pall Mall Gazette*. Stephenson subsequently became involved in a rather dubious financial deal in which he and a man named Marsh sought to exploit their belief that a Dr Morgan Davies was Jack the Ripper. In 1890 Stephenson was living with Mabel Collins, the editor of *Lucifer*, the Theosophical Society magazine. In partnership with Baroness Vittoria Cremers, the couple embarked on a cosmetics venture, while Stephenson supplemented their income from commerce with lecturing on matters occult.

In the late 1920s, the Baroness told author and journalist Bernard O'Donnell that in Stephenson's room she had unintentionally come across some neckties caked with dried blood, which he later told her had belonged to Jack the Ripper. He explained that Jack was in the habit of secreting the organs of his victims beneath his tie. The ties eventually found their way into the possession of arch-magician Aleister Crowley who kept them at his Abbey of Thelema in Sicily. Crowley claimed that they had formerly belonged to a magician who was also Jack the Ripper. He was described as a prominent surgeon who had achieved 'the highest power of magic and could make himself invisible'. This man, so Crowley said, was none other than Robert Donston Stephenson, and his motive had been to ritually murder his victims at locations in East London which, when plotted on a map, mark the points of a five-pointed occult star. This was so that he could secure invisibility and thus evade detection.

Despite the rather fanciful nature of this claim, at least one prominent Ripperologist, Melvin Harris, has supported Stephenson as one of the candidates for the identity of Jack the Ripper. (It must be said in closing that plotting the murder sites on a map of Whitechapel produces a very odd-shaped star indeed.)

K

KASPRZAK, Nadia Was Nadia Kasprzak a sorceress? If you had asked Serge Pognon he would certainly have said yes. He came under her spell, so he claimed, in July 1982 at Saint Raphaël, where he and his lover, Agnès Bouvier, shared their holiday flat with her. Pognon was a twenty-two-year-old of mixed ethnic origin, who had deserted from the army – in Mademoiselle Bouvier's favour – with only a week of military service left to complete. Not, one might think, a very clever thing to do; but then, the reluctant conscript had already been assessed by the army doctor to be slow-witted and easily led. The ideal recruit, though, for conscription into the service of Nadia Kasprzak.

At that time Nadia's first wish in life was for a divorce; her second was for some money. Both, coincidentally, from the husband she had left one month earlier. Henri Kasprzak was a highly successful but rather dull engineer; a man who, for the most part, shunned what might be called the good life. His wife was almost the opposite, an attractive socialite with no interest in being either mother or housewife. Her greatest passion lay in the occult, and she acquired a considerable reputation as a fortune-teller. To Serge Pognon she was more than that – she was a Witch; one who had bound him with her spells.

So it was that when Henri Kasprzak entered his apartment at 27 rue Claude Debussy in the district of Evry-Corbeil-Essonnes, south of Paris, on the evening of 1 August 1982, he was pounced on by a young man of uncertain race. The engineer shook off the hands which tried to throttle him; deflected the wine bottle which nearly came down on his head; thrust aside the hypodermic needle. Then he booted the young man out, bolted the door and called the police.

Kasprzak had no explanation for the attack. He had no enemies, had never seen the man before, and had no idea how he could have let himself into the flat. The strangest thing was how the intruder seemed so uncoordinated, his eyes glazed, like . . . That was the word; he was like a zombie!

A subsequent police investigation discovered nothing remarkable in the past lives of either Kasprzak, the victim, or the obvious suspect, his wife, and the case was filed. And there the matter rested until the evening of Tuesday 23 November. At eight o'clock Jerome d'Estrel went to collect his car from the garage in the basement of Kasprzak's apartment block. The car next to his was the engineer's expensive Renault, and it appeared to have been vandalised, because two of the windows were shattered. Taking a closer look d'Estrel was shocked to discover the inert form of his neighbour's body slumped in the driver's seat, blood running down his face. He was, in a word, dead.

The autopsy found Kasprzak had been shot with three bullets from a .22-calibre rifle. Three bullets, each inscribed by a knife with the number 7. Three sevens . . . the trail led to someone with more than a passing interest in the occult. Nadia Kasprzak.

The susceptible Serge Pognon was only too willing to confess to the two attacks on Monsieur Kasprzak. But it had only been to frighten him – Nadia had never told him to kill her husband. It was the bullets. She had bewitched the bullets.

On 10 February 1984 Pognon was sentenced to fifteen years' imprisonment, while Nadia got off with twelve. It was one of the judge's last trials, for he was to die of a heart attack just five months later – at seven o'clock, on the seventh day of the seventh month of the year.

KASSO, Richard Ricky Kasso was born in March 1967 and despite – or perhaps because of – his secure affluent background, he soon went to the bad, and before he had entered teenage was experimenting with drugs. By the time he reached high school, Kasso (which he delighted in telling people rhymed with 'asshole') was described as 'socially handicapped'. At age seventeen Ricky, known on the streets around Northport, Long Island, as the 'Acid King', had become obsessed with black magic and

Satanism (after reading LaVey's *Satanic Bible*) to the point where fantasy and reality overlapped dangerously.

Although he never became a full member, Ricky hovered around on the periphery of the Knights of the Black Circle, a drug 'n' orgy cult based at Northport High School, and he was fond of initiating his own circle of druggy hangers-on into his brand of immature Satanism. Ricky's closest friend at this time was James Troiano (called 'Dracula'), less dominant, but Kasso's equal in almost every other brand of unpleasantness. One of Ricky's biggest fans was seventeen-year-old Gary Lauwers, who followed the Acid King rather as a dog follows its master.

In 1984, Ricky Kasso led his merry men on a pilgrimage to the notorious house at Amityville where Ronald 'Butch' DeFeo (see p.96) had massacred his family ten years earlier. It was 30 April, the witches' feast of Walpurgisnacht, so Ricky knocked together an altar and they all shouted a few praises to Satan.

A month or so later, at the start of June, Kasso found he was missing several twists of 'angel dust', and repeatedly accused Gary Lauwers of having stolen the drugs. On 16 June Kasso, Troiano, Lauwers and a youth named Albert Quinones hid themselves away in Newport's Aztakea Woods to partake of some mescaline. During the course of subsequent reveries they renewed the dispute over the allegedly pilfered drugs. The result was a vicious attack by the dope-crazed Kasso on the disciple who in trying to escape was felled by Troiano and held down while Ricky repeatedly drove a hunting knife into his body; Lauwers' disinclination at the time to embrace the church of Satan in his hour of need resulted in Kasso gouging out his eyes. Ricky and 'Drac' covered the body with leaves, though poor terrified Albert had long since taken to his heels.

Despite the fact that Ricky Kasso was openly boasting of his human sacrifice, it was not until 5 July that anybody had the courage to tell the police. That day Kasso and Troiano were arrested and held in a cell. Two days later the Acid King hanged himself with a bed sheet. Albert Quinones turned state's evidence, but having been out of his head on drugs at the time of the 'sacrifice', proved a very unreliable witness against James Troiano at his trial in April 1985. This, combined with some irregularity in Dracula's confession, led to his eventual acquittal.

KOHLER, Maria Magdalena It was as unlikely a scenario as even the most fertile mind of a crime-fiction writer could dream up. Imagine a quiet country road; this one leads alongside the woodland outside Singen, Germany, to the shores of Lake Constance on the border with Switzerland. On Saturday 12 July 1986, an early morning walker came across a small Volkswagen parked by the side of the lane. Nothing unusual in that – there are, after all, quite a lot of small Volkswagens in Germany. It was the plastic tube leading from the exhaust through the driver's window that caught Herr Egger's bright eye. Uncommon enough, as were the crosses painted on the door panels. But in opening the door, the unfortunate fellow staggered back, not only from the effects of the smell of decomposing flesh, but from the fact that the occupants were dressed in black robes with carved crosses hanging round their necks. Priests?!

They were not priests, as the police summoned by Herr Egger discovered. They were twenty-one-year-old Jose Ferrero and seventeen-year-old Patrick Heilmann, members of a local offbeat sect calling themselves the International Association for the Preservation of World Peace; who just happened to affect the habits of priests. And when detectives visited the cult's headquarters (called Noah's Ark) in Erzbergstrasse, they found it inhabited by similarly robed individuals under the direct control of a woman the devotees knew as 'Holy Mother'. So far there was nothing to contradict the obvious explanation of a suicide pact, and the case was shelved.

It was a piece of strange coincidence, supported by shrewd police work, that finally made the link between the deaths of Ferrero and Heilmann, late of the IAPWP, and the leader of that group, 'Holy Mother'. A certain Frau Anna Wermuthshauser, a sixty-six-year-old widow, disappeared from her expensive home in 1982. Although the house was locked and barred and the services had been disconnected at the owner's request, Frau Wermuthshauser continued to be fleetingly seen around the Erzbergstrasse for a few months. And she had taken to wearing black clothing – only black clothing; and wearing a cross.

It was this connection that led the Singen police team back to Erzbergstrasse and the International Association for the Preservation of World Peace. And to the Holy Mother, now identified as Maria Magdalena Kohler. A check of police records showed that Frau Kohler had quite a history of 'religious' activity. She and a male partner named Josef Stocker had once been involved in running a very suspect group in Switzerland and had acquired quite a name for themselves as exorcists. At least once, in May 1966, the subject of the exorcism died. Despite trying to shift the blame on to God who, they claimed, instructed them, Kohler and Stocker were convicted by a court and sentenced to ten years apiece. On their release, Stocker founded another sect on his own, and so did Maria Magdalena. It began to make the Ferrero and Heilmann suicides look distinctly suspicious, and the 'disappearance' of Frau Wermuthshauser too.

It was on 7 February 1988 that the mystery of Erzbergstrasse was eventually solved. Quite out of the blue one of the followers of IAPWP had telephoned police headquarters to announce that somebody had died there. When detectives arrived they found the Holy Mother and another crone, who turned out to be her sister, taking a leisurely breakfast, while several disciples prayed. One of them led officers down to the basement chapel where they found the pitiful remains of Anna Wermuthshauser. The poor woman remained tied naked to the altar, her almost skeletal body unrecognisable from years of continual beatings. Once the story had been prised out of the inhabitants of Noah's Ark, it proved as ghastly a tale as any of those case-hardened detectives had ever heard.

Frau Wermuthshauser had joined the sect in 1982 – which is why she disappeared from her house. It was indeed her who had been seen in black robes around Erzbergstrasse. However, the Holy Mother became convinced that her new convert was possessed by devils and sought, with regular beatings and privations, to banish them. Sadly for Frau Wermuthshauser the imps proved stubborn, and even following five years of increasingly violent treatment they had not been exorcised. Eventually, of course, the

Albert De Salvo, self-confessed Boston Strangler (*Topham*)

Peter Hurkos, the Dutch psychic who became involved in the case. He remained convinced until the day he died that De Salvo was not the Strangler (*Topham*)

Ernest Dyer

Eric Gordon-Tombe

'The Welcomes', where the body of Eric Gordon-Tombe was found covered with rubble at the bottom of the well

This etching by Francisco de Goya represents a psychic attack. Many believe Norah Farnario to have suffered a similar attack on a bleak island moor

James Greenacre

A contemporary portrait of
James Greenacre

William Clark's encounter with a restless ghost in 1675 led to the discovery of a hidden store of money and documents which, the ghost claimed, had to be distributed among his relatives before his soul could rest in peace

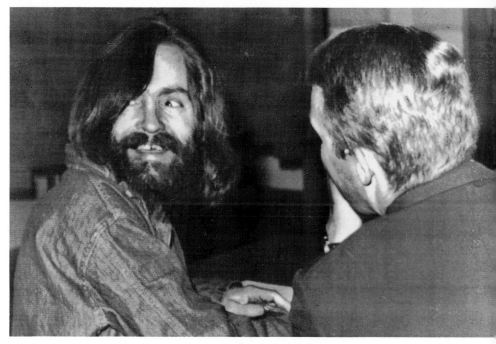

Charles Manson (*Associated Press*)

J. STENNETT, PRINTER, NEWARK.

NEWARK BOROUGH POLICE

Telephone No. 26

CHIEF CONSTABLE'S OFFICE,
TOWN HALL,
NEWARK-ON-TRENT.
11th JANUARY, 1937

MISSING FROM HER HOME

at 11, Thoresby Avenue, Newark-on-Trent, since Tuesday, 5th January, 1937, MONA LILIAN TINSLEY. age 10 years (rather short for age), dark hair, (bobbed with fringe), rosy cheeks, four prominent teeth at front. Dress, when last seen, light blue woollen jumper suit, brown double breasted tweed coat (frayed at bottom of sleeves), black Wellington boots, no hat, white half hose, dark blue knickers, white liberty bodice, white cotton underskirt, woollen combinations. was carrying a brown or grey handbag which contained a birthday card with figure " 10 " thereon. It has been established that this girl was seen at Hayton Smeath, near Retford, Notts. at about mid-day on Wednesday, 6th January, 1937, since when all trace of her has been lost. It has been suggested that she travelled to Sheffield on a bus leaving Retford at 6.45 p.m.

Any person who has seen this girl, or the clothing described above, since Wednesday mid-day is asked to get in touch with the nearest police officer immediately.

HARRY BARNES,
CHIEF CONSTABLE.

The missing person notice issued by the Nottingham police for ten-year-old Mona Tinsley

Spirit medium Estelle
Roberts. She accurately
predicted that Mona
Tinsley's body would be
found in a river
(*Popperfoto*)

Frederick Nodder, who
was hanged for the murder
of Mona Tinsley on 30
December 1937 at Lincoln
Prison (*Popperfoto*)

'Night Stalker' Richard Ramirez. From June 1984 until August 1985 he terrorised suburban Los Angeles. He invariably left an occult symbol at the scene of his crime (*Associated Press/Topham*)

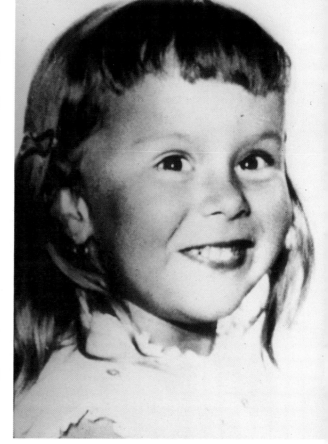

Four-year-old Edith Kiecorius, whose body was found in a shabby tenement room in New York. She had disappeared from her uncle's home on 22 February 1961 (*Associated Press/Topham*)

Dutch clairvoyant Gerard Croiset, who described Edith's killer as: 'Small, about fifty-four or fifty-five years of age; having a sharp face . . . He wears something grey.' His predictions were to prove a good description of Fred Thompson, the man who was later found guilty of Edith's murder (*Press Association/Topham*)

Fred Thompson, surrounded by journalists, following his confession to killing Edith Kiecorius (*Associated Press/Topham*)

Charles Walton, whose body was found impaled on his own hay-fork – symbols resembling crosses had been carved on his cheek, throat and body

Alfred Potter. Although no one was charged with Walton's murder, Detective-Superintendent Fabian, who was in charge of the investigation, told a friend many years later that he was sure that Potter had committed the crime

victim died; indeed, it was a matter of great surprise that she had not succumbed earlier.

Maria Magdalena never stood trial – she was considered far too mad, and was committed to an institution. As for the faithful of the struggle for World Peace, they too escaped justice as it was thought that they had become so brainwashed that they no longer were responsible for their actions. It remains unexplained why the two unfortunate disciples took their own lives, though with hindsight it may have had something to do with guilt – guilt at not exposing the terrible torture being suffered by Anna Wermuthshauser.

L

LABBÉ, Denise, and **ALGARRON, Jacques** Denise Labbé had met Algarron at the Rennes Mayday festivities in 1954. At the time she was the unmarried mother of a baby girl, Cathy, and Algarron was a cadet at the prestigious military academy at Saint-Cyr. The couple danced, and arranged to meet the following week, though perhaps the warning lights should have gone on in Denise's head when, in the meantime, she received a letter from Jacques stating his intention of making her his mistress. It happened that he too was an unmarried parent of not one, but two children.

The relationship, odd though it may have been, seemed to work for both of them – he enjoyed treating her roughly, and she appeared to lap it up. Certainly there is some indication of her attitude in a letter she wrote to Algarron in which she 'noted with despair' that the scratch marks he had inflicted on her back had begun to heal. But if Denise Labbé had fallen under his spell, then Jacques Algarron had fallen under an equally unhealthy spell – that woven by the German philosopher Friedrich Nietzsche. Algarron believed that he was one of the breed of 'Supermen' discussed in Nietzsche's celebrated work *Thus Spake Zarathustra* who dictated: 'Let man fear woman when she loves. Then she bears every sacrifice and every other thing she accounts valueless.'

The long and the short of it was that Jacques Algarron decided to put this philosophy, and Denise, to the test – could he persuade her to commit the ultimate sacrifice; that of her baby daughter? On 29 August 1954, as they dined out in Paris, Jacques announced: 'The price of our love must be the death of your daughter . . . an innocent victim must be sacrificed.' The idea seemed to be that only through suffering could their union become strong. Naturally, Denise refused at first, but after being worn down by her seriously psychopathic consort, she eventually made two abortive attempts to kill the child. Once she dangled the infant over the balcony of her mother's apartment, but quickly pulled herself together and took it inside. A few days later Denise dropped little Cathy over a bridge into the canal. Again she regretted it in time and summoned the lock-keeper to pull the baby out. Needless to say the obvious display of weakness did not meet with the approval of 'Superman' Jacques Algarron.

It was in November, while she and two-year-old Cathy were staying with her sister in Vendôme, that Denise Labbé made her final, successful, attempt; on the eighth she pushed Cathy's head under a bucket of water. Then she wrote to Algarron: 'Catherine deceased. See you soon.' To which he, rather churlishly under the circumstances, replied: 'It is all very disappointing. It means nothing to me now.'

But by this time the police were already investigating the child's mysterious death and it was not long before Denise, then twenty-eight years old, was taken in for questioning. At first she claimed that the baby had met with an accident. She had, she said, tried to save the child, but the image of Algarron's eyes appeared and blinded her, and she fainted. Silly, loyal Denise steadfastly avoided incriminating her lover, and it is possible that she would have held her tongue and suffered alone for their terrible crime. However, the arrogant Jacques was cavorting with other women in night-clubs at the time Denise was languishing in prison, and when she found out about it via her brother-in-law, she was understandably put out – put out enough to tell the truth. So Jacques Algarron found himself in the male wing of the Blois prison, with Denise in the female section, awaiting their trial.

The process finally opened on 30 May 1956. There was little dispute over the facts, and most of the court's time was taken up by arguments from legal representatives of Denise Labbé and Jacques Algarron, each trying to shift the major blame on to the other. Although his expertise in matters of witchcraft and Satanism was not called on, Denise's attorney, Maurice Garçon, was a specialist in such occult matters and it was clear from his choice as a defender that these were relevant to the case. After much squabbling between the two defendants, the jury retired, and after just three hours returned verdicts of guilty of murder on both of them. Denise Labbé was given a lifetime of penal servitude, Algarron picked up twenty years' hard labour.

LANCASHIRE WITCHES   Of the many pamphlets, broadsides and chapbooks recounting the trials and executions of Britain's witches, the most remarkable – for its style, accuracy and detail, and its retention of atmosphere – is the *Wonderful Discoverie of Witches in the Countie of Lancaster*. It was written by Thomas Potts, Clerk to the Court, at the suggestion of one of the trial judges, Mr Justice Bromley, who later testified as to its reliability. Apart from being a 'guide' to the conduct of witch trials, Potts' introduction provides some useful observations on the underlying causes behind the case. In 1591, Potts wrote, the Great Council had made strenuous efforts to suppress Roman Catholicism, and Ecclesiastical Commissioners were charged with eradicating Jesuits and recusants; a task at which they were noticeably unsuccessful around Lancashire.

In his study of the Lancashire witches (*Stories of Great Witch Trials*), Ronald Seth adds:

The ministers of the Church of England had no authority over their flocks; the law was defied, the churches were empty, the people refused instruction, preachers were few, drunkenness and bastardy were rife, marriages and baptisms were celebrated by Catholic priests in secret. In such conditions secret societies flourished, and it was at this time that Elizabeth Sowthern, alias 'Old Demdike' first became a witch.

In her 'voluntary confession' to the assizes, Old Demdike described the incident like this:

About twenty years past I was coming homeward from begging and there, near a stonepit in Gouldshey, in the Forest of Pendle, did meet a spirit or devil in the shape of a boy, the one half of his coat black and the other brown. He said that, if I would give him my soul, then I should have anything that I would request.

The bargain was sealed and over the next five or six years the spirit, whose name was 'Tibb', appeared at various times as a brown dog to take instruction from his new mistress.

At about this time Mrs Sowthern persuaded her neighbour and friend Anne Whittle (called 'Old Chattox') to: 'agree to become subject unto that devilish abominable profession of witchcraft'. Both these crones were now in their eighties and it seemed only right that they should train up a few apprentices. Old Demdike initiated her daughter, Elizabeth Device, and grandchildren Alison and James Device; Old Chattox introduced her daughter Anne Redfearne to the art of sorcery. Later an odd assortment of other locals joined the group, and they began to make a nuisance of themselves, and many of those that crossed them seemed to meet with fatal accidents or illnesses. Richard Baldwyn, for example, and Robert Nutter . . .

So ill was her reputation – 'the rankest hag that ever troubled daylight' – that in March 1612 Old Demdike was hauled before a local magistrate. Never one to suffer silently – or alone – she happily implicated the rest of her family, friends and associates. The result was that Demdike, Alison Device and Chattox were committed to Lancaster Castle to await the next assize. Alison in particular was charged with laming a pedlar so that: 'by a devilish art of witchcraft his head is drawn awry, his eyes and face deformed, his speech not well understood, his thighs and legs stark lame; his arms lame, especially the left side, his hands lamed and turned out of their course . . .'

Old Demdike, Elizabeth Device, Alison Device and Anne Redfearne were indicted for the bewitching to death of Robert Nutter, and various other charges – including some relating to a plot to release the prisoners from confinement by blowing up the gaol – resulted in there being no fewer than twenty alleged witches before Mr Justice Altham and Mr Justice Bromley when the Lancaster assize opened on 17 August 1612. The one conspicuous absentee was Old Demdike herself, who had in the meantime died in gaol; thus leaving Old Chattox the chief defendant.

A great part of the prosecution evidence relied on the testimony of Elizabeth Device and two of her children, James, aged about twenty-two, and nine-year-old Jennet. Jennet obligingly told the court how her mother's familiar, 'a spirit in the likeness of a brown dog' called 'Ball' had helped kill people; and James recalled the fashioning of clay images.

At the end of the trial only Old Chattox 'weeping tears' admitted the charges laid against her; Elizabeth Device had at one time confessed but retracted her statement later. All the other accused maintained their innocence. At the close of the fifth day's proceedings the jury returned guilty verdicts against twelve of the defendants, and not guilty against the remaining eight. Ten of the twelve sentenced to death were hanged shortly afterwards, including Elizabeth Device, Alison and James Device, Anne Redfearne, Jennet Preston (see page 183), and, surprisingly, for there was little enough evidence against her, Alice Nutter. The two others convicted were sentenced to one year's imprisonment and four appearances on the pillory.

LA VOISIN There lived in Paris, towards the end of the seventeenth century, a certain widow named Catherine Deshayes, who had forsaken the menial occupation of the midwife for the more profitable one of fortune-telling. We know little of Deshayes' early life, but for the fact that she claimed to have recognised her 'powers' in childhood. Those powers would soon extend their malignant influence to embrace the French Court, and even to threaten the 'Sun King' Louis XIV.

It so happened that Madame's specialty – the specialty which gives her an unrivalled place in this book – was the prophesy of death. More specifically, the death of husbands. This being so, it was not unnatural that she should attract to her by no means modest cottage at Villeneuve-sur-Gravois a number of discontented wives, anxious to learn the worst. And it is a remarkable thing that by looking into a crystal ball, or consulting the cards, without any intimate knowledge of her subject, her predictions were unerring. She would simply concoct some innocent-looking philtre intended to, for example, make the husband blind to the lady's amorous indiscretions, instruct her client to administer it, and remark: 'The cards foretell your husband's death within the week.' Pure magic. As one great literary mind described it: 'Madame Voisin's [the name she adopted] clients were generally in a hurry and so were willing to take any little trouble or responsibility necessary to ensure success. They had two qualities which endear customers to those of La Voisin's trade; they were grateful and they were silent.'

To cut a long story short, word of Madame's high rate of success rapidly spread outwards and, more importantly, upwards. So that soon the very rich and the very powerful were also beating a path to her door – the Duchesse de Bouillon, for example, and Olympe de Mancini, the Comtesse de Soisons, and her most illustrious client of all, Françoise-Athenais de Rochechouart de Mortemart, Marquise de Montespan, mistress of King Louis XIV. A woman who, with no difficulty, overshadowed both the queen, Marie-Thérèse, and Louis' other mistress, Mademoiselle de la Vallière. Sadly the Marquise, apart from being exceedingly beautiful, was also exceedingly paranoid, and not content to overshadow she desperately wanted to eliminate all possible rivals. So very soon the Marquise was on the old fortune-teller's doorstep. It is true to say that the royal mistress fell totally for La Voisin's hocus-pocus, and was a regular customer for the philtres and potions with which Madame had so long ensured the accuracy of her predictions. Some say that one of these deadly cocktails was meant for the king himself, but was eventually used to dispose of de la Vallière. But the more deeply she became involved in her own mischief, the more excessive did de Montespan's demands become. It is a matter of record that she paid vast sums of money to have special rituals enacted which would ensure her supreme control over the king; black masses performed by the defrocked hunchback Abbé Guilbourg.

But in this the Marquise was not alone, for many of society's brightest stars were thought to be involved in similar necromantic practices – at some of which, it was rumoured, children were sacrificed. Guilbourg himself later described one such ceremony, and it was afterwards confirmed by La Voisin's daughter Marguerite:

> He had bought a child to sacrifice at the mass, said on behalf of a great lady. He had cut the child's throat with a knife, and drawing its blood, had poured it into the chalice; after which he had the body taken away into another place, so that later he could use the heart and entrails for another mass. He said this second mass in a hovel on the ramparts of Saint-Denis, over the same woman, and with the same ceremonies. The body of the child would, he said, be used to make magic powders.

Such was the scandal that swept through the French Court over its members' involvement in black magic, witchcraft and poisoning that for a while even Louis' own reputation seemed at risk. Many arrests were made in high places in an attempt to stifle the almost rampant spread of sorcery and murder, and many cases came before the so-called *Chambre Ardente* (similar to England's 'Star Chamber'). After that, Police Commissioner Reynie – in charge of the cleaning-up process – turned his attention to the little band of dedicated sorcerers and poisoners who were servicing the lucrative trade. During the purge there were 319 arrests, of which 104 came to trial – thirty-six were sentenced to death, four to slavery in the galleys, thirty-four to banishment and thirty were acquitted.

Among those sentenced to death was La Voisin. In February 1680 she was dragged to a public square in the centre of Paris and burned alive at the stake.

LEE, John John Lee was the son of a farmer, and lived with his mother in the village of Abbotskerswell, in the county of Devon. When he had passed his fifteenth birthday, young Lee was taken into the service of a Miss Emma Keyse, of Babbacombe in the same county. Miss Keyse had once been a maid to Queen Victoria and was known locally as a kind and generous woman; except by her servants, that is – among them she was known for her strictness and her parsimony.

About eighteen months after his appointment to the Keyse

household, John Lee was struck by wanderlust, and left service to join the Royal Navy. Alas, John's youthful enthusiasm was not matched by his physical strength, and a weak chest made him fit for only the lightest of duties. Finally he developed pneumonia and was necessarily invalided out of the Navy. Back on shore, the formerly open, honest lad became a changed person. From his first employer, John began to steal – and was rewarded by six months' hard labour. However, Miss Keyse hearing of his predicament interceded on his behalf and persuaded the governor of the prison to release him back into her service. An act of generosity she had cause to regret. Indeed, she paid for it with her life.

In the early hours of Saturday 15 November 1884, one of the maids woke to the smell of smoke. When the household had been roused, it was discovered that there was not one but five separate fires, all accelerated by paraffin. With horror and disbelief, the servants found the body of Miss Keyse in the dining room. Her head had been terribly bludgeoned and her throat had been cut through to the vertebrae. Around the body, like a ghastly funeral pyre, were smouldering newspapers soaked in blood and paraffin. When John Lee's bloody knife and towel were found next to the body he was immediately taken into custody and charged with murder. He admitted later that the killing had been revenge for having his weekly wage reduced by sixpence on account of some minor lapse.

John Lee was scheduled to be executed for his crime by the official hangman James Berry, whose competence had never been held in doubt. The prisoner was led to the drop, positioned over the trap and with the customary white hood over his face, the noose was secured around his neck. As he had done scores of times before, executioner Berry pulled the lever to release the trap. It remained stuck fast with Lee still standing on it. Berry pulled the lever again; still it would not budge. And again. Still the prisoner could not drop. James Berry stamped several times on the doors of the trap, and so did the warders; still they remained firmly together.

With some embarrassment, prison officers removed James Lee from the gallows. The executioner and his assistant tested it – and it worked perfectly. Until they tried to hang John Lee for the second time.

A very bewildered Berry again completed a successful test drop; and was once again unsuccessful in launching John Lee into eternity. To the evident dismay of the observers, the trap refused to open for a third time. The chaplain recorded: 'The lever was pulled again and again. A great noise was heard which sounded like the falling of the drop, but to my horror, when I turned my eyes to the scaffold I saw the poor convict standing on the trap as I had seen him twice before. I refused to stay any longer.'

The only person not surprised by this bizarre turn of events was John Lee himself. In fact he had predicted it, when he told warders of a dream that he would not hang: 'The Lord will never permit me to be executed,' he said. And indeed, he did not. In recognition of his dreadful ordeal Lee's sentence was commuted to life imprisonment and he was released in 1907.

There were many suggestions for the cause of this apparent miracle – including more than a few invoking Divine Intervention. The most rational explanation was that the flaps of the trap had become swollen as a result of soaking up the recent heavy rain, and when a weight was put directly on them the edges bound.

In fact a similar prosaic explanation was favoured by the red-faced Mr Berry, when invited to explain the incident to the Under-Sheriff of Devon. He wrote:

It was suggested to me that the woodwork fitted too tightly in the centre of the doors, and one of the warders fetched an axe and another a plane. I again tried the lever but it did not act. A piece of wood was then sawn off one of the doors close to where the iron catches were, and by the aid of a crowbar the catches were knocked off, and the doors fell down. You then gave orders that the execution should not be proceeded with . . . I am of the opinion that the ironwork catches were not strong enough for the purpose, that the woodwork of the doors should have been about three or four times as heavy, and with ironwork to correspond, so that when a man of Lee's weight was placed upon the doors the iron catches would not have become locked, as I feel sure they did on this occasion, but would respond readily. So far as I am concerned, everything was performed in a careful manner, and had the iron and woodwork been sufficiently strong, the execution would have been satisfactorily accomplished.

Or perhaps it was different. Perhaps God *was* smiling down on John Lee after all.

LIM, Adrian, *et al.* A self-styled spirit medium Lim, with his wife Catherine Tan Mui Choo and his mistress Hoe Kah Hong, earned his place in the annals of infamy through the murders of two children at his apartment in Toa Payoh, Singapore.

The first victim, nine-year-old Agnes Ng Siew Heok, failed to return home from the religious school she attended in January 1981. On the twenty-fifth of the month her body was found stuffed into a bag beside a lift in the apartment block adjoining Lim's home; the child had been asphyxiated and the post-mortem examination suggested that she had been sodomised and that rape had been attempted.

While investigations were proceeding into the murder of Agnes Ng, a second corpse, that of ten-year-old Ghazali bin Mazurki, was found under a tree outside the same apartment block on 7 February. There was no indication of sexual assault, but there were three burns on the boy's back and a puncture mark on his arm which confirmed post-mortem findings of a tranquilliser in blood and tissue samples. Cause of death had been drowning.

Subsequent enquiry established that Ghazali had been enticed away from a playground by a 'Chinese' woman. Furthermore, small blood spots were found leading from the young victim's body to the adjacent flats – the flats in which Adrian Lim lived with his ménage of wife and mistress, and whose quarters were similarly spotted with Ghazali bin Mazurki's blood. Under questioning, all three confessed their participation in the two murders, supplemented by a catalogue of other unsavoury activities – rape, unnatural sex, blood drinking, child abduction and various practices of supernatural hocus-pocus and deception. Investigations were now reopened into the death twelve months earlier of Benson Loh Ngak Hua, who had been found 'accidentally' electrocuted in Lim's apartment. Adrian Lim and his wife were subsequently charged jointly with his murder.

During their forty-one-day trial in 1983, the two women pleaded that Lim had forced them to help with the sacrificial murders aimed at invoking the goddess Kali's intervention so as to effect escape from an earlier charge of rape brought against him.

The proceedings were held, according to Singapore practice, before a panel of three judges without a jury, and concluded with convictions against all three defendants and death sentences accompanying each conviction. The two female prisoners made a desperate sequence of unsuccessful appeals, first to the Singapore Court of Criminal Appeal, then to the Privy Council in London and the President of Singapore. Adrian Lim did not bother to appeal at all. The result was the same: Lim, Tan and Hoe were hanged at Changi Prison on 25 November 1988. The *Straits Times* recorded that Adrian Lim went to the gallows with an inscrutable smile on his face.

LOZA UCEDA, Camilo   On 1 April 1988, shepherds watching their flocks on the grassy slopes of Mount Kapia in the Yunguyo province of Peru were the first to stumble on the badly mutilated body of a young man. Although they had heard of the sudden disappearance from home on 15 March of twenty-year-old Camilo Loza Uceda, the shepherds did nothing – they dared do nothing but leave the corpse where it was and keep quiet. This, they could see, was a ritual slaughter, a sacrifice.

Six weeks later two young boys, roaming the hillsides, also stumbled upon the by now badly decomposing remains of the human sacrifice. Fearing to touch the corpse itself, the lads picked up one of its shoes and ran down to the village, where the shoe was identified by Loza's anxious relatives. But the power of magic is strong within these rural communities, and just as the shepherds had closed their eyes to what, after all, was murder, so did the local police. In short, they made the right sympathetic noises, but did nothing, leaving Camilo Loza's mourning family to hike up the side of Mount Kapia to retrieve his earthly remains. As if this were not distressing enough, having gathered a basket full of bones, the family returned to the village to be told that this sun-bleached skeleton was far too old to belong to

Camilo Loza – this was a different sacrifice entirely.

When they did eventually locate what was left of him, Camilo's relatives found that his head had been enclosed in a plastic bag which was secured tightly round his neck with string. This had had the effect of retarding putrefaction, and when the bag was removed it was still possible to see that the skin of the face had been carefully stripped off – a feature consistent with sacrificial practice in earlier cases.

Although the police were now obliged to undertake a rudimentary enquiry, the mayor decided that it was a hopeless task and the investigation was terminated with no charges being made.

Although there was no shortage of theories, the two most favoured were that the 'sacrifices' were warnings given against interference with the powerful cocaine gang that operated in the area, or that they were the victims of magic rituals carried out by local sorcerers called *liquichiri*. Indeed, it was even rumoured that Camilo Loza's own family, known to be involved with *liquichiri*, had far more information on Camilo's death than they were letting on. The death of this unfortunate youth remains officially unsolved.

LYLES, Anjette   Well known around Macon, Georgia, as a practitioner of voodoo and Satanic rituals, Anjette Lyles nevertheless relied on the deadlier power of poison when it came to disposing of her family.

The sudden death of her husband Ben in January 1952 was a great disappointment to Anjette Lyles – or rather, the death was a success, but she had felt sure he was insured for more than the measly $3,000 she got. Nothing ventured, she supplemented this modest sum by taking out a loan in order to open a restaurant which she called, not without a certain black humour, the Gay Widow.

One of the restaurant's regulars was an airline pilot named Joe Neal Gabbert who became as fond of Anjette as he was of her cooking, and after a whirlwind romance they married in June 1955. Three months after the wedding, Gabbert was taken seriously ill and Mrs Gabbert with the help of a hired nurse failed to effect any improvement. Joe Gabbert was hospitalised and died soon afterwards. Of course, he was insured.

And so was Anjette's former mother-in-law, Julia Young Lyles. She died on 29 September 1957, and eight months later nine-year-old daughter Marcia Elaine Lyles suffered an agonising death in hospital.

So alarming had the child's death been that an autopsy was ordered by the hospital, and the cause of death attributed to arsenical poisoning. A police search of Anjette Lyles' home uncovered six bottles of arsenic-based rat poison together with several empty poison bottles; most of which formed parts of the concoctions used in her 'potions'. Although Anjette insisted that little Marcia must have taken the poison while playing doctors and nurses, it surprised nobody when the Gay Widow was arrested and charged with murder.

It was stated in the evidence against her at trial that Anjette Lyles had altogether netted some $47,750 from the four deaths, including the estate of her mother-in-law which had been secured with a forged will. The money was spent mainly on men and supplies and equipment for her black-magic practices.

Although she was sentenced to die in the electric chair, Mrs Lyles was eventually declared insane and committed to the State Hospital at Milledgeville, Georgia.

M

McLAUCHLAN, Sheena, and **PORTER, Alan** In the first month of 1986, an extraordinary trial opened in the Glasgow High Court of Justiciary which would shock the most hardened of that city's hearts. Standing in the dock were twenty-three-year-old Sheena McLauchlan and her twenty-eight-year-old boyfriend Alan Porter. They were jointly charged with the murder of Sheena's baby daughter Kether.

Sheena McLauchlan had acquired a reputation for being a wee bit peculiar and spent a number of her early adult years dabbling on the fringe of various occult practices. It seemed entirely in keeping, then, that when she became pregnant in the early eighties Sheena claimed that it was an 'immaculate conception' – the result of an other-worldly experience while walking across the lonely and mysterious Salisbury Plain, host to the Stonehenge and Avebury stone circles. The cynical may feel that Sheena concocted this story because she was unmarried at the time and living at home with her mother. The child's name – Kether – is one of the points on the Qabalistic Tree of Life – and reflected Sheena McLauchlan's preoccupation.

Shortly afterwards Sheena met Alan Porter and they began to live together. Then baby Kether disappeared, a fact explained by her mother as a tragic cot death. The truth of the matter was no less tragic, but infinitely more bizarre, and in the end Sheena McLauchlan's uneasy conscience prodded her two years later into confiding to her mother that Kether had been killed and at that moment lay buried on the bank of Loch Lomond. Although police searchers subsequently found baby clothes and a pram at the spot, there was no body. Whether it was, as suggested, devoured over the period by scavenging local fauna we will never know.

The tale Sheena told to the police, and later the court, was that she had been instructed by her 'spirit guide' – described as an ethereal Tibetan monk in saffron robes – to murder three-month-old Kether as a sacrifice. According to Alan Porter's recollection, when the couple and the child had reached the desolate lochside Sheena was unable to strangle her daughter and he, Porter, was obliged to step in and finish the job – a gesture he described as designed to 'put her out of her misery'. Though what misery the child was in, apart from having a dangerously unbalanced mother, is not clear. For his part in this wicked crime, Alan Porter was convicted of murder and sentenced to life imprisonment. Sheena McLauchlan pleaded diminished responsibility and admitted culpable homicide.

MANSON, Charles, *et al.* An ex-convict and all-round drop-out, Manson is generally considered to have dominated his equally unattractive disciples with a mish-mash of corrupted Biblical philosophy and mistaken interpretations of the lyrics of Beatles songs. However, there is also a considerable body of evidence that Manson was deeply involved in various occult and satanic cults, which underpinned the Family's killings. Notably, it has been suggested that Mad Charlie was a member of the notorious 'Four P Movement', an offshoot of the Satanic Process Church of Final Judgement. There is some support for this suggestion from Ed Sanders, author of the definitive study of *The Family* (Signet, New York, 1989) who reports that Manson's followers referred to him as 'Grand Chingon' – the title given to the Four P Movement's leaders. This, combined with his magnetic sexual attraction for the female members of his Family, ensured Manson's complete physical and spiritual control of the group.

The first publicised murders took place in the summer of 1969, at which time the Family were occupying a disused movie-set ranch owned by George Spahn. While at the ranch, Manson organised the 'Land Armada', a fleet of armoured dune buggies that would protect the homestead during what he called 'Helter Skelter'. It is characteristic of Manson's retarded educational development that for him Helter Skelter was a simple misinterpretation of the words of a song written by the Beatles – he had no idea that the reference was to a fairground ride. Charlie had already decided that the Fab Four's earlier song, *Blackbird*, represented a call to the blacks of America to rise up against the whites, and he now believed it was time to get the holocaust started which would lead to mutual annihilation of the races and leave the Family in control.

Just after midnight on Saturday 9 August 1969, four shadowy figures were skulking about the grounds of the secluded mansion at 10050 Cielo Drive in Beverly Hills. At this stage, Manson was not doing his own killing; tonight it was the turn of 'Tex' Watson, Patricia 'Katie' Krenwinkel, 'Sadie' Atkins and Linda Kasabian to do their master's will. 10050 Cielo was occupied that night by actress Sharon Tate (her husband, the film director Roman Polanski, was away on business), who was heavily pregnant, and four friends. In an orgy of overkill, the Family left all five victims horribly butchered. Voytec Frykowski alone was stabbed more than fifty times, slashed, shot and so savagely bludgeoned with the butt of a gun that the weapon shattered. On the front door to the house the word 'Pig' was painted in blood; not one of the murderous gang had had the slightest idea of whom they had killed – they were just random victims.

Only one person back at the Spahn Ranch was not pleased – Charlie Manson. When the news came through on television of the bloodbath it apparently offended Charlie's sensibilities that it had been such a messy job. He decided to show everybody how it should be done.

On 11 August, just two days after the Tate murders, after motivating themselves with drugs, Manson led a group consisting of 'Tex' Watson, Susan Atkins, Katie Krenwinkel, Linda Kasabian, Clem Grogan and Leslie van Houten on a second murder spree. At shortly after 1.00 a.m. the Family invaded the Silver Lake home of businessman Leno LaBianca and his wife Rosemary; as with the Cielo Drive victims, the choice was entirely random. After stabbing and slashing the LaBiancas to death, Manson and his disciples inscribed the mottoes 'Death to the Pigs', 'Rise' and 'Healter [*sic*] Skelter' in blood on the walls; as a final act of gratuitous violence, the word 'War' was carved into Leno LaBianca's abdomen.

Following these utterly mindless killings, the Family went to ground. Susan Atkins was later arrested on a prostitution charge and while she was in custody admitted her part in the Tate murders to a cellmate. The information filtered back to the prison authorities and, on 1 December 1969, the Family were rounded up and charges of murder were laid against the principal members. Manson, Krenwinkel, Atkins and van Houten were tried together and, on 19 April 1971, after one of the most extraordinary trials in California's history, they were convicted and sentenced to death for the Tate/LaBianca murders.

At a later trial, Manson, Bruce Davis and Clem Grogan were convicted of murder and conspiracy in the murder of Hinman and a cowboy actor named 'Shorty' Shea. Charles 'Tex' Watson was tried separately and found guilty on seven counts of murder and conspiracy; he too was sentenced to death. Susan Atkins pleaded guilty to Gary Hinman's murder and was sentenced to life imprisonment and Bobby Beausoleil was given the same sentence. Mary Brunner and Linda Kasabian turned state's evidence and no charges were brought against them. In view of the state of California's suspension of capital punishment, the death sentences were subsequently reduced to life imprisonment.

Although no further charges were brought, there is reason to believe that many other murders could be laid to the account of Charles Manson's Family, including several of their own members. Vincent Bugliosi, prosecutor in the Tate/LaBianca trial, in his book *Helter Skelter* does not dismiss Manson's own claim to have committed thirty-five murders – indeed, he now feels that it may have been an uncharacteristic understatement.

And if everybody thinks that Charlie is evil – and crazy, too – then Charlie is the first to agree with them. Since he became eligible for parole a dozen years ago, Manson has insisted on his right to a regular hearing. Not that he seems to take these occasions terribly seriously – certainly not seriously enough to stand a hope in hell of ever being released – but it is the one time every eighteen months or so when he can guarantee that a mass media committed to keeping the cult of Manson alive will be assembled *en masse* in an adjoining room listening to the proceedings and hanging on Charlie's every word. He rarely disappoints.

In an article on Stephen Kay, the Los Angeles County deputy district attorney whose mission it has been to oppose each and every one of the Manson Family's bids for parole, Martin Kasindorf related how, at the 1981 parole hearing, Manson predicted that Stephen Kay himself would be murdered in the San Quentin car park as he left the meeting. Of course, Kay suffered no such dramatic fate, and was there facing Manson across the wooden table at the next parole board. But the point was that everybody expects something like this from Mad Charlie – so who is he to disappoint them?

Then there was the time when Stephen Kay asked Manson why it was he spent so much of his time making scorpions out of the thread unravelled from his socks. By way of explanation, Manson rose in his seat and intoned: 'From the world of darkness I did loose demons and devils in the power of scorpions to torment!' Needless to say, this put the 'Messiah's' parole chances back by a few years.

The year 1986 found Charlie reading his twenty-page hand-written statement, described as 'bizarre and rambling', when parole was opposed by no less an authority than California's governor George Deukmejian. In 1989, Manson decided that he would not face the parole board with manacles on his wrists because: 'They'll think I'm dangerous.' They probably did anyway – but in his absence Charles Milles Manson was predictably denied the opportunity to join the world at large for a few years more.

Ironically, Manson made his latest appeal for freedom on 20 April 1992 – it was within hours of the death sentence, the first in California for decades, being carried out on Robert Alton Harris. Manson's own death sentence could not be reinstated, nor, it seemed, was he destined to win his freedom. According to one newspaper correspondent in New York, Charlie surprised his new parole board by announcing: 'There's no one as bad as me. I'm everywhere – I'm down in San Diego zoo; I'm in the trees; I'm in your children. Someone has to be insane, we can't all be good guys. They've tried to kill me thirty or forty times in prison; they've poured fire over me. They haven't found anyone badder than me because there is no one as bad as me – and that's a fact.'

Charlie had blown his chance yet again.

MARTI, Enriqueta The world's folk-lore is full of stories of unrequited love being requited by the simple introduction into the equation of a love potion. Throughout the ages in every corner of the earth cunning men, witches, sorcerers and shamen have assembled amatory concoctions as part of their daily stock-in-trade. Usually the ingredients are no more exotic than a few wild flowers, herbs, nuts and berries – all put together with the appropriate spells and gesticulations, black cats and broomsticks, of course.

But there have been some whose enthusiasm for the perfect potion has crossed the line between mumbo-jumbo and criminal madness. One such was Enriqueta Marti, in the first decade of the present century a resident of Barcelona. In March 1912 a young girl named Angelita escaped after being kidnapped by what she described to the police as a witch. She had been abducted, it turned out, by a well-known local sorceress named Enriqueta Marti, who offered a specialist service in potions and philtres. She had taken the child to her home and invited her for supper; the meal, Angelita learned later, was comprised of the left-overs of an earlier little captive. The prime parts of the child's body had already found their way into the potions cauldron.

Under investigation Enriqueta Marti disclosed that to date half a dozen local children had been dispatched and their bodies boiled down to make her deluxe, irresistible love potion, for which, it seemed, her regular clients were prepared to dig deep into their purses. Señora Marti seemed to look on this activity as all part and parcel of her calling, leaving the court with little option but to convict her of multiple murder; she was sentenced to death and executed.

MSOMI, Elifasi   In South African tribal folk-lore the equivalent of the European *bogle*, or bogey-man, is the 'tokoloshe'. From August 1953, for a period of twenty-one months, Elifasi Msomi embarked on a series of fifteen murders of men, women and children claiming that it was not he, but the tokoloshe that was responsible. Msomi was a native of Richmond, Natal, and carried on the profession of witch doctor – though how successful he was may be judged by his declining practice. Taking, so to speak, some of his own medicine, Msomi established that it would require the blood of just fifteen freshly slaughtered humans to boost his flagging fortunes and restore his business to its peak.

The first step in self-improvement was taken in August 1953, when Msomi, in the presence of his mistress, raped and stabbed to death a young girl. The woman, understandably shocked and disillusioned, reported her lover to the police and he was arrested. Perhaps Msomi was receiving a little advance reward from the tokoloshe, since he managed to escape from custody.

Soon afterwards, posing as a labour agent at a village in the Boston district, Msomi persuaded parents to let him take five children with him to work as servants for Europeans in the city. Having stabbed the unfortunate mites to death, Msomi had the audacity to return to the village, assure the parents that their offspring were well placed, and demand money to provide them with extra comforts. He seems to have continued to murder almost at will, frequently employing the 'labour agent' ruse to lure children from their families. The police, convinced that an unbalanced Zulu was responsible for the disappear-ances, could only advise the tribespeople in the area to be on their guard.

In April 1955, Elifasi Msomi was reported to the police for theft, arrested and placed in custody. Almost as quickly – and this may be attributed either to the power of the tokoloshe or the lax procedures of the native Natal police – he was away again.

Recaptured the following month, Msomi found himself in the embarrassing position of being in possession of some property formerly belonging to one of his victims, and the very knife with which he had committed his first murder. Not that Msomi was uncooperative; he was quite prepared to lead the police to the last resting grounds of all the victims – not of himself, but of the tokoloshe!

The court would entertain none of this mumbo-jumbo. As far as they were concerned Elifasi Msomi was a multiple murderer, and accordingly, in September 1955, he was sentenced to death for his crimes.

But there are powers abroad that transcend the judgement of a mortal court. So terrified were the local people that the tokoloshe would step in once again and lift Msomi from captivity to wreak further havoc that, to convince them that Msomi was dead, the prison authorities were obliged to arrange for a deputation of chiefs and elders to view Msomi before and after his appointment with the hangman at Pretoria Central Prison on 10 February 1956.

MULLIN, Herbert   Mullin began to establish his credentials as a multicide on the instruction of the voices which he heard in his head – voices which he was later to acknowledge as Satan's, but which nevertheless convinced him that by shedding blood he would save California from a cataclysmic earthquake and a giant tidal wave. What was more, the voices told him, the victims would be inexpressibly grateful for being given the opportunity to help in this way. A matter of the 'small disasters' (the murders) being justified in averting the 'great disaster'.

Herb's first sacrifice was a vagrant named 'Old Whitey', whom he battered to death with a baseball bat on 13 October 1972; eleven days later he butchered a young girl student called Mary Guilfoyle. By the beginning of the following year the voices were still there. They were always there now, some telling Herb to kill, others begging him to kill them. Mullin had got hold of a gun and was killing more randomly, and more frequently – as many as five murders in a single day in January. Then on 13 February 1973, Herb Mullin shot an elderly man in his garden; what the voices hadn't told him was that the victim's neighbour would see it happen. Within the hour Mullin was in custody. Among his first words were: 'Satan gets into people and makes them do things they don't want to do.' Then he confessed to thirteen murders.

In many ways Herbert Mullin is the stereotypical 'visionary' psychotic killer. His reason for murder was that he genuinely believed that the voices and 'telepathic messages' were directed to him as a saviour of the world. Despite a history of in-patient treatment for paranoid schizophrenia, and a long-established pattern of responding to 'voices', Mullin's plea of insanity at his trial was rejected, and he was sentenced to various terms of imprisonment for eleven murders. He will be eligible for parole in the year 2025.

N

NEW, Harry S., junior It was something of a surprise when Harry New presented himself at the Los Angeles Central police headquarters on 5 July 1919. Not because he was claiming to be the son of a high-profile Indiana senator, but because he had come to give himself up. For murder.

According to Harry he had quarelled with twenty-one-year-old Frieda J. Lesser somewhere up in Topango Canyon. The cause of the disagreement was the young woman's refusal to marry him, and to show just how peeved he was, Harry New shot her through the head. The police had no difficulty believing New's story because he had brought Frieda's body back with him – it was in the car outside the police station. 'We didn't understand each other,' New confided to Detective-sergeant Davidson, 'and so I shot her, and here I am.' With a wistful nod towards his car, he added: 'And there she is too.' Thirty-year-old Harry S. New, junior was without more ado charged with murder.

Later, Harry made a full written confession to the effect that:

Frieda and I were engaged to be married for a long time. Yesterday, accompanied by others, we drove to Hermosa Beach and after our return I took her for a ride to discuss our marriage, which was due to take place tomorrow night. We drove to a lonely canyon several miles away and talked over our future. During our conversation Frieda told me the wedding would have to be postponed as she intended seeking a nurse for an operation which would prevent our child being born. Enraged at her stand, I took a revolver from a pocket of the car and shot her through the temple. She dropped to the bottom of the car. I picked her up but she had died almost instantly . . . I remember driving about for four hours, holding her hand in one of mine while with the other I steered the car. Often I stopped and kissed her cold face, as if that would bring back to me the spirit I had sent to eternity.

By Tuesday the eighth, Senator New of Indiana was on record claiming that, although he did have a brief liaison with Harry junior's mother it was thirty or more years ago, and he had since 'made amends'. He emphatically denied, though, that he had ever married the lady. Quite a different story, in fact, from that still being told by young Harry, who insisted that the senator and his mother were married and then divorced.

At the same time Harry New was arraigned before Justice of the Peace Howard Hinshaw on 8 July, and on the twelfth he was indicted by the Los Angeles County Grand Jury. Already Harry's defence was stated to be one of not guilty by reason of insanity.

On 16 December 1919 this plea was formally advanced by Harry New's counsel Lecompte Davis when he addressed the jury of nine men and two women. District Attorney Thomas Lee Woodwine responded for the prosecution by saying that, while he was not intending to prove that Harry was 'an intellectual giant', he would be seeking to show that he was intelligent enough to be responsible for his actions.

Mrs Alice Lesser, the victim's mother, made a brief, hysterical appearance in the witness box on Thursday 18 December, to tell the jury of the relationship between her daughter and Harry S. New. Mrs Lesser had been escorted from her home to the courthouse by detectives, though as she approached the trial room she fainted. According to one eyewitness, when she was revived 'her screams penetrated the courtroom and several other women became hysterical'.

In support of Harry's insanity plea, a fellow prisoner at the county jail, E.W. McCumber, testified that his cell-mate would spend hours on end, silent and motionless, looking out of the window – an observation which was backed up by New's commanding officer while he was serving in the artillery; Colonel Tyndall referred to Harry New as being 'morose' and 'mentally unsound'.

Perhaps the most curious piece of evidence to come from Harry's defence team – though what possible relevance it could have had seemed to evade the jury – was that a seance had been held during the early days of the trial at which Miss Frieda Lesser, or at least her shade, appeared and announced that Harry had not, she was sure, intended to kill her, and that she forgave him.

When it came time for the jury to decide on Harry New's guilt they had obviously rejected the insanity plea altogether. Not that it made things any easier, because by 14 January they were deadlocked. Despite a lengthy retirement, the foreman announced to Judge Craig that they were split between a verdict of second-degree murder and one of manslaughter. A request for further instruction on the distinction between the crimes was, unaccountably, refused. Finally, following a further forty-two hours of deliberation, the jury returned a unanimous verdict of murder in the second degree.

Although Harry New's counsel pressed for a retrial it was a forlorn hope, and Harry was packed off to San Quentin to serve a term of imprisonment of not less than ten years and a maximum of life.

NEWELL, Andrew According to his own evidence, twenty-one-year-old Newell fled from the flat he shared with Philip Booth after Booth became violent and attacked him with a knife after a bout of heavy drinking and eating quantities of 'magic' mushrooms. When he returned to the house at Telford in Shropshire, so he said, he found twenty-year-old Booth had unaccountably been stabbed to death.

Not so, claimed Crown prosecutor Mr Timothy Barnes QC when Andrew Newell appeared before Shrewsbury Crown Court charged with murder in December 1987. According to prosecution evidence, Newell was a practising devil-worshipper who had deliberately knifed his unsuspecting friend after they returned from a Guy Fawkes' night bonfire party the previous year. Not only that, but it was believed that after bludgeoning Philip Booth with a heavy chain and repeatedly plunging a knife into his body, Newell performed some homespun Satanic ritual over the dying man's body. Police had found a 'black magic box' (in reality a modest plastic record storage holder) at the scene of the crime, which contained Newell's paraphernalia – candles, a ceremonial dagger, an altar cloth, and a number of books on ritual magic, including the *Grimoire of Magick* and *The Grim War of Chaos Magic*. It was suggested that the box also served as a makeshift altar; painted on to the base of it in blood was an inverted cross.

Aside from his excursion into murder – for which, incidentally, he was convicted and sentenced to life imprisonment – it seems that Andrew Newell was more generally, how to put it . . . unstable. His diary, found in the murder flat, recorded how he would gaze into a mirror while 'turning into a werewolf'. Scene-of-crime officers had also recovered a slip of paper bearing the words of his favourite heavy-metal band Iron Maiden's song *The Number of the Beast*, one verse of which read, appropriately, 'The sacrifice is going on tonight; I am coming back; I will return.'

It may possibly have been just as Newell's bewildered family claimed, a drunken prank, but his sleeping inside a centuries-old tomb in the disused graveyard at Stirchley 'to be surrounded by the dead', could hardly have helped the jury accept his father's claim that Andrew was not involved in black magic.

'NIGHT STALKER', *see* **RAMIREZ, Richard**

NODDER, Frederick   The case, as far as the police were concerned, began on 5 January 1937. In the afternoon of this chilly Tuesday, shortly after ten-year-old Mona Tinsley left the Methodist School in Guildhall Street, Newark, she had been seen in the company of a man at the bus station near the Robin Hood Hotel. This sighting was of vital importance, because Mona never returned home. Despite the rather sketchy descriptions of the man – the most prominent feature being his staring eyes, leading the more imaginative of the tabloid newspapers to call him the 'Phantom with Staring Eyes' – it was enough for the police to identify him as Frederick Nodder.

Nodder had deserted his wife some years previously, and had gone to Sheffield where he lodged with a Mr and Mrs Grimes. For no honest reason he had adopted the name Hudson and claimed to be a car mechanic, though his intemperate habits resulted in his being for the most part unemployable. After a year with the Grimeses, in 1935, Frederick Nodder took lodgings with Mrs Grimes' sister, Mrs Tinsley, at Thoresby Avenue, Newark, where for some unaccountable reason he was a popular figure with the many Tinsley children (including Mona) to whom he became 'Uncle Fred'.

When he left the Tinsleys, Nodder moved on his own to a scruffy semi-detached house in Smeath Road, Hayton; it was rather inappropriately named 'Peacehaven'. When Frederick Nodder was picked up by Harry Barnes, Chief Constable of Newark, he at first denied having seen Mona for fifteen months. That was his story on the night of 6 January. By the eighth, Nodder had decided to cooperate – though not with the truth of course.

According to his new statement, Mona had asked Uncle Fred to take her to visit her aunt (Mrs Grimes) and new baby cousin, Peter, in Sheffield. He persuaded Mona to stay the night at 'Peacehaven', and the following evening Nodder took his young charge by bus from East Retford to Worksop and then put her on another bus to travel alone to Sheffield.

Frederick Nodder was charged with abduction, and in the absence of Mona Tinsley's body – still missing despite a massive search operation – he found himself facing the lesser charge when he appeared before Mr Justice Swift at the Birmingham Assizes. On 10 March 1937 Nodder was convicted, and in sentencing him to seven years, the judge observed: 'What you did with that little girl, what became of her, only you know. It may be that time will reveal the dreadful secret you carry in your breast.'

And that is exactly what did happen.

The search continued for little Mona Tinsley's body, but it was only eventually found by chance. It was in the river, as the spirit medium Estelle Roberts had predicted by psychometry, but had escaped detection becoming lodged in a drain culvert. It was three months into Frederick Nodder's sentence, on Sunday 6 June, that a party of people boating on the river Idle, just below Bawtry, saw the floating bundle which contained Mona's corpse. She had been strangled with a ligature, such as a bootlace, but the advanced state of the body's decomposition made it impossible to tell whether or not she had been sexually assaulted.

Now it was impossible for Frederick Nodder to escape the full and awful might of British justice. His defence was a repetition of that given at his first trial, and the jury did not believe it this time either. Passing sentence of death on him, Mr Justice Macnaghten told Nodder: 'Justice has slowly but surely overtaken you.'

At Lincoln Prison on the morning of Thursday 30 December 1937 the degenerate Frederick Nodder took his last breath of air before plummeting, unlamented, into the pit below the scaffold.

In her autobiography, *Forty Years a Medium*, Estelle Roberts recalled being asked by a friend to help in the search for Mona Tinsley. At first she was reluctant to become involved in anything which might, as she put it, 'be condemned as a stunt'. However, her natural concern for Mona's anxious parents overcame Mrs Roberts' apprehensions and she wrote to the Chief Constable at Newark, who obtained a pink dress from Mrs Tinsley and put it in the post along with a note ending: 'I shall be glad if you will refrain from giving my action any official interpretation.' Estelle Roberts remembered with sorrow her instant knowledge that Mona was dead as soon as she touched the child's dress.

Through her personal spirit guide, Red Cloud, Mrs Roberts contacted Mona Tinsley who told her that she had been strangled. 'She gave me a picture of the house, with a water-filled ditch on one side, a field at its back, a churchyard close by, and an inn within sight. In my vision I was taken to a graveyard, over a bridge, and across some fields to a river beyond. There I stopped, unable to go any further.' So impressed were the police by the accuracy of this description of the place from which Mona disappeared that they invited Estelle Roberts up to visit the site.

Their first stop was 'Peacehaven' (though Mrs Roberts did not know that at first). The building had been stripped of furniture, but the medium felt the strong presence of Mona Tinsley in one of the empty rooms upstairs, and in the downstairs front room. It was her belief, she told detectives, that the child had been strangled in the upstairs room, then the body had been put in a sack and taken out by the side door.

'Why not the front door?'

'I don't know. All I can say is it was the side door he used.'

'Actually,' one of the policeman admitted, 'the front door won't open. Nodder screwed it up so that it is permanently closed.'

'This is Nodder's house?' I asked.

'Yes.'

'I thought it might be.'

Next, Mrs Roberts tried to trace the route given to her in her spirit contact with Mona – through the graveyard, over the bridge to some fields, where she asked the police: 'Beyond those fields there is a river?' There was – the river Idle. 'The river holds the secret of the child's whereabouts. If you've dragged it already and found nothing, you must drag it again.'

In discussing her part in the Nodder case, Mrs Roberts concludes by expressing her dislike of dealing with murder cases: 'It is a harassing experience for a medium to relive the impressions of the victim's last moments on earth. It has happened several times that I have embarked unknowingly on a case in which murder was involved, but it has required only a few seconds of spirit communication before I am aware that the victim died by violence.'

P

PONESSA, Domingo   To Chief Inspector Matteoli of the Florentine police and his team of experts it was by no means rare, if not
exactly an everyday scene. After all, bodies were their business.
But hardly the stock-in-trade of the unfortunate Signor Capelli
who had discovered this one.

It had been a sunny Sunday afternoon in March 1986, and Luigi
Capelli was wandering in a leisurely Sunday afternoon sort of way
in the countryside outside Florence when his attention strayed to
the eyesore of a number of bulging rubbish bags discarded in the
middle of a field. More curious than perhaps he should have been
for his own peace of mind, Capelli landed the nearest offending
bag a determined kick with his right foot, splitting the plastic and
revealing the badly decomposed human head inside.

So putrefied was the collection of twenty-nine assorted
remains found in the rubbish sacks that it was impossible for
the police surgeon even to determine gender at the scene of the
discovery. Later, on the post-mortem slab where the body had
been reassembled, it became clear that the victim had been
killed around the middle of the previous month, February;
cause of death was bludgeoning with a heavy cylindrical
weapon, possibly a walking stick. That much the police had
been prepared for as they reacquainted themselves with the
corpse at the mortuary. What momentarily stunned Inspector
Matteoli and the sergeant was the doctor's announcement that
the victim had been neither man nor woman – but both. Not a
true hermaphrodite, but a male who had undergone a sex-
change operation. It did at any rate present the probability that
the murder had some sexual motive, and the fact of the
sex-change greatly limited the field of search for the victim's

identity. It proved, in fact, to be remarkably easy. Underwear dumped with the remains was traced to an exclusive lingerie shop in the city which catered for what the manageress liked to describe as 'folk in the entertainment business' – in other words, female impersonators who worked the night-clubs and bars, and prostitutes. Of their many regular customers, the sales staff recalled the names of two who had not been shopping for 'costumes' recently. One had simply taken his custom elsewhere, but the second one, whose stage name was Jackie, had not turned up in the clubs since the middle of February. Ominous indeed.

It transpired that 'Jackie' was in reality Alfreda Tolaba (formerly Alfredo Tolaba), and he/she was a thirty-four-year-old stripper and whore. A painstaking search of Alfreda's luxury apartment resulted in a lengthy list of names and addresses among which was The Great Garbanzo, a stage magician to whom the victim had played his 'lovely assistant'. They had apparently both dabbled in the periphery of the occult, and Alfreda possessed a sizeable library of books on arcane subjects. Other men, a lot of them, with whom the victim may or may not have been having affairs, were gradually traced and eliminated from the enquiry. It began to look as though this would be one of those long-drawn-out murder investigations where no stone dare be left unturned.

And it was one of the unlikely stones that led Inspector Matteoli to his man. As detectives progressed through Alfreda's address book, a letter had been sent to the police in Argentina asking them to check on a Maria Ponessa. When the Florentine police received word of Mrs Ponessa, she could not help with Alfreda Tolaba – never heard of her – but did ask for help in tracing her husband Domingo Ponessa, who had been living in Florence and had not been heard from since February – not since he had sent his wife a photograph of himself dressed as a woman. It was this last fact that had caught the Inspector's attention – just such a snap had been found in Alfreda's apartment.

Eventually, the wandering Domingo Ponessa was located in his native Sicily, performing in a strip-tease joint in Palermo. The rest was easy. Back in Florence in custody, Ponessa confessed to killing Alfreda Tolaba whom he had first encountered in October 1985. Clearly impressed by Alfreda's lifestyle, Ponessa was encouraged to try a bit of cross-dressing himself. What followed was almost too bizarre for description. Because Ponessa could not afford a sex-change operation himself, his new friend, who boasted knowledge of occult practices, offered to work a bit of magic. The long and the short of it was that Domingo Ponessa became convinced that every time he dressed and made-up as a woman he was transformed into one. And after some hocus-pocus ceremony, Domingo truly believed that he did. Their personal and business relationship might have continued much longer had Alfreda not, in a fit of pique at some imagined slight, sent the photograph of Ponessa to his wife. So Ponessa beat Alfreda to death, cut the body up with a saw and dumped the resulting shambles for Luigi Capelli to trip over a month later.

On 20 March 1987 Domingo Ponessa was judged sane and guilty of murder. However, for some unaccountable reason, the court exercised great leniency and sentenced him to just four years' imprisonment.

PRESTON, Jennet   Although she committed her alleged murder in Yorkshire, was held in York Castle prison and tried there at the York Assize, Jennet Preston is most frequently associated with the Lancashire Witches (see page 154) because, so it is said, Mistress Preston attended the notorious Lancashire coven meeting at Malking Tower where the plot to blow up Lancaster Gaol was mooted.

Thomas Potts, in his *Wonderful Discoverie of Witches in the Countie of Lancaster* adds as a postscript: 'The Arraignement and Triall of Iennet Preston . . . with her Execution for the murther of Master Lister by Witchcraft'. The following text is abridged from an even earlier published record than Potts', printed for the London bookseller John Barnes in 1612:

INDICTMENT

This *Jennet Preston* was accused that shee felloniously had practised divers wicked and devilish arts, called Witchcrafts, Inchantments, Charmes, and Sorceries, in and upon one *Thomas Lister* of Westby in

Craven, in the Countie of Yorke, and by force of the same witchcraft
the said *Thomas Lister* had killed. To this Indictment shee pleaded
not guiltie.

The Evidence for the Kings Majestie [prosecution]
Anne Robinson and others were examined, who upon their Oaths
declared that Mr *Lister* lying in great distress, upon his death-bedde,
cried out unto them that stood about him that *Jennet Preston* was in
the House, look where she is, take holde of her; for Gods sake shut
the doors, and take her, shee cannot escape away. Look about for
her, and lay hold of her, for she is in the house: and so cried very
often in his great paines, to them that came to visit him during his
sicknesse.

Being examined further, *Anne Robinson* gave this evidence against
her: that when Master *Lister* lay upon his death-bedde, hee cried out
in great extremitie; *Jennet Preston* lays heavy upon me, *Preston's* wife
lays heavy upon me; helpe me, helpe me: and so departed, crying out
against her.

Many other witnesses deposed, that *Jennet Preston*, being brought
to Mr *Lister* after he was dead, and layed out to be wound up in his
winding-sheet, the said *Jennet Preston* comming to touch the dead
corpse, it bled fresh blood in the presence of all that were then
present: which hath ever been held a great proof to induce a Jurie to
hold him guiltie that shall be accused of murther, and hath seldome or
never, failed in the Tryall. But this was not all; the Friday following,
being Good-Friday, shee rode to the great meeting at *Malkin-Tower*
[see *Lancashire Witches*, page 154], and there asked help in the
murther of *Thomas Lister*.

And whereat all gave their consents to put the said Master *Thomas
Lister* of Westby to death: and after Master *Lister* should be made
away by witchcraft, then all the said Witches gave their consents to
joyne altogether to hancke Master *Leonard Lister*, when he should
come to dwell at the Sowgill, and so put *him* to death.

Before
After these many Examinations, Confessions, and Evidences, delivered in open Court against *Jennet Preston*, his Lordship commanded
the Jurie to observe that: Master *Lister* in his sickness to complaine
hee *saw* her, and requested them that were by him to lay hold on her;
that he cried out, shee laying heavie upon him even at the time of his
death.

But the conclusion is of more grave importance than all the rest, that *Jennet Preston* being brought to the dead corpse and touching it, the openings bled freshly. Then, in Lent, it was proved she rode upon a white Foal, and was present in the great assembly at Malkin-Tower with the [Lancashire] Witches, to intreate and pray for aide to kill *Master Lister*.

After which the Gentlemen of the Jurie delivered up their verdict, and found *Jennet Preston* guiltie of the murder by Witchcraft of *Thomas Lister*.

Afterwards, according to the Lawes, his Lordship pronounced Judgement that she should be hanged.

One thing more I shall add, which I saw, and was present in the Court at Lancaster, when it was done at the Assizes held in August following.

My *Lord Bromley* being very suspicious of the accusation of the little wench, *Jennet Device*, commanded her to look upon the prisoners that were present, and declare which of them were present at *Malkin-Tower*, at the great assembly of Witches. Shee looked upon and tooke many by the handes, and accused them of being there, and when shee accused all that were there present, shee told his Lordship there was a woman that came out of Craven that was amongst the Witches at that feast, but shee saw her not among the Prisoners.

What a singular note was this of a Child, amongst many to misse her, that *before that time was hanged for her offence*, which shee would never confesse or declare at her death? Also present was old *Preston*, Jennet's husband, who then cried out and went away: being fully satisfied his wife had Justice, and was worthie of death.

And for this great deliverance, let us pray to GOD
Almightie, that the memorie of these worthie Judges may
bee blessed to all posterities.

R

RAKOWITZ, Daniel Dan Rakowitz was what you might call a 'well-known personality' around New York's Lower East Side. This was mainly because he pushed dope; nothing heavy – marijuana, a bit of hash and a few amphetamines. But it was also because he was weird; in fact he was *very* weird.

At the time we are interested in him – 1989 – Texas-born Rakowitz was twenty-eight years old and conspicuous around the East Village for the cockerel which he carried, after the fashion of Long John Silver and his parrot, on his shoulder. He was also noted for his peculiar views on religion. Dan had passed through the phase when he believed he was God, and had just developed a new religion based on a revelation that came to him that Satan, the Beast of the Apocalypse, had changed his number from 666 to 966. There was probably a reason for this somewhere in his head, but this is a matter best left to Dan and his psychiatrist. The important fact at this time was that his Swiss girlfriend, a student at the Martha Graham Contemporary Dance School, was becoming mightily fed-up with Dan's 'peculiarities'. In short, she had threatened to throw him out on his ear.

And so, on 19 August 1989, having failed to convert the unfortunate Monika to the Church of 966, Rakowitz killed her. Then he dismembered her body; then he boiled the flesh off the parts and put the skull and some assorted bones into a bucket to keep as a souvenir – for old times' sake.

But such activities do not go unnoticed by the authorities for very long – especially as Dan Rakowitz had let his disciples into the secret. Some of these followers were not quite as faithful as Dan might have wanted, and it was not long before he and his bucket of bones were in police custody. Daniel Rakowitz (or 'The

New Messiah' as he was now calling himself) made a full confession and, on 14 September 1990 he was convicted of murder and sentenced to life imprisonment.

RAMIREZ, Richard   From June 1984 to August 1985, twenty-five-year-old Richard Ramirez, a drifter out of El Paso, Texas, and serious disciple of the Devil, terrorised the middle-class homes of suburban Los Angeles. Detectives soon dubbed the crimes the 'Valley Intruder' murders and felt confident in attributing them to a single killer because he always left an occult symbol at the scene – sometimes on the victim's body, sometimes on the walls. The most common sign was the one known as a pentagram, or witches' star, consisting of a five-pointed star in a circle.

With skill and stealth, entering through an open window or an unlatched door, the killer crept through the sleeping houses: first to strangle or shoot the male occupants before turning his terrible attention on to the women and children – brutal rape and vicious mutilation of victims of both sexes and all ages fuelled the fire of his demon-driven blood lust. Sometimes he would compound the terror by turning child victims loose miles from home and family, barely alive, to wander in search of help.

The first of Ramirez' victims was seventy-nine-year-old Jennie Vincow, whose throat was slit on the night of 28 June 1984. Dayle Okazaki was next, shot through the forehead on 17 March 1985; thirty-year-old Tsai Lan Yu was dragged from her car and shot the very same night.

The most brutal murders were those of sixty-four-year-old Vincent Zazzara and his wife Maxine. Zazzara had retired as an investment adviser to pursue his dream of opening a restaurant; his wife was a successful lawyer. On the night of 26 March 1985, Mr and Mrs Zazzara were at home in their luxury ranch-house by the San Gabriel River, when an intruder broke in and shot them both. Then in an orgy of sadism he hacked at Maxine Zazzara's body with a knife, carving ragged wounds in her chest, neck, face, abdomen and groin. Worse still, the killer had gouged out both her eyes and taken them with him.

Although he went on to kill again in the middle-class suburban areas around the city, it was not until June 1985 that the Los Angeles police officially announced that they had a serial killer on the loose; the press christened him the 'Night Stalker.'

Two months after the Zazzara killings, William Doi was killed at his home in Monterey Park and his wife was raped and battered. This was followed by the murders of Mabel Bell, Patty Elaine Higgins, Mary Louise Cannon and Joyce Lucille Nelson. On 20 July the Night Stalker claimed no fewer than three victims – an elderly couple, Maxson and Lela Kneiding, shot dead, Chainarong Khovananth shot dead and his wife raped after being forced to promise Satan she would not scream. Elyath was shot dead on 8 August and his wife was raped and beaten. On the seventeenth of the same month Peter Pan and his wife Barbara were shot dead, and before he left their home the Stalker scrawled his familiar inverted pentragram on the wall in Barbara Pan's pink lipstick – with the words 'Jack the Knife' written underneath. The final victim was twenty-nine-year-old William Carns, shot dead on 24 August; his fiancée was forced to recite the words 'I Love Satan' as she was sexually violated.

Desperation and a belief that the Stalker was invincible were reducing the community to panic, when FBI officers at Quantico, checking out a getaway car, discovered the smudged fingerprint of a petty crook named Ramirez. Photographs were circulated to the media, and at nine o'clock on a Saturday morning in August 1985, a well-heeled LA suburb, as usual busy with its weekend shoppers, became the scene of a drama that ended the fear.

A man had been observed unsuccessfully trying the doors of parked cars; he attempted to pull a woman out of her car and was attacked by her husband. Then everybody recognised the man whose face had been staring at them from the front page of the morning papers. Richard Ramirez had come shopping for another victim and found himself the victim of the mob. Bruised and bloody, the Night Stalker was rescued by the police just in time to save him from being lynched.

Throughout his trial, Richard Ramirez was by turns sullen and explosive; at one moment flashing the Devil's pentagram scrawled on his hand to the eager press photographers, then falling silent for hours before placing his fingers to the sides of his head like a demon's horns and intoning, 'Evil, evil . . .'

It almost seemed at one point as if his invocation of demonic help might be bearing fruit as two juries in succession had to be dismissed – one because a member, who was clearly unimpressed by the honour of sitting in judgement on the Devil's disciple, fell into a deep sleep, the other because one of the members was murdered in a quite unconnected incident.

As he was convicted of twelve first-degree murders, one second-degree murder, and thirty other major offences of rape and burglary, Ramirez summed up for himself. 'You maggots make me sick,' he spat at the court. 'I will be avenged. Lucifer dwells within all of us!'

Richard Ramirez dwells on Death Row; and as California carries out the death penalty very sparingly (only twice since reintroduction in 1975) he is likely to dwell there for some years to come.

RED BARN MURDER, *see* **CORDER, William**

RESTLESS GHOST   One of the joys of compiling a book such as this is the number of completely unexpected gems that can be found lurking in dusty corners during research. Such a precious find was the following story of the Restless Ghost which appeared to William Clark, and which was preserved in a pamphlet published in 1675.

The man Clark was known as an honest, sober citizen, a stonemason by trade, living at Old Pells Farm, Hennington, a village four miles outside Northampton. Until the date of this most curious occurrence, the farmhouse had not in living memory been disturbed by anything which could be described as 'supernatural'. And then, around the beginning of 1674, the unfortunate Clark family were frequently put in fear by a sequence of mischievous hauntings. Sometimes, during the night, the doors would be unlocked and unbolted, at other times windows would be smashed. Whenever William Clark rose from his bed to investigate this confusion, there would be nothing and nobody to be seen. That is until the end of December.

Around this time the good maulster was walking close to the

house when he saw what he later described as 'a Spirit, which on a sudden became visible, at first in a very horrid, but immediately afterwards a more familiar and human shape'. Putting aside his understandable apprehension, Clark demanded of the shade what it was and what it was up to. To which the apparition, 'with a pleasant, friendly countenance and distinct voice', replied: 'I am the disturbed spirit of a person long since dead. I was murdered near this place two hundred and sixty-seven years, nine weeks and two days ago, to this very time. Come along with me, I will show you where it was done.'

It was the kind of request Will Clark felt it better not to refuse, and so followed the ghost to a hedge in the adjoining field where it announced: 'Here was I killed, my head being separated from my body.' For the sake of politeness, Clark asked his companion how it was he came to be murdered, and was told it was done by those greedy to inherit his estate. It also came to light that the unhappy fellow had at the time been a resident of Southwark, in London. In fact, he still had a hidden store of cash and documents in that place which he needed to unearth and dispose of before his soul could rest. 'Why,' Clark wanted to know, 'have you waited so very long a space of time to do it?' 'Ah,' wailed the soul in torment, 'I did for several years after my murder haunt that place, but was laid, bound down, by the exorcism of a certain friar and banished from the earth for two hundred and fifty years.'

Now, it seemed, the time had elapsed, and the phantom wanted William Clark to accompany him to London and help recover the treasure. Clark, worthy man, agreed, and they arranged to meet upon London Bridge in a fortnight.

Somewhat bewildered by his encounter with the other world, William Clark hastened to tell his story to the local parson, who advised him to keep his word, and not fail to meet with the troubled ghost – 'but do not eat or drink in any place where he might lead you'.

Over the succeeding couple of weeks the phantom appeared to Clark regularly to remind him of his promise, and the pair became as friendly as man and ghost could reasonably expect to be; though the spectre declined to describe at any length the quality of life on 'the other side'.

And so it happened that on 9 January 1675, a Saturday, William Clark set off for London, arriving the following day, and going straight to London Bridge and that district known as the Borough, he saw the phantom. At first William did not recognise him, for he had exchanged his customary winding-sheet for a suit of clothes. So, after a friendly greeting, the odd couple made for that area of Southwark where their work was to be done. Arriving at the house, the shade went in, fully visible to a number of people living there and told them his story, and that they were numbered among his heirs.

It was early on the following morning that Clark and the occupants were put to digging a hole – it must be inferred from this that having no corporeal body, ghosts are incapable of manual labour, or else that this one was somewhat lazy. When they had excavated to a depth of some eight feet, the diggers came upon a pot containing a large quantity of gold coin and a bundle of documents – the paper sheets 'mouldered away and crumbled to dust when they were touched', but the parchments were well preserved, their dates proving that the spirit's tale had been true, and that the pot had lain hidden for upwards of two hundred and fifty years. William Clark was entrusted with distributing the bounty among the murdered man's friends and heirs according to his instructions.

This being effected, the grateful phantasm returned to Will Clark and said: 'Thou hast done well, and henceforth I shall be at rest, so as never more to trouble thee.' And with that he disappeared.

RIVA, James P. Jimmy Riva's life was a spiral of increasingly bizarre and horrifying acts of bloodlust, which led him eventually to kill his own grandmother and drink her blood. He had been a deeply disturbed child, who filled his days drawing fantasy pictures – first of witches and goblins, then scenes of increasing violence, women with punctured necks, blood dripping from the wounds. At the age of four he rigged up a fiendish death trap as a revenge against his father, whom he believed had cheated him out of two dimes and a nickel. Fortunately the booby trap was discovered before anyone was injured.

Things got worse as Jimmy crossed the threshold of adolescence. His mother recalled how he would 'cook up concoctions on a hot plate of parts of animals with oil and entrails and raw fish and birds'. He would eat birds whole. Once James killed a cat, cut off its head and dissected the brains 'because he wanted to fix his own brain'. When the mother asked why his teeth were stained, he told her – he drank the cat's blood.

Jimmy Riva was in and out of mental institutions between 1975 and 1978, but emerged more weird than he went in. From 1977, he began to hear voices which dictated what he should do. He became totally preoccupied with blood, sex and violence, and began to claim that he had become a full-blown vampire, who kept company with other two-hundred-year-old vampires. Meanwhile, his family slept behind locked doors, and took turns to keep vigil during the long, ominous nights.

On a cold and rainy day in April 1980, twenty-four-year-old James Riva took off on a visit to his grandmother, Carmen Lopez, in the small town of Marshfield, Massachusetts. He took with him not flowers or chocolates, but a knife, a gun, and nine gold-painted bullets.

Riva parked his car fifty yards down the road from the house at 19 East Street, walked back, let himself in, and assaulted the frail seventy-four-year-old in her wheelchair. This was the point at which Jimmy believed his problems would end. Either his grandmother was a vampire who was stealing his blood, or else he was a vampire himself, who would gain strength from supping the old woman's blood. Anyway, he would be blessed with eternal life, would come back as a handsome man, with girls and smart cars. If only . . . He fired two bullets into the old woman's body, and finished her off with the knife. And then the sucking of the blood . . .

Riva made a crude attempt to cover his tracks by dousing his grandmother's body with petrol and torching her and her home. But it took the police no time at all to discover the bullet holes in the corpse, and the other seven gold bullets hidden in a box upstairs in the partially burned house. And it was a very short time indeed before they came knocking on Jimmy Riva's door.

The case was heard before Judge Peter F. Brady at the Superior Court at Plymouth, Massachusetts, in October 1981. A string of psychiatrists disagreed whether the defendant was a paranoid schizophrenic, or a manic depressive, or suffering a borderline personality disorder, or just plain crazy. But the jury followed the prosecution's line that the young man was 'aware of wrongdoing' and therefore criminally responsible for the murder. James P. Riva II was found guilty of second-degree murder and arson, and was sent to Walpole State Prison for life.

ROLLINGS, Peter   Described in court as 'a pagan who dabbled in witchcraft', twenty-three-year-old car cleaner Peter Rollings was standing trial at St Albans Crown Court for the murder of John Blair. It astonished the court, as well it might, that the reason Blair ended up on the sharp end of Rollings' knife was because he wished him 'Merry Christmas'. Rollings later told the police: 'We [presumably he meant pagans] don't believe in Christmas.'

It happened on Christmas Day 1978, Crown prosecutor Mr Francis Irwin QC told the jury. Peter Rollings and his victim lived in separate flats in the same house in Ashburnham Road, Luton, and on the day in question the two men had a drink together in another of the flats, occupied by Blair's brother. Rollings and his girlfriend subsequently left and went home; however, as John Blair and his girlfriend left, Rollings wandered into the common hallway. Blair – innocently enough one might think – called out a cheery 'Merry Christmas, Peter'. Rollings, who had in the meantime changed his clothes and was now dressed entirely in black, pounced on his former drinking partner, punched him viciously in the face and stabbed him thirteen times with a sheath-knife. When told by police officers later that Blair had died in hospital, Peter Rollings commented: 'I knew he was dead. My sixth sense told me.' Rollings also told detectives that he and his girlfriend were pagans, which meant they believed in God but not in Christ – therefore Christmas Day was much like any other; until 1978 that is. Thus had John Blair's seasonal greeting been perceived as an insult.

The jury at Rollings' trial in July 1979 were told that he was a 'dabbler in the occult' and that they might think 'there are undertones of black magic in the case'. Certainly there was evidence in his flat of witchcraft paraphernalia. Not that any of this mumbo-jumbo did Peter Rollings very much good; though he might have felt the pagan gods were smiling benevolently on him when the jury rejected the charge of murder in favour of one of manslaughter. He was sentenced to five years' imprisonment.

S

SAN DWE The interest of this case is that it is a crime of intense passion – the passions of two men from the East; their mutual passions for money and for elephants; and in particular for the great Sacred White Elephant. Surprisingly, the saga takes place in the heart of London, at the Zoological Gardens in Regent's Park.

Said Ali was an Indian, a *mahmout*, or elephant-driver, by profession, and his intimate understanding of that animal's habits and temperament had developed throughout his early life in the jungles of his homeland. He first came to England in 1922, and found his singular achievements were warmly welcomed by the Zoological Gardens in London. Over the next two or three years Ali endeared himself not only to his employers – among whom his knowledge of elephants was legendary – but also to the many thousands of young visitors who came to look at and ride upon his charges. For the entertainment of these children, Said Ali had taught the elephants a remarkably profitable trick. With their trunks, these huge beasts would delicately pick up pennies thrown on to the pathway by visitors and deposit them, unfailingly, into their trainer's pocket – considerably boosting his weekly wage of two pounds and ten shillings.

As Said Ali was the son of a warmer climate than England could offer, his health suffered from the damp, foggy London winters, and he liked to return to Calcutta during the colder months and come back to the zoo for the summer season.

In 1925 he returned to find himself faced with a potential rival. The newcomer was a Burmese elephant trainer named San Dwe, who had been sent over in charge of the Sacred White Elephant belonging to a religious sect in his native country. After a very popular stay in the London Zoo this valuable elephant was returned to its far-away home suffering, like Said Ali, from the English climate. San Dwe decided to stay on at the zoo as assistant to Said Ali.

The two keepers were, on the face of it, good, if not close companions, and shared the modest accommodation above the Tapir House as well as the day-to-day pleasures and problems of caring for the elephants. And everything might have remained in equilibrium if the daily routine had not been changed.

When he returned from his winter trip of 1928, Said Ali was given back the charge of the children's elephant ride, while San Dwe (who by now had been anglicised to 'Sandy Wee') was appointed to the back-room responsibilities of looking after the baby elephants in the zoo's sanitorium. But Sandy Wee's passions did not stop at elephants – they embraced money too, money which he hoped one day would take him home to a life of luxury. And he had looked to the tips that he received from a generous public to supplement his £2-a-week wage. Sandy Wee was passionately aggrieved.

While police constables Buzzy and Evans were on their midnight patrol of the Outer Circle road around the zoo on 25 August, they heard the unmistakable sounds of a human voice in distress coming from the thick bushes that grew on the zoo side of the railing just beside the Tapir House. Prompt investigation revealed the pathetic sight of San Dwe clutching his ankle in pain and groaning on the grass. He was gibbering incoherently (or perhaps he had lapsed into his native Burmese), but gave the officers to understand that he and Said Ali had been attacked in their quarters and that he, San Dwe, had been obliged to jump out of the window to safety.

After alerting the zoo's superintendent, Dr Geoffrey Marr Vevers, and his assistant Mr Hicks, the policemen ran to the Tapir House, and the unfortunate Sandy Wee was removed to St Pancras Hospital where he was patched up and detained – for some reason best known to the authorities – in a mental ward.

Meanwhile the police party had discovered Said Ali lying on his bed cruelly battered about the head and body, the blood-stained murder weapons (a heavy sledgehammer and a pickaxe) on the floor beside him. When Detective Inspector Walter Hambrook arrived on the scene it was obvious to him that a ferocious struggle had taken place, amply supporting San Dwe's story of having been attacked by four men. On the face of it, the intruders had used the sledgehammer to break down the entrance door before employing it to attack the occupants. Closer examination, however, showed bloodstains in the indentations where the door had been battered down, which could only mean – even to a less experienced eye than Hambrook's – that the door had been attacked *after* Said Ali. Somebody was telling lies; and it could only be Sandy Wee.

The young man's story was that they had been standing by the open bedroom window when Said Ali became involved in some abusive banter with a group of people outside on the Outer Circle. Some time later San Dwe was awakened by a flashlight roving around the bedroom, and Said Ali shouting 'Who are you?' Whereupon four men set upon him. It was only by launching himself from the window and rolling to the place where the policemen had found him that San Dwe was not as dead as his companion, or so he said. The rest of the story lapses into virtual incoherence:

> I saw two lights but I think three or four men. I cannot see the men. I only heard his voice. If they ask me if I like Said Ali I say no, I don't like him. I play my music and Said Ali do not like it. I want to see my friends to tell them what happen. I should be satisfied if I died with Said Ali. I know the people won't believe me. I know Said Ali was dead from the noise. I know everybody will say I killed him because they know I live with him. Me no kill Said Ali. Me no fight Said Ali . . .

At his Old Bailey trial in November before Mr Justice Swift, San Dwe's jealousy was exposed as motive, and despite the best efforts of Sir Henry Curtis Bennett in his defence, the carelessness of his activity with the sledgehammer and door persuaded the jury to return a guilty verdict. Sentenced to death (as was mandatory) San Dwe was subsequently reprieved and committed to life imprisonment. Four years later the little elephant trainer was compassionately released and returned to his native land.

It was with relish that the popular press seized on the story of Said Ali's unfortunate death; not only for the saga's colourful 'oriental' protagonists, but because of the *Romance of the Sacred White Elephant*.

The rare white elephant was generally regarded as a holy animal in the religions of Burma and Siam (modern Thailand); they were revered as incarnations of the Buddha. The animals were not allowed to work, or to be ridden, and in an elaborate ceremony, at a time appointed by the Court astrologer, the king of Siam anointed the baby elephant, naming it 'Most Magnificent White Elephant Lord', and fed the animal pieces of fine red sugar cane with its name inscribed on it.

This particular Sacred White Elephant, the one that was in the care of San Dwe, was called 'Pa Wa' (meaning Mr White), and was caught and owned by Dr Saw Durmay Po Min, President of the National Karen Association of Burma. Dr Po Min describes the capture of the creature:

> He was then only a baby of about twelve months old, and less than four feet high. No sooner had the stockade been erected than the white elephant and his retinue entered of their own accord. With the retinue of the white elephant was a big male elephant over nine feet high. He looked after the others, especially protecting the little white one. It is said that sometimes he carried the white one on his tusks in the jungle.

A further intriguing twist not missed by the press was that Pa Wa died in Calcutta on exactly the same day as its former keeper committed his horrible crime in London – giving credence to the legend that misfortune always follows when a white elephant leaves its own country.

SHARP (or SHARPE), Mark The following text appears on an English broadsheet under the banner 'Apparition of a Ghost to a Miller to Discover a Hidden Murder'. The original is unreliably dated, and not attributed to a publisher or place of publishing.

This may simply be because in reproduction the publication details have been lost; or it may mean that the story is apocryphal and sold on as a pot-boiler to any printer who cared to buy it and add his own imprint. It does, however, have the virtue of that tone of moral retribution so characteristic of these sheets.

About a year of our Lord, 18–, near unto Chester-in-the-Street, there lived one Walker, a yeoman of good estate, and a widower who had a young woman to his kinswoman that kept his house, who was by the neighbours suspected to be with child; and was towards the dark of the evening one night sent away with one Mark Sharp, who was a collier, or one that digged coals under ground, and one that had been born in Blackburn-Hundred, in Lancashire: and so she was not heard of a long time, and little or no noise was made about it. In the winter time after, one James Graham, or Grime (for so in that country they called him), being a miller, and living about two miles from the place where Walker lived, was one night alone very late in the mill grinding corn; and at about twelve or one o'clock at night he came down stairs, having been putting corn in the hopper, the mill doors being fast shut, there stood a woman upon the midst of the floor with her hair about her head hanging down all bloody, with five large wounds on her head. He being much affrighted and amazed, began to bless himself, and at last asked her who she was, and what she wanted? To which she said, 'I am the spirit of such a woman, who lived with Walker; and being got with child by him, he promised to send me to a private place, where I should be well looked to, until I was brought to bed, and well again, and then I should come again and keep his house. And accordingly,' said the apparition, 'I was one night late sent away with one Mark Sharp, who, upon a moor (naming a place the miller knew) slew me with a pick (such as men dig coals withal) and gave me these five wounds, and after threw my body into a coal pit hard by, and hid the pick under a bank: and his shoes and stockings being bloody he endeavoured to wash them, but seeing the blood would not wash out, he hid them there.' And the apparition further told the miller that he must be the man to reveal it, or else she must still appear to haunt him. The miller returned home very sad and heavy, but spoke not one word of what he had seen, but eschewed as much as he could to stay in the mill within night without company, thinking thereby to escape the seeing again of that frightful apparition.

But notwithstanding, one night when it began to be dark, the apparition met him again, and seemed very fierce and cruel, and threatened him, that if he did not reveal the murder, she would continually pursue and haunt him. Yet for all this, he still concealed it until St Thomas' Eve, before Christmas, when, being after sunset, walking in his garden, she appeared again, and then so threatened and affrighted him, that he faithfully promised to reveal it next morning.

In the morning he went to a magistrate, and made the whole matter known, with all the circumstances; and diligent search being made the body was found in a coal pit, with five wounds in the head, and the pick and shoes, and stockings yet bloody, in every circumstance as the apparition had related unto the miller: whereupon Walker and Mark Sharpe were both apprehended, but would confess nothing. At the assizes following they were arraigned, found guilty, condemned, and executed, but we could never hear that they confessed the fact. There were some who reported that the apparition did appear to the Judge, or foreman of the jury (who was alive at Chester-in-the-Street, about ten years ago), as we have been credibly informed.

SHOWERY, Allen   This extraordinary case was reported for the *New York Times* on 2 September 1978, though due to the lengthy newspaperworkers' strike it was never published.

Allen Showery had been accused of killing forty-eight-year-old Teresita Basa in February 1977 and had made a confession after his arrest. Miss Basa, who worked at the Edgewater Hospital with Showery, was discovered beneath a pile of smouldering clothing in her apartment; she had been stabbed in the chest with a butcher's knife.

After making little progress in the investigation, detective Joseph Stachula was advised by local police to have a word with a Dr and Mrs Jose Chua – Mrs Chua also worked at the Edgewater Hospital. It transpired that on several occasions the good lady had been possessed by a spirit voice which identified itself as that of Teresita Basa, and accused Allen Showery of her murder. Through his wife, the voice pleaded with Dr Chua to take the story to the police, and when he declined, fearing ridicule, the voice told him that Showery had taken some jewellery from the victim and given it to his common-law wife Yanka Kamluk. It was at that point that the Chuas took their bizarre story to the local police.

The result was that detective Stachula paid a visit to Allen Showery's apartment to interview him. At first Showery denied visiting the victim's home, but eventually admitted that he had. When some of Miss Basa's jewellery was found in Yanka Kamluk's possession – as the spirit said it would be – Showery confessed to the killing.

So far so good, and one might be grateful to officer Stachula for his enterprise. However, when thirty-two-year-old Allen Showery faced a Circuit Court hearing in September 1978, defence counsel moved to have the arrest and confession quashed on the grounds that his client had been improperly arrested. Assistant Public Defender William Swano argued that there was no evidence linking Showery with the crime except 'the claimed supernatural contact with Teresita Basa's spirit'. He added that if Showery was taken from his home and arrested without a warrant of sufficient evidence, it would make his confession inadmissible. Without some concrete evidence placing him at the scene of the crime, it seemed that Showery would go free. The police stepped up their efforts to locate the murder weapon, but their searches were ultimately to prove unnecessary when, for no obvious reason, Showery changed his plea to guilty.

Allen Showery was convicted of the murder of Teresita Basa and sentenced to fourteen years in prison.

SIBROL, Oswald   There have been some strange motives for murder in the dark history of world crime, and it is inevitable that in a book such as this the motives are a little stranger than usual. But there can be few to match the explanation given in court by Oswald Sibrol for the brutal killing of two elderly women.

It began as a series of thoroughly cowardly muggings of old ladies in the Austrian capital of Vienna (where there are rather more old ladies than in most cities) during the summer of 1983. There was nothing remarkable about this – most capital cities (and more than a few smaller ones) play host to their share of layabouts; idle vicious young men (and women too) who would rather steal than work, and would rather rob the elderly and infirm because they are unlikely to put up much resistance. Sometimes these muggings and burglaries go too far, and the victim dies – either from their injuries or from some associated cause such as shock or heart failure. But sometimes it is clear that the killer had murder in mind. That seemed to be the case when, on the morning of the last day of the year 1983, one elderly Viennese lady visited her equally venerable friend and found her murdered and the apartment ransacked.

The next murder of an old lady took place on 18 April 1984, and the victim was eighty-year-old Franziska Spengler. She had been strangled and stabbed in the chest with a pair of scissors and a kitchen knife. There was something distinctly odd about this one. Despite the fact that Franziska Spengler had been dead for more than twelve hours, there was clear evidence that somebody had spent the night lying in bed next to her corpse. In fact the mattress was still warm. Strangely, nothing appeared to have been taken from the flat, though there was a tidy sum of money in Frau Spengler's handbag. Quite the reverse, the killer had left something behind – something that left the police team wondering whether Christmas had come early that year. He had left behind his wallet containing all his identity papers!

Twenty-year-old Oswald Sibrol had been looked after by the Juvenile Care Service during a life spent in one institution after another. He had run away in July 1983, and was arrested while trying to snatch an old lady's handbag. Back at police headquarters Sibrol confessed to two murders and to the string of muggings that had recently terrorised the city.

When Oswald Sibrol stood before the judge to face his trial, the court could hardly believe its collective ears. It was all the fault of his late grandfather, Gottlieb, Oswald explained. Gottlieb Sibrol, despite his eighty-four years, had retained a remarkable virility; indeed, when he died three years previously, he appears to have taken his sex drive with him. At any rate, granddad Sibrol took to returning to the land of the living in spirit form and made use of the opportunity to plead with Oswald to, as it were, send him a few old ladies to enjoy himself with. Which Oswald dutifully did – twice. Whether his grandfather was happy with Oswald's fatal handiwork he has not yet returned to say. As for young Sibrol, on 14 June 1985 he was sentenced to twenty years in jail.

The night spent with Frau Spengler's dead body? That was easy – Oswald was simply tired.

SMITH, Francis One of the capital's most celebrated hauntings was once associated with the churchyard at Hammersmith, in the year 1803 just one of the small villages skirting London. The restless spirit first displayed its malevolent nature to an unfortunate local who was quietly making her way home across the graveyard at ten o'clock at night. Halfway through the tombstones, she was accosted by something 'very tall and very white', rising as though from the grave. Understandably terrified, the poor woman fled as fast as her legs would carry her; the ghost was quicker, overtaking his prey and enveloping her in its spectral arms. She remained in a faint until carried home by neighbours to her bed; a bed from which she never again rose.

Though this is the only record of a fatal encounter, enough people were sufficiently badly frightened for there to be formed an *ad hoc* watch committee determined at least to discover whether the nuisance was caused, as some said, by the shade of a suicide who had cut his throat a year earlier or, as the cynics had it, by a misguided prankster.

Numbered among the courageous band of watchers was one fated to be the only man to appear before the bench at the Old Bailey charged with murdering a ghost.

On the night of Tuesday 3 January 1804, a young excise officer by the name of Francis Smith was supping happily in the White Hart tavern when general conversation turned to the subject of The Ghost – in truth, a subject never far from anybody's lips in those parts of Hammersmith where the spectre stalked. Suddenly Smith stood up and left for his lodgings close by, where he loaded his fowling-piece with powder and shot and struck out for Black Lion Lane, a favourite haunt of The Ghost. The time was just approaching eleven o'clock, and it is unlikely that Smith was entirely sober. As he moved cautiously along Cross Lane, at the far end of Black Lion Lane, the intrepid exciseman encountered a white figure before him . . .

'Who goes there?' challenged Smith.

There was an eerie silence.

'Who goes there?' asked Smith again, adding: 'Speak up or I shoot.'

No reply.

Whereupon Francis Smith levelled his gun at the apparition's head and fired, the ball entering the mouth and exiting through the back of the head. Too late did Francis Smith realise his mistake. Too late did he discover that his ghost was in reality a man.

It was not then – as it is not now – etiquette to shoot a man; however much like a ghost he may look. And this was the victim's only crime, poor fellow; for twenty-three-year-old Thomas Mill-wood was a bricklayer, and as a bricklayer wore the traditional clothing of his trade – white trousers, white apron, and a white linen jacket!

On the following morning Francis Smith was escorted by some Runners from Bow Street from the White Hart to Newgate Prison, where he was confined awaiting his trial.

It was Friday 13 (oh unlucky day!) January 1804 that Smith stood in the dock of the Old Bailey in front of the Lord Chief Baron. For the prosecution Mr John Locke, a wine merchant, and William Girdler, the local watchman, were called upon to describe how, on the evening in question, they had been accosted by Smith, who confessed the deed to them and placed himself in their custody. The victim's sister, Ann Millwood, told the court that on the night of the third she had a dreadful premonition that something was about to happen to her brother, so she went out of the house to look for him. As she was peering into the darkness, Miss Millwood heard a voice say: 'Damn you, who are you? Stand, else I shoot you.' Followed by the loud report of a gun.

A surgeon by the name of Flower gave medical evidence to the effect that Thomas Millwood had died of a single gunshot wound in the lower part of the left jaw which had penetrated the vertebra of the neck and injured the spinal marrow of the brain. Mr Flower observed that the deceased's face had been blackened with gunpowder, indicating that he had been shot at close range.

However, perhaps Millwood's death could have been avoided together, if only he had listened to the advice of his mother-in-law. When she gave evidence at Smith's trial it transpired that 'on the Saturday evening before his death Millwood told her that two ladies and a gentleman had taken fright at him as he was coming down the terrace, thinking he was The Ghost. He told them he was no more a ghost than any of them, and asked the gentleman if he wished for a punch in the head.' Upon which the mother-in-law recommended that he wear a greatcoat to avoid further trouble.

As to Francis Smith, although he was able to call a number of character witnesses in his defence, each describing him as a mild and gentle man in the extreme, according to one contemporary report:

> The Lord Chief Baron, in his address to the jury, said that however disgusted they might feel in their own minds with any abominable person guilty of the misdemeanour of terrifying the neighbourhood, still the prisoner had no right to construe such misdemeanour into a capital offence, or to conclude that a man dressed in white was a ghost. It was his own opinion, and was confirmed by those of his learned brethren on the bench, that if the facts stated in evidence were credible, the prisoner had committed murder.

The jury took a more lenient view, as juries often do, and returned with a verdict of 'guilty of manslaughter'.

On hearing this verdict the bench responded that 'such a judgement cannot be received in this case, for it ought to be either a verdict of murder or of acquittal. In this case there was a deliberate carrying of a loaded gun, which the prisoner concluded he was entitled to fire, but which he really was not; and he did fire it, with a rashness which the law did not excuse.'

Chastened, the jury reconsidered their verdict. 'Guilty of murder.'

And so it was that the man who shot a 'ghost' was himself

sentenced to die. Happily, history has provided a less austere ending, for Francis Smith earned an eleventh-hour reprieve, and was sentenced instead to one year's imprisonment.

SOLIS, Magdalena, *et al.*   It was in the industrial city of Monterrey in north-east Mexico that Magdalena Solis eked out a risky living as a prostitute, engaging her homosexual brother Eleazor as pimp. In 1962 they were approached by the Hernandez brothers, Cayetano and Santos, with a proposition so bizarre that it would defy the talents of a novelist to invent. The brothers had set up some kind of sex cult in Yerba Buena, and desperately needed a god and goddess – did Eleazor and Magdalena want the job? Of course they did.

The Hernandez brothers had been using the cult in order to squeeze money out of the gullible local farmers and, as an added bonus, had persuaded them that submitting to sexual molestation by the priests (themselves) was essential to the purging of demons. With the recruitment of the Solises, activities were expanded, and Magdalena satisfied the lesbian tendencies of the priestesses, while Eleazor and Cayetano Hernandez indulged their homosexual appetites with the farmers. Things could not be expected to continue in so idyllic a fashion for ever; sooner or later the peasants were certain to tire of giving body and soul as well as their meagre income to the cult.

At this point Magdalena developed the idea of revitalising interest with a couple of human sacrifices, and ordered two men stoned to death and their blood collected for a kind of unholy communion. After the success of this venture, blood sacrifice became a regular feature of cult life, and before many months had passed eight members had given their lives in the interests of purification. Magdalena then offered the ultimate sacrifice and gave her lesbian lover up to be beaten to a pulp, accompanied by another member who had his heart cut out.

These two ritual murders had been unwittingly observed by a teenage boy who took his horrifying tale as fast as his legs would carry him to officer Martinez, the local policeman. Martinez followed the lad back to Yerba Buena to investigate, and they themselves were hacked to death by devotees.

A few missing peasants were one thing, but when a policeman disappeared the authorities wanted to know why, and an armed police squad was sent to investigate. During the battle that followed, members of the cult were routed, and after the shooting of Santos Hernandez they surrendered.

On 13 June 1963, eleven days after their arrest, Magdalena and Eleazor Solis together with twelve members of the cult were tried on charges of multiple murder, convicted and given the maximum sentence of thirty years in the state prison. One face notably absent from the court line-up was that of Cayetano Hernandez, founder of the cult. He had been murdered by a disaffected follower after the killing of officer Martinez.

'SON OF SAM', *see* **BERKOWITZ, David**

SPREITZER, Edward, *et al.*   In Chicago during 1981 and 1982 women were being kidnapped, raped, mutilated and murdered by a gang who became as notorious in the Windy City as the original Jack the Ripper had been in London a hundred years before. In fact they became known as the 'Chicago Rippers'.

The first victim, Linda Sutton, was attacked in May 1981 by three men who gang-raped and stabbed her to death, compounding their sickening crime by mutilating her body and cutting off her left breast. Just over a year later, in separate incidents, two girls, Lorraine Borowski and Shui Mak, disappeared from their homes; it was not until September that their mutilated bodies were found. Meanwhile, in August, in the north tributary of the Chicago river, the body of Sandra Delaware was found strangled and with the familiar trademark of a severed left breast. The attacks began to escalate in their savagery and the next victim, Mrs Rose Beck Davis, was found between two apartment blocks in the Gold Coast district raped, bludgeoned, axed, stabbed, strangled and her breasts mutilated.

In September 1982 an eighteen-year-old prostitute was attacked by a client in a red van, raped, slashed and left for dead beside the North Western railroad tracks. The girl was found, miraculously still alive, and rushed to hospital where emergency treatment saved her life – and at the same time the lives of countless potential victims of the Chicago Rippers.

A few nights later a police patrol stopped a red van answering the description given by the victim and took in for questioning the driver Edward Spreitzer, aged twenty-one, and his nineteen-year-old passenger Andrew Kokoraleis. Spreitzer claimed the van belonged to his employer, Robin Gecht, and Gecht was picked up and detained when records revealed convictions for sexual assault and violence. It was Gecht who was later identified by the teenage prostitute as her attacker and he was charged with rape and attempted murder. (A bizarre sideline to the case was the discovery that Robin Gecht had once been employed by Chicago's most notorious serial killer, John Wayne Gacy.)

Under questioning during 5 to 8 November 1982, Spreitzer and Kokoraleis eventually admitted their involvement in the series of mutilation murders and in doing so implicated Thomas Kokoraleis, Andrew's eighteen-year-old brother. Andrew also confessed to the random shooting of a man earlier in the year. They all described the sickening rituals that went on in Robin Gecht's 'satanic chapel', where the women victims were tortured with a variety of instruments, subjected to multiple rape, and then sacrificed to Satan. One breast was severed with a thin wire garrotte, and as part of the ritual was passed around the circle of celebrants, each eating a piece; what was left over, Gecht put away in a box. Robin Gecht alone denied having done anything wrong at all.

In view of the lack of direct evidence implicating him in murder, Gecht was put on trial only for attempted murder and rape – enough, though, to earn him a total of 120 years' imprisonment.

Edward Spreitzer was indicted on six murder charges, and after being found guilty in 1986 of the aggravated kidnap and murder of Linda Sutton, he was sentenced to die by lethal injection. In addition each of the other murder chargers carried a life sentence.

Andrew Kokoraleis was sentenced to death for the murder of Lorraine Borowski, with thirty years' imprisonment for her aggravated kidnapping, life for the Davis murder, and concurrent terms of sixty and thirty years for rape and aggravated kidnapping.

Thomas Kokoraleis was convicted of the Borowski murder, but won a reversal from the Appeal Court on a technicality. Plea-bargaining before his second trial ensured a sentence of seventy years' imprisonment.

T

TEUFEL, Karl Retz is the largest of a group of villages scattered among the pine woods forty or fifty miles to the north of Vienna, not far from the border with Czechoslovakia. It serves as a shopping centre, seat of local government, and home to the biggest – perhaps the only – event on the region's social calendar, the carnival before Lent. And the climax of the carnival is the fancy dress ball.

In 1973 Karl Teufel was a relative newcomer to the district, having arrived just two years earlier from . . . well, nobody knew quite where. Even on his identity papers the place of birth had been left blank. But being a good mechanic he had found work easily enough, at the garage owned by Anton Schelzer; and being tall, strong and handsome, he had experienced as little difficulty in wooing a partner. Karl fell for the charms of the attractive Gertrude Felsenbock, two years his junior at the age of thirty-two. When the couple married, they moved into a cottage on the edge of the forest, which Gertrude paid for with some money she had inherited.

That year Karl Teufel attended the fancy dress ball with Gertrude, his bride of two weeks. He wore a red suit with forked tail, cloven boots, a horned masked and trident. Very apt, for Teufel is the German word for devil.

Devilishly attractive he may have been, but now Karl Teufel was married he had lost some of his impish appeal. The local girls teased him, one of them giving his tail a tug and laughingly proclaiming it 'limp'. (The word for tail in German has an obvious *double entendre*.) All the girls laughed, and Gertrude laughed with them. Karl did not laugh.

Anton Schelzer became alarmed when the usually punctilious

Karl was absent from work for two days after the ball. He drove out to the cottage and found Teufel's car outside, but there was no answer to the doorbell. Herr Schelzer found the door unlocked; crept inside; called Karl's name. No reply. He tried the kitchen, living room, bathroom. Empty. So was the first bedroom. The second bedroom was in darkness, and when Schelzer turned on the light he found himself confronted by Gertrude's almost naked body. Her face was black, eyes bloodshot, and purple tongue protruding. She had been strangled.

Schelzer ran back into town, and alerted Inspector Josef Eichendorf at the Department of Criminal Investigations. The body was taken to the morgue, where Doctor Peter Graff performed an autopsy. Gertrude had died about two hours after returning home from the ball; had died after a prolonged session of love-making, with the red imprints of the hands that had killed her blemishing her slender neck.

Karl had still not appeared the following day, so a posse set out to search the forest for him. And it was not long before one of the volunteers spotted a red figure frolicking among the trees. 'Beware,' it cried. 'I am the devil! My home is hell!' But the 'devil' surrendered meekly enough to Inspector Eichendorf, who took him back to Retz for a much-needed meal and interrogation. He had killed his wife, Teufel admitted, because she had laughed at him, and one should not laugh at the devil. He had shown his tail was not so limp, and then delivered the devil's own punishment.

Karl Teufel was found unfit to stand trial, and was committed to an institution for the criminally insane.

THOMPSON, Fred J. Four-year-old Edith Kiecorius (affectionately known as 'Google') had been playing outside the home of her uncle, Manuel Duclat, on Eighth Avenue, Manhattan. It was the early evening of Wednesday 22 February 1961, and Edith had been taken there by her mother on a visit from their home in Brooklyn. At around 4.45 p.m. the child simply vanished.

Although a massive search was mounted involving more than 350 New York police officers and helicopters, and despite a methodical dragging of the local stretch of the Hudson River, there was no trace that would explain Edith's disappearance. After a few days during which the mood of the city grew ever darker, thoughts began to turn to less orthodox methods of tracing missing persons. One of these methods was the use of clairvoyance, and through the mediation of writer and journalist Jack Harrison Pollock, friend and biographer* of the Dutch psychic Gerard Croiset, the Dutch national airline KLM offered to fly Croiset to New York to take part in the investigation.

Although he immediately agreed to do whatever he could, Gerard Croiset refused the trip across the Atlantic and asked instead for a photograph of the child and a map of New York to be sent to him in Utrecht. That same day Croiset received the documents and sent back his first impressions to New York. The information staggered police chiefs there; the clairvoyant had described, with unbelievable accuracy, the area from which little Edith had been snatched. The rest of the news was bad – the child was dead. And Croiset appended a broad description of her killer: 'Small, about fifty-four or fifty-five years of age; having a sharp face; and originally from southern Europe. He wears something grey.'

Next day, Gerard Croiset was handed a detailed map of New York showing house numbers, which he found mentally confusing. Eventually he had a picture of a dark woman who was sitting by a window; two houses down there was a laundry and presser . . . then he saw the first house again, which was grey and had five storeys. More information also about the killer – he had a small, sharp, tawny face, and was a little older than Croiset previously thought – fifty-four to fifty-eight. The psychic then received a strong emotion about the second floor of the building: 'In this room I see the child with the man . . .'

At about the same time that Gerard Croiset was receiving his mental pictures, two New York police officers were breaking down the door of a second-floor room in a squalid four-storey rooming-house on West Twentieth Street. The building had been visited before during the extensive house-to-house enquiries, but nobody had answered the door. Now Patrolman John Megrini

* *Croiset the Clairvoyant*, J.H. Pollock, W.H. Allen, London, 1965.

and Detective James Peterson knew why. Scattered around the grimy room were about three dozen empty beer cans and hundreds of cigarette butts. On the bed was the bruised and broken body of Edith Kiecorius; she was naked and had been beaten and raped.

It did not take long to track down Fred J. Thompson, the man who had rented the eight-dollar-a-week room – he was picked up two days later in New Jersey, where he confessed to little Edith's murder. He had been drinking, he said, and wanted sex. Older women just laughed at him, and so for that matter did younger ones. So he abducted a child.

At his trial, Thompson was convicted of first-degree murder, but was considered to be so mentally unstable that he was committed to the Matteawean Hospital for the Criminally Insane.

Although he was too late to be of any direct assistance to the police team investigating Edith Kiecorius' disappearance, Gerard Croiset was materially correct in a number of his predictions. Thompson was a small man, with a sharp nose and a tawny complexion. He was not, however, from the south of Europe, but from England.

V

VAN BUUREN, Clarence Gordon Eighteen-year-old Myrna Joy Aken was last seen by her friend leaving the office in Durban at which they both worked in the company of a man who had picked Myrna up from work; they had driven off in a light-coloured car. It was the evening of 2 October 1956, and Myrna Aken would not be seen alive again. Indeed it was beginning to look as though the police effort to trace her was going to be unsuccessful when Myrna's family called on the assistance of Dale Palmer, a respected and successful medium. The psychic went into a trance during which he described a woman's body lying in a drain under the road at a spot sixty miles away. Palmer accompanied the Aken family, directing them to a place just outside the village of Umtwalumi. There, just as he had 'seen', Palmer pointed out the exact spot where Myrna's naked body lay. She had been raped and shot.

While the search for the victim's body had been going on, police officers had been successful in tracking down the light-coloured car. It was registered to the owner of a Durban radio store, and on the day of Myrna Aken's abduction he had lent the vehicle to one of his salesmen, thirty-three-year-old Clarence Van Buuren. Van Buuren returned it the following day and then promptly disappeared himself.

A little over a week after Myrna's body was found, detectives traced the fugitive Van Buuren to Pinetown. They were clearly interested to know why he had taken to his heels less than twenty-four hours after a young woman seen in his company had disappeared. Panic, Van Buuren explained, sheer panic. It was true, he said, that he had visited Myrna Aken at her office, true that he had invited her out for a drink. But she refused and he went into the bar alone. When he returned, he saw to his puzzlement that the car he had borrowed had inexplicably been driven fifteen yards down the street. When he opened the car door he came face to face with the corpse of a young woman, her face covered with blood. In desperation he had dumped the remains in the ditch and got away as fast as he could.

Although he had no record of violence, Clarence Van Buuren had been known to the South African police since he was a teenager and had collected a number of penalties for theft, forgery and passing dud cheques; he had escaped several times from various penal institutions.

The main evidence against Van Buuren when he came to trial in February 1957 consisted of his being the last person seen in the company of Myrna Aken, and that he possessed a quantity of .22-calibre ammunition of the type used to kill her. It may have fallen far short of overwhelming proof, but it was sufficient for a jury to convict on. Clarence Gordon Van Buuren was hanged on 10 June 1957 at Pretoria Central Prison.

VOLLMER 'DELIVERANCE'   Some people would have called it an exorcism, but for the Vollmer family, adherents of the Charismatic cult of Christianity, it was known as a 'deliverance'.

It was on 22 January 1993, in the hamlet of Antwerp, near Melbourne, that Joan Vollmer's deliverance began. Her ordeal would last until Saturday the thirtieth, climaxing with – so the exorcists claimed – the expulsion of evil spirits. The only problem was that in getting rid of the demons Mrs Vollmer died; and not only did Mrs Vollmer die, but she died in acute agony.

But let us start at the beginning of this strange tale – a tale that is the stranger because the action takes place in the late twentieth century.

Ralph and Jean Vollmer had been married for four years, but they had lived together for a number of years before that; Ralph was a fifty-four-year-old pig farmer, and the couple had lived in Antwerp for five years. The Vollmers were devoutly religious, Ralph almost to the point of fanaticism. Around 1990, fifty-year-old Joan had been admitted for treatment to the Lakeside Psychiatric Hospital at Ballarat. When she was discharged Ralph

Vollmer suggested that she submit to a 'deliverance'; in fact he mentioned it several times. Sensibly, Joan's view was that if the hospital had discharged her she was in no need of exorcism.

At around this time Ralph Vollmer, then a Salvationist, began to attend 'home church' meetings at the house of John and Leanne Reichenbach, who had gathered around them a dozen or so like-minded 'Charismatic Christians'. The Charismatics, according to one description, are 'typified by talking in tongues, a vivid belief in supernatural evil, and an intense, almost obsessive, religious commitment'. It would be the Reichenbachs and members David Kligner and Matthew Nuske who would assist Ralph Vollmer in the deliverance.

On 22 January 1993 the ritual began. Because, according to Ralph, his wife had begun 'behaving strangely', she was not consulted on the matter and was simply tied to a kitchen chair at the Vollmer home. While Leanne Reichenbach pushed against Joan's stomach and chest, twenty-two-year-old Matthew Nuske, who seems to have been in charge of the proceedings, ordered the demons to leave immediately 'in the name of Jesus Christ'. When the spirits proved stubborn, the treatment was tried again and again with increasing brutality. When she was not being pummelled and pushed, Joan Vollmer was having uplifting texts from the scriptures read and sung at her. 'When you are being led by the Lord,' John Reichenbach said later, 'you feel at peace about it and you act.'

The end of Mrs Vollmer's torture came on the afternoon of 30 January. This is how Ralph Vollmer described the climax: 'It was just the last few moments before the evil spirits released their hold on Joan's tongue. By this time they were on the tongue, there was a hissing and frothing of the mouth, and then a groan when they finally released her.' It is worth adding that the spirits were described as manifesting themselves as a pig, a dog, a man, and two females calling themselves Princess Joan and Princess Baby Joan. The demons may have departed, but so had Mrs Vollmer's life.

Undeterred, the assembled exorcists received a message from God (oddly enough over the telephone) saying that Joan would be resurrected. And over the next couple of days, as the Charismatics prayed, and the summer heat soared, the exposed body lying on a mattress in the back yard began to putrefy. According to Ralph Vollmer it became very smelly, and 'there were a lot of blowflies and things around'. Quite how long the earthly remains of Joan Vollmer would have been left awaiting resurrection is anybody's guess, had Ralph not received another telephone instruction from God – notify the authorities!

And that is how the Homicide Squad from Melbourne became involved. According to the most recent reports Ralph Vollmer has been charged with manslaughter, though there is no information on the fate of the other exorcists involved in delivering Mrs Vollmer from her life.

W

WALTON, Charles, Murder of Charles Walton lived with his niece Edith in a cottage in the medieval village of Lower Quinton, located between Chipping Norton and Stratford-on-Avon in the English county of Warwickshire. Although Charlie Walton was no longer young – seventy-four and a martyr to rheumatism – he still insisted on eking out a scant living as a hedge-cutter. And that is what Charlie had in mind when he left home at nine on the morning of Wednesday 14 February 1945. A familiar sight in the neighbourhood with his slash-hook in his hand and double-pronged hay-fork over his shoulder, the shambling figure hobbled his way up Meon Hill to attend to the hedges bordering Alfred Potter's farm about a mile from the Walton cottage.

At six o'clock that evening, when Charlie had not arrived home, Edith began to worry. He was never later than four, and bearing in mind the pain that was crippling his legs she feared he might have had a fall. She picked up a neighbour, Harry Beasley, for company and in case old Charlie needed lifting, and they hiked up the hill to Potter's farm, 'The Firs'. Potter said that he remembered seeing somebody across the fields earlier in the day, and as he was cutting hedges on his land it had to be Charlie Walton. And so, walking briskly behind the beam of a flashlight, farmer Potter, Harry Beasley and Edith Walton made their way over the fields to the lower slopes of the hill where Walton had last been seen.

They came upon it quite suddenly, picked out by the torch's beam as though it were caught in a spotlight; the figure of a man lying on the ground. One look was enough for Potter, and shielding Miss Walton from the sight with his arm, he hurried her back home and summoned the police. Beasley, meanwhile, had the unappetising responsibility of standing guard over a corpse in the middle of a dark field.

When the police arrived at the scene later they could fully appreciate Alfred Potter's shock and horror. Charles Walton had been impaled with his own hay-fork, the twin prongs of which had been driven with such force through his neck that the points penetrated the ground fully six inches. On his cheek, throat and body symbols resembling crosses had been carved with the slash-hook. Close to the corpse lay the old hedger's trusty walking stick, bloody from the savage bludgeoning it had dealt his head.

Realising that this might just be a tricky one, the Warwickshire force put in an immediate call for help to Scotland Yard, and were rewarded by the assistance of Detective Superintendent Robert Fabian – celebrated throughout the nation simply as 'Fabian of the Yard'. From the outset Fabian and his assistant, Detective-Sergeant Albert Webb, were inclined to treat this as an ordinary case of murder. Brutal, yes; seemingly pointless, yes. But Robert Fabian was not yet prepared to have his first impressions clouded by superstition – and there was plenty of that in the atmosphere.

Wartime xenophobia resulted in the close scrutiny of the several thousand enemy prisoners of war incarcerated in a camp over at Long Marston, about two miles away. But however many deaths they may have been responsible for on the field of battle, the pathetic rag-bag of Italians, Slavs and Germans were clearly innocent of the death of Charlie Walton.

Perhaps that tangible air of something more sinister even than murder was beginning to penetrate the usually thick skins of the two experienced London detectives. Perhaps Robert Fabian was beginning to realise that there is a trace of atavistic superstition in all of us. This is how the Yard man described his encounter with the supernatural:

I climbed Meon Hill, a bleak and lonely spot, to examine the scene of the crime for myself. A black dog, a retriever, sat on a nearby wall for a moment, then it trotted past me. I did not look at it again. Shortly afterwards a farm boy came along.

'Looking for your dog?' I asked him.

'What dog?'

'A black dog . . .'

The lad didn't wait to hear any more. He fled down the hill. Instantly, word spread through the village that I had seen the Ghost.

Next, Fabian was presented with a piece of information in the form of a passage from a work entitled *Folk Lore, Old Customs and Superstitions in Shakespeare Land*. It is a volume of modest pretensions from the prolific pen of a Warwick parson named J. Harvey Bloom (he is, I believe, father of Ursula, the actress and author), and it was published in 1930. The text we are concerned with reads:

> At Alveston a plough lad named Charles Walton met a dog on his way home nine times in successive evenings. He told both the shepherd and the carter with whom he worked, and was laughed at for his pains. On the ninth encounter a headless lady rushed past him in a silk dress, and on the next day he heard of his sister's death.

Charles Walton! The same Charlie Walton!

It was a local man who presented Bob Fabian with his next excursion into the folk-lore of the district. He had been talking over the case with Detective-Superintendent Alex Spooner of the Warwickshire CID, when Spooner drew his attention to a paragraph in Clive Holland's *Warwickshire*. It told that in the nearby village of Long Compton, in 1875, a similar murder had taken place. In this case a simple-minded youth named John Haywood slew an old woman named Ann Turner who, he was convinced, was a member of a coven of witches who held their sabbats at Long Compton. At his trial, Haywood explained: 'Her was a proper witch. I pinned her to the ground [actually with a hay-fork] before slashing her throat with a bill-hook in the form of a cross.' Long Compton, so local gossip had it, was still an important centre of witchcraft.

Whether such ingrained fear of the supernatural, of witches and ghosts and ghouls, was the reason that the local people were so tight lipped, or whether it was just prejudice against a couple of 'flash' London coppers stalking about the village, Fabian and Webb never knew. The fact was, nobody felt like talking. In the end, even the experience and determination of one of the country's finest detectives found they had met their match in the stubborn silence at Lower Quinton. Knowing that they could get no further, Detective-Superintendent Fabian and Detective-Sergeant Webb retreated to London, and less spooky investigations.

It was strange, therefore, to read, in Robert Fabian's autobiographical account of the Walton case (*The Anatomy of Crime*, Pelham, London, 1970), this warning:

> I advise anybody who is tempted at any time to venture into Black Magic, witchcraft, Satanism – call it what you will – to remember Charles Walton and to think of his death, which was clearly the ghastly climax of a pagan rite. There is no stronger argument for keeping as far away as possible from the villains with their swords, incense and mumbo-jumbo. It is prudence on which your future peace of mind and even your life could depend.

Now far be it from me to cast a cynical eye over the words of one of the country's most successful detectives. But it is a fact that while he was penning this warning of possible death at the hands of witches, Fabian was certain that he knew exactly why Charlie Walton, the hedger of Lower Quinton, died; and what is more, who killed him. Of course Fabian was quite correct in warning the idly curious about embarking on flirtations with the occult. And he was quite correct in keeping to himself any unprovable suspicions as to who was responsible for Charlie Walton's untimely death; the laws of slander and libel dictate this. But before he died in 1978, Robert Fabian confided in his friend, the crime historian Richard Whittington-Egan, that he was sure that Alfred Potter had committed the crime. Potter, who died in 1974, had borrowed a large sum of money from Charles Walton, and Charlie, so it was said, wanted to be repaid. So – motive for murder?

Or do witches still dance in circles at Lower Quinton?

WARBOYS WITCHES It was around the tenth of November 1589 when Mistress Jane, daughter of the Master of Throckmorton, at Warboys, being ten years of age suddenly fell sick with a mysterious complaint. Sometimes she would sneeze loudly for as long as half an hour, followed by a fainting fit which would last as long. Then her belly would swell and heave, and she would shake one leg as though with palsy; or she would shake an arm or her head. She had suffered this sickness for several days when old Alice Samuel visited the child, and sat at her sickbed. Immediately Jane called out to her grandmother: 'Look, the old witch sits by me; did you ever see anybody more like a witch than that; tell her to take off her black cap.'

Despite the speedy exit of Mother Samuel, and despite the best efforts of the physicians, the small patient grew more poorly by the day, so that in the end there was only one explanation that fitted the bill – the child was the victim of witchcraft! When all four of the Squire's other daughters fell victim to the same strange malady as Jane it became obvious that old Alice Samuel was at the bottom of it. Then several of the Throckmorton servants took sick, and they too blamed the same unfortunate old woman.

Eventually the children and staff recovered their former health and everything might have been forgotten, had not the girls' uncle, Mr Gilbert Pickering, paid a visit and interfered in what would have been best left alone. Pickering took himself off to the wretched cottage of Mother Samuel and insisted on her returning with him to the Big House to confront the lately sick children. In spite of her protests, the old woman, along with her daughter Agnes and one Cicely Burder, was dragged into the company of the girls, whereupon, so it is recorded: 'They all fell down upon the ground strangely tormented, so that if they had been let lie still on the ground, they would have leaped and sprung like a quicke pickerel newly taken out of the water' – whatever a 'quicke pickerel' might be.

The narrative takes a worse turn for the ridiculous when, in 'one particular instance which the reader will excuse our inserting' the unfortunate Jane Throckmorton becomes an unwilling tool for anti-Catholicism. When Jane was in one of her 'fits', she was asked if she loved the word of God; 'whereat she was sore troubled and vexed'. Then she was asked if she loved witchcraft; 'she seemed content'. The rest of the conversation is recorded thus:

'Love you the Bible?' Again she shook.
'But love you Popery?' She was quiet.
'Love you prayer?' She raged.
'Love you the Mass?' She was still.
'Love you the Gospel?' Again she heaved up her belly.
So that whatever good thing you named it disliked; but whatever concerning the Pope it seemed peaceful and quiet.

In March 1590 the children were visited by Lady Cromwell, who also entered into her own kind of mischief by summoning the now much maligned Alice Samuel and accusing her of witchcraft. Not unnaturally the old woman was 'cross'. Whereupon 'Lady Cromwell suddenly pulled off her [Mother Samuel's] kerchief, and taking a pair of shears clipped off a lock of her hair' which she gave to Lady Throckmorton with instructions to burn it. Woe to poor Lady Cromwell, for it is recorded that that night 'she was strangely tormented in her sleep by a cat' (the implication being that it was Mother Samuel's familiar) which 'tried to pluck off all the skin and flesh from her arms and body'. The following day her Ladyship fell sick, and within a year and a quarter died.

It was clear, to the Throckmorton clan at least, that Alice Samuel and her familiars had been responsible for this devilment in their house, and to add a touch of comedy to the already bizarre, those familiars were given substance and names – according to one contemporary account:

The names of the first six were Pluck, Blue, Catch, White, Calico and Hardname . . . and that of the other three Smack, they being cousins, for be it known that relationship exists even amongst the inhabitants of the nether regions. The favourite form under which they appeared was that of dun chickens.

In fact these familiars, and in particular the Smack cousins, became close confidants of the Throckmorton girls and frequently visited for a chat – most often to malign their mistress 'Dame' Samuel.

A few days before Christmas 1592 one of the children – it was Jane – was stricken by a more violent fit than any of them had suffered previously. Her father sent for Mother Samuel and insisted that she remove the spell her familiars had woven around Jane which, strange to say, she did, and the child recovered immediately. The upshot was that, according to record: 'Mother Samuel fell on her knees before Mr Throckmorton, entreating him to forgive her, and confessing that she was the cause of all this trouble to his children.' However, back in the safety of her own home the old woman retracted her confession, obliging the Squire to take her before the magistrates, and for good measure her daughter Agnes was arraigned with her.

To a panel consisting of the Bishop of Lincoln and two Justices of the Peace, Alice Samuel confessed to various acts of witchcraft carried out by her 'spirits', or familiars, and alongside with her daughter was clapped in Huntingdon gaol.

When the assize opened in January 1593, there was a lamentable lack of evidence against young Agnes Samuel, whereupon Robert Throckmorton begged the court's indulgence and took the woman back to his home where, as soon as she had crossed the threshold, the Throckmorton children obligingly fell into one of their familiar 'fits'. Proof indeed, if any were needed, that Alice's familiars worked for the family business. But they evidently were not above a touch of counter-espionage, because cousin Smack, in a *tête-à-tête* with Jane Throckmorton, added the name of John Samuel – Alice's husband, Agnes' father – to the list of culprits. Which is how the whole of the Samuel family found itself on trial accused, effectively, by the uncorroborated words of the Throckmorton children (and Smack, of course).

We are told that: 'On 5 April 1593, these three wicked offenders, John Samuel, Alice Samuel and Agnes their daughter, were arraigned before Mr Justice Fenner, "for bewitching of the Lady Cromwell to death, and for bewitching of Mistress Jane Throckmorton and others".'

The evidence in court consisted mainly in bringing the luckless Jane in and watching her throw a fit at the sight of the Samuel family standing in the dock. It need hardly be said that the verdict of the court was guilty, and that the sentence was death. On the gallows old Mother Samuel again confirmed her confession and implicated her husband and daughter – both of whom strenuously protested their innocence. And much good it did them, all three strangling at the end of the hangman's rope.

So what are we to make of this strange story? Given the fact that poor, simple old Mother Samuel was unlikely to have held any power of enchantment, the most likely explanation is that Jane Throckmorton suffered from a form of epilepsy. Canny Jane, knowing more about superstition than medicine, was ready to blame her fits on witchcraft and so excuse her destructive behaviour and make herself the centre of attention. As for the younger sisters, what more natural than to want to share in Jane's glory? And for the servants – who must surely have been rewarded for their 'suffering' even if only by a few days of lighter duties – it was surely worth keeping the myth going. And so it is more than likely that due to a sick and spiteful child, a few envious sisters, a gaggle of lazy servants and a family steeped in the fashionable fear of witchcraft, the Samuels died an excruciating death on the scaffold.

Or perhaps it was different . . .

WATERHOUSE, Scott The body of twelve-year-old Gycelle Cote was found floating in the Mousam river at the point where it meandered through the small New England town of Sandford, Maine. It was 30 April 1984, and Gycelle had been reported missing the previous evening when she failed to turn up for supper after going to meet friends. She had left her home in Jackson Street late in the afternoon to keep her regular Sunday rendezvous with friends in the wooded area around Pike's Hill; when they arrived she couldn't be found.

It is always distressing when a young innocent child is robbed so prematurely of its life, but for the residents of Sandford it seemed like confirmation of another fear – that Satan was stealing their children. Early the previous year there had been steadily growing rumours that a group of devil-worshippers was actively recruiting local teenagers, who met together for orgiastic rituals.

A police investigation failed to find evidence of any such activity, but this did nothing to dispel the atmosphere of unease that was spreading through the town.

In the weeks leading up to Halloween a number of young girls began to receive death threats signed by 'The Cult'. At last the police had something tangible to investigate, and as the result of their enquiry, a dozen or so youths were arrested on charges of issuing death threats and criminal mischief. And that seemed, officially at least, to be the end of the matter – there was no predatory Satanist cult, just a gang of thoughtless kids feeding off local fears. Then little Gycelle Cote's strangled body was found floating through town.

Perhaps it was the sheer horror of it that kick-started people's memories, but within hours of their pleas for help from the community the police received reports of four sightings of the same person near Pike's Hill on the afternoon of Sunday 29 April. One witness recalled seeing a youth in a combat jacket with his hand on the shoulder of a girl fitting Gycelle's description walking close to the river. The youth was Scott Waterhouse, eighteen years old, a high school junior with a record of abetting theft.

On the afternoon of 3 May Waterhouse was pulled in for questioning at the station in Alfred while a team of officers exercised a warrant to search his home. What they found would vindicate the fears of the past twelve months. In Waterhouse's room at home and his locker at school, detectives discovered items proving the youth's deep psychological involvement with Satanism: a notepad listing what he called 'The Satanic Rules', another containing 'Questions about Satan', a bizarre letter purporting to be written to Waterhouse by Jesus Christ, and a manuscript sheet of 'Notes about Satanic/Christian Beliefs'. A glimpse into the background of Scott Waterhouse revealed that he had first become attracted to devil-worship after reading a copy of Anton Szandor LaVey's classic *Satanic Bible*; though he was clearly so emotionally disturbed that almost anything could have pushed him over the edge, particularly as he had begun to use LSD and marijuana. As he became more obsessed with the ritual of black magic, so Scott Waterhouse began to develop an active streak of malevolence – in particular he enjoyed threatening teenage girls with death – 'Make the most of your every waking moment because your days are numbered' was a favourite.

Waterhouse pleaded not guilty to the charge of murder when his trial opened in November. The jury did not agree and convicted him as charged. On 20 December 1984, in sentencing him, Judge William Broderick told Waterhouse: 'The evidence indicates that you enjoyed killing. And there is every reason to believe you could do it again given the chance. Thrill killing deserves the maximum penalty of life imprisonment.' Perhaps the good people of Sandford rest a little easier now, because in Maine life for first-degree murder means life, with no possibility of parole.

WIGGINTON, Tracy, *et al.* When the news broke at the end of October 1989 even the British press took an interest and beneath the sensationalist headline 'Satan Girls' Bloodlust', the murder was reported of Edward Baldock in Brisbane, Australia, by what were described as 'a gang of Satan-worshipping women who drank pints of blood' and 'hacked the naked man to death in their evil lust for thrills'. Sergeant Pat Clancey, a detective for twenty-five years, said, 'I thought I had seen everything – now this.'

By the time the case came to trial in February 1991 a new twist had been added and the press had a field day with 'Lesbian Vampire Trial'. The court heard how twenty-five-year-old Tracey Wiggington, said to be the ringleader, had already confessed to her part in the brutal murder of Edward Baldock, a forty-seven-year-old road worker. Wiggington and three other women – her lover Lisa Ptaschinski, aged twenty-five, twenty-four-year-old Kim Jervis and Tracey Waugh, also twenty-four – picked a very inebriated Baldock up and drove him to a deserted yacht club where Wiggington made a frenzied attack on him with a knife almost severing his head from his body. Although nobody actually saw her do so, Wiggington claimed to have drunk her victim's blood, and Tracey Waugh told police she had smelled blood on her breath. She added: 'Tracey [Wiggington] has mind power, you can't stop yourself from doing what she tells you to do.'

Further accolades were offered to the jury by Lisa Ptaschinski who described her lover as 'a vampire who lives on human blood and has the ability to disappear – except for her cat-like eyes'. Needless to say, in the best vampire tradition, Wiggington had a loathing of mirrors and a fondness for putting spells on people. Although she did not give evidence during the trial, two psychiatrists who had examined her testified that Tracey Wiggington claimed to have been sexually abused by her grandfather between the ages of eight and eleven. The doctors also reported that she demonstrated four distinct personalities. In former days Wiggington might have been punished with a stake through the heart and burial at the crossroads; in 1991 she was merely sentenced to life imprisonment.

For her part in the Satanic revels, Lisa Ptaschinski was also found guilty of murder and given a life sentence. Kim Jervis was convicted on the lesser charge of manslaughter and jailed for eight years, while Tracey Waugh, allegedly Jervis's lover, was acquitted.

WISE, Martha Hasel　Martha Hasel, born in 1885, had married somewhere along the line to a Mr Wise, been widowed, and was living in poverty with her mother on a broken-down farm in Medina County, Ohio. Then she fell in love. It was 1924, and to look at Martha, with her long, plain face, heavy brows and staring eyes, you would have found it difficult not to agree with her mother that romance with the much younger Walter Johns was indeed 'capricious'. We do not know what Mr Johns thought about it, but he seems to have had no strong objections to such talk; but Martha was peeved as hell. In fact, on New Year's Eve 1924 she poisoned the old lady.

There was no reason at the time to suspect foul play, and the local *Medina County Gazette* simply announced:

HASEL. At Liverpool on December 31, Mrs Sophie Hasel, aged 72 years 13 months and 16 days. Funeral at Zion Lutheran Church, burial Hardscrabble Cemetery.

By now, Martha's 'cradle-robbing' had become something of a family joke, especially among the Geinkes – her aunt, uncle and cousins. During January and February 1925, Lily and Fred Geinke died suddenly; Martha had slipped arsenic into their coffee. Then she thought she might as well get rid of the whole damn family and have done with it, so out came the poison bottle again. This time Martha misjudged her doses, or the robustness of her victims, and although the remainder of the Geinke family were very ill indeed, they all lived to tell the tale. And it was to the police they told it.

And in its turn the modest *Medina County Gazette* excitedly passed on the story to their eager readers. Although in order to preserve calm during their investigations the police had announced that the post-mortem on Fred Geinke revealed no reason for suspicion, it now turned out that the analysis of his stomach contents indicated arsenical poisoning. Despite heavy speculation of the type common in such communities, there was considerable surprise that, on 19 March, the *Gazette* was able to tell its readers that the killer had already confessed – her name was Martha Wise. One journalist who visited Martha in the local jail reported that she was hiding under a blanket on the bed, weeping and wailing, and 'pointing a bony finger at the vision of the devil which she seemed to see standing in the corner of her cell'. Martha Wise then began to ramble on about this persistent demon: 'He came to me in my kitchen while I was baking bread, and he said "Do it" . . . He came to me when I walked the fields in the cold damp night, trying to fight him off. He said "Do it" . . . He came to me when my children were around me. Everywhere I turned, I saw him, grinning and talking at me.'

Of course nobody really believed Martha's story about being followed around by the devil, and even when Walter Johns loyally tried to give it some credence by telling the court that during their love-making Martha barked like a dog, it served to make Martha look more comic than demonic. And the coroner felt constrained to observe that, in his opinion, she should be classed as 'a mental and moral imbecile whose normal side knew little of her subconscious acts'.

At the end of her trial, Martha Wise, the woman they were calling 'America's Borgia', was convicted of first-degree murder and sentenced to life imprisonment; she died in the Marysville Reformatory in 1971, and was buried there.

Z

'ZODIAC' The first killings took place near Vallejo, outside San Francisco. On the Lake Herman Road, a 'lovers' lane', two teenagers, David Faraday and Bettilou Jensen, were found shot close to their station wagon. Bettilou had managed to run a few yards before falling dead, David was alive when help came but died shortly after his arrival in hospital.

On 5 July 1969, a man with a 'gruff' voice telephoned the Vallejo Police Department to report a second double murder: 'If you will go one mile east on Columbus Parkway to a public park, you will find the kids in a brown car. They have been shot with a 9mm Luger. I also killed those kids last year. Goodbye.' As they had been warned, the police found twenty-two-year-old waitress Darlene Ferris dead of gunshot wounds, and Michael Mageau seriously injured from a bullet in the neck. When he had recovered sufficiently from his ordeal, Michael Mageau described their assailant as about twenty-five to thirty years old, stockily built, with a round face and wavy brown hair.

On 1 August, the *Times-Herald* of Vallejo and two newspapers in San Francisco received letters signed with a kind of cross superimposed on a circle which is the symbol of the zodiac. The letters began: 'Dear Editor, This is the murderer of the two teenagers last Christmas at Lake Herman and the girl on the 4th of July . . .' They also contained sufficient details about the guns and ammunition used to exclude anybody but the killer from being their author. At the bottom of each of the letters were lines of cipher which, the writer claimed, if the code was broken would reveal his identity. In fact when military experts had failed, Dale Harden, a teacher at Alisal High School, Salinas, did crack the cipher. Although it gave no clues as to the identity of the killer, it opened a bizarre window into his clearly sick mind:

> I like to kill people because it is so much fun. It is more fun than killing wild game in the forest, because Man is the most dangerous animal of all. To kill something gives me the most thrilling experience. It is even better than [sex]. The best part [will be] when I die. I will be reborn in Paradise, and then all I have killed will become my slaves. I will not give you my name because you will try to slow or stop my collecting of slaves for my afterlife.

In a further letter to a newspaper, the writer introduced himself: 'Dear Editor, This is Zodiac speaking . . .' and proceeded to give accurate information about the murder of Darlene Ferrin. The man with the gruff voice telephoned the Napa Police Department on 27 September to report another double killing. It was almost as he had described it; in a parked car on the shore of Lake Verriesa, Cecilia Shepherd and Bryan Hartnell, students at Pacific Union College, were lying bound and soaked in their own blood. The girl was dead, but Mr Hartnell survived and was able to tell the police that the man who had stabbed them was wearing a black mask with eye-slits and the zodiac sign painted on it in white. Through the eye-holes he could see a pair of spectacles, and the stocky build and light brown hair matched the description of 'Zodiac' given by Michael Mageau. He approached the couple and demanded money, claiming that he was an escaped convict. Then he tied his victims up and said matter-of-factly: 'I'm going to have to stab you people.' At his own request, Hartnell was the first to be stabbed, and as the attacker moved on to Cecilia Shepherd he seemed to go berserk, repeatedly thrusting his knife into her body. When the police arrived at the scene after being alerted by a fisherman who heard the couple's screams, they found that the killer had left his signature. With a black felt-tip pen he had scrawled the zodiac sign on the door panel of Bryan Hartnell's car.

The last known victim was a twenty-nine-year-old taxi driver named Paul Stine, who was shot dead in his cab and robbed in San Francisco in broad daylight. On the following day the editor of San Francisco's *Chronicle* received a Zodiac letter threatening to kill a bus-load of children, and enclosing a piece of bloody cloth that had been cut from Paul Stine's shirt.

Zodiac now began to manipulate the media as never before. On 21 October he telephoned the Oakland police offering to give himself up if he could be represented by a famous lawyer – he suggested somebody of the distinction of Melvin Belli or F. Lee Bailey. Then he demanded air-time on an early morning television chat show. Ratings had never been so high as viewers tuned in to watch the Jim Dunbar show. At 7.41 a man with what was described as a 'soft, boyish voice' came on the phone line and discussed the murders and his own health problems (it appeared he suffered from severe headaches, the implication being that they were the cause of his violence). He spoke at length with Melvin Belli who was in the studio, and whom Zodiac agreed to meet in a public place in Daly City. He failed to keep the appointment.

Although the few people who had heard Zodiac speak before could not identify him with the voice on television, it is likely that any impostor would have been vigorously denounced by the real killer; Zodiac was clearly not the sort of man to share his limelight. Besides, Melvin Belli subsequently received an identifiable Zodiac letter which began: 'Dear Melvin, This is Zodiac speaking. I wish you a happy Christmas. One thing I ask of you is this, please help me . . . I am afraid I will lose control and take my ninth and possibly tenth victim.' The note also contained a second piece of the taxi-driver's shirt. Although the letter threatened to kill again, nothing more was heard from Zodiac until the *Los Angeles Times* received a letter in March 1971, commenting, 'If the blue menaces are ever going to catch me, they had better get off their fat butts and do something.' In 1974 , the San Francisco Police Department received a Zodiac letter claiming a total of thirty-seven killings (almost certainly an exaggeration) and threatening to 'do something nasty'. All these letters were proved to have a common origin, and despite his self-publicity and that given to him by an eager media machine, Zodiac was never caught, nor, as far as we can know, did he kill again.

As a postscript, I am grateful to Nicholas Warren, the editor of *Ripperana*, for this snippet from the London *Sunday Times* of 14 August 1994. It reported that a letter signed with a zodiac had been received by the *New York Post*, claiming 'NYPD 0, Zodiac 9'. Although the letter described four unsolved killings which are on New York police files, and the NYPD received similar letters in 1990, the common theory is that these are copy-cat letters and killings.

Alphabetical Index

Geographical Index

Australia

DALE, Rodney (1990)
VOLLMER 'DELIVERANCE' (1993)
WIGGINTON, Tracey, *et al.* (1989)

Austria

SIBROL, Oswald (1983)
TEUFEL, Karl (1973)

Belgium

BOUCK, Claude and Nicole (1987)

Canada

BOOHER, Vernon (1928)

Canary Islands

ALEXANDER, Harald and Frank (1970)

Chile

CATRILAF, Juana (1953)

England

ALLAWAY, Thomas Henry (1921)
BASHIR, Mohammed (1991)
BATEMAN, Mary (1809)
BEECHOOK, Mirella (1985)
BOSTOCK, Paul (1986)